C000068466

Acknowledgements

Thanks to all those who have helped to transform the ideas in this book. My appreciation goes to Dr Andrew Willis of Department of Criminology, Leicester University for the initial guidance that helped me better understand this project. I also acknowledge the contribution of Dr Jonathan Taylor of Leicester University, whose advice has contributed to the publication of this book.

Preface

As many countries struggle to meet vast demands for security services from their citizens, this book hopes to complement public policing duties while stimulating an increase in entrepreneurship in the private security industry in the relevant countries.

This book focuses on work processes in the United Kingdom; which shares many common law features with other countries such as Kenya, Australia, New Zealand, South Africa, Canada, Nigeria, other English-speaking countries and the United States. Nevertheless, individuals should always seek appropriate legal guidance to adapt the procedures suggested in this book to local culture and national laws.

This book provides possible solutions to the problems of how to protect people, property, and premises. It is expected to serve as a resource to security entrepreneurs and managers. It is also intended to serve as a teaching handbook and instruction manual for teachers. It contains detailed information on how to start and run a security business.

This book is aimed at improving security and the feeling of safety in business premises and communities. It addresses the issues of crime and fear of crime throughout. The later chapters are specifically dedicated to dealing with the threats of terrorism and organised crime through risk management strategies. Central to the crime reduction strategies is the partnership between the police, the community and the private sector. It explains the importance of 'territoriality' and how people can take responsibility to protect their territories through vigilance and access control. In this regard, it deals with patrolling, access control, CCTV, and electronic security systems.

It also covers how to provide private security in the hospitality industry; hotels, nightclubs, bars, restaurants and sports venues. It covers how the public police can work with managers of these venues to provide policing in these areas and other high crime areas. It covers the need for effective communication between partners and between personnel. It contains recommended operational procedures for radio use in communication. Other areas covered are; the civil and criminal law, arrest, searching, Health and safety procedures, fire awareness and emergency procedures.

Towards the end, the book discusses 'business continuity management'. This aims to reduce the post-incident impact of disasters and emergencies in organisations. The book finishes with instructions on how personnel can report and record incidents in the workplace. It also deals with issues of evidence and how to preserve a crime scene. The summary chapter in tabular form, summarises the functions security personnel are expected to perform in various roles and venues. The book is well researched and academic references are provided in the last pages.

In the end readers will find that this book not only identifies contemporary security problems, but offers solutions. In an era where businesses are hit by drops in profit and security companies are either closing down or merging, this book provides an opportunity for the business owner to train his own in-house security team. For the businesses that want to transfer risks to third parties, it provides an opportunity for individuals to set up as entrepreneurs and compete for contracts with established security firms.

Overall the book aims at expanding private sector policing, especially in countries with limited policing budget. There is need for professionalism in the private security sector around the world. It is vital that owners of land and property can afford the services of the private security to complement the role of the public police. It is hoped that, if widely and correctly implemented, the number of ungoverned spaces will reduce. Shrinking the number of ungoverned spaces would displace certain organised crimes such as terrorism and kidnapping. It is only then that surveillance and vigilance could play a meaningful role in the crime prevention.

Finally, this book is based on UK security principles. It is hoped that countries will adapt it to their own social, cultural and economic context. It is also intended to make it easy for countries to adapt contents to their own rules and regulations. The author, to the extent possible limits any reference to law to the common laws applicable in common law countries, with little or no emphasis on statutes. The writing style adopted in this book is intended to make it easy to understand by anyone with or without prior knowledge or experience of working in the private security industry.

About the Author

The author, Chike Onyeari is an entrepreneur and a security instructor with over fifteen years' experience. He provides security services in the United Kingdom. He specialises in the risk management discipline; providing services ranging from training and consultancies in both corporate and national security sectors.

At the end of his secondary education Chike Onyeari felt compelled to further his education. He obtained a bachelor's degree in Pure and Applied Chemistry from the University of Benin. Since then, Chike Onyeari has worked in the UK security industry where he has completed several training programmes and enjoyed steady success in his career to become a security instructor.

Chike Onyeari obtained his Master's degree in Security and Risk Management from University of Leicester in the United Kingdom (UK). He later proceeded to obtain his law degree from the University of Westminster in the UK. Chike Onyeari completed his Legal Practice from the Westminster Law School. He is also a regulated Adviser on UK Asylum and Immigration matters.

As an instructor, Chike Onyeari has personally provided training to thousands of students in the UK. His students come from various backgrounds, which include re-settlement soldiers from Sandhurst Military Academy Camberley England. The scenario-based and practical intensive courses cover; conflict management; roles and responsibilities in the private security industry; risk management; working in the hospitality and leisure industry; self-defence; terrorism and emergency procedures.

He has also produced academic research works covering the areas of access control, natural surveillance, terrorism, territoriality and designing out crime in residential environment initiatives. The author also did research work on accountability in the private and public police; the impact of CCTV surveillance; evaluating the nature and severity of risks posed by terrorism and how leaders could manipulate organisational culture to achieve improved performance.

Table of Contents

Introduction

Main aims of the Private Security Industry

- To protect persons, property, premises
- To improve public feeling of safety and security
- Enhance public confidence in the private security industry through skills and professionalism

Fig 1. Gated private property

Objects

To achieve the aim, the private security industry specifically:

- Provides personnel
- Provides systems (also known as technologies of control)
- Provides physical barriers or gates
- Provides personnel training to meet sector requirements
- Forms a partnership between public police and private security

> **The private security industry has expanded in recent years due to many factors amongst which are (Johnston, 1999):**
>
> - High levels of reported crime
> - Increased public fear of crime
> - Threats from public demonstrations
> - Threats from terrorism (bombings) and organised crimes (hijackings and kidnappings)
> - Mass privatization of public property coupled with increased property ownership resulting from growth of private and corporate incomes
> - Increased demand for protection of properties and increase in availability of money to pay for security protection

Previously owned public properties could no longer be manned by public police; thereby enabling private security to blossom. Today, public police and the private security can both compete for private sector contracts and the police are able to sell their services in the same way as a private security firm; hence the shift to customer oriented policing, (Kinsella and McGarry, 2011).

In Britain, much of the private security policing powers of the public police are derived from the Police Reform Act (National Archives, 2002). This law allows the police to enter into contract with any individual or organisation for the provision of detention or escort services for arrested suspects or prisoners. It also enables chief police officers to delegate powers to private security agents as detention or escort officers. There is also the power to run 'community safety accreditation schemes' in their respective localities for the purpose of fighting crime and disorder, public nuisance and anti-social behaviour. These powers have brought the private security agents closer to the public police prompting sharing of information and intelligence between the private security sector and the public police, (Wakefield, 2006:403).

Consequently, commercialised policing has become inevitable as decisions are driven by costs and efficiency implications. This has resulted in the growth of private security and hence the involvement of the private security sector in policing and law enforcement, (Walsh and Conway 2011).

As operational activities of most criminal gangs mimic activities of legitimate enterprises, private sector involvement in security and policing is inevitable. While the private police are understood to have ordinary powers like other members of the public, the public police have special powers, (Stenning, 2000). Again, the public police are paid by the state whereas the private police are paid by the person with whom they have contract.

However, the presence of private security agents in a state will make little or no difference to policing unless the services offered by these organisations are organised in a strategic sense to help the public police in their fight against crime. Private security operatives have their primary assignment on the premises of those who pay them.

But it is for the public police and other federal agencies to find out how to make the most out of these privately paid personnel. In advanced economies, this is done through approved training programmes and state regulations with a view to creating lines of accountability.

Crime Reduction Initiatives

Safer Community Partnerships

The security industry comprising of security firms, vigilantes or neighbourhood watch and suppliers of security products are supported by Local Authorities, the police, trade associations, professional bodies, professional institutes and inspectorates.

Key Partnerships:

- Local Authority (Councils)
- The Police

Key objectives of the initiative

- Reduction of crime
- Reduction of fear of crime
- Public disorder
- Anti-social behaviour
- Drug misuse
- Vandalism

Examples of how the initiatives can be achieved:

- Physical presence to deter opportunistic crimes
- Extra lighting in areas to improve natural surveillance (visibility)
- Access control to certain areas
- CCTV schemes
- Radio communication links between partnership organizations
- Pub-watch and shop-watch initiatives

The main functions of security personnel can be grouped under:

- The protection of life
- The protection of property and premises
- The prevention of loss and waste
- The prevention and deterrence of crime

See appendix A for a breakdown of how these roles can be carried out in practice.

Security operatives participate in the partnership through:

- Vigilance
- Observations and reporting to their employers.
- Communication with other partners or agencies via radio or phone

Partnering with the local police service

Fig 2 Surveillance is about watching people and spotting unusual activity and behaviour. In this picture a person stopping or looking behind will be unusual behaviour

The relationship between the private security personnel and the public police has never been more relevant. Increase in the number of privately controlled public spaces such as shopping centres, gated communities, parks (and outsourcing of policing functions within the public sector), has increased the role of private security personnel in law enforcement.

CCTV control room operations and public space patrol duties can now be carried out by private security personnel. This private security expansion of the role brings the public police and private security personnel into regular contact with each other as partners.

Public police/private security partnership will enhance:

- Exchange of information
- Intelligence sharing
- Joint operations
- Response to emergency calls
- Assistance to private security personnel in areas they lack authority to deal with problems independently; such as dealing with disorder, breaches of peace, knives and firearms cases.

The law allows the police to establish both business and professional relationships with the private sector and underwrite activities of the private security personnel in public policing functions. Private security personnel must take direct instructions from their employers and not from the public police.

Regulation of the Private Security industry

Regulation is a concept of management in accordance with rules, guidance and directions. It is a means of ensuring accountability.

Regulatory Functions:

- Licensing of security personnel and approving security companies
- Continuous review of the private security industry
- Monitoring activities and effectiveness of those working in the private security industry
- Carrying out inspections
- Setting and approving standards of conduct, training and supervision within the industry
- Making recommendations to improve standards

Regulatory object will usually aim to:

- Improve skills
- Raise professionalism
- Reduce Criminality
- Enhance public trust in those providing security services.

Security personnel are expected to be:

- Fit
- Proper persons
- Properly trained for the job

Security personnel are required to provide:

- Proof of Identity - A photo ID and two forms of proof of address
- Proof of Competence – obtain a nationally recognized qualification
- Criminality Check – Applicants background checks carried out to ensure that any recent offences and convictions have been disclosed.

Qualities expected of security personnel

Security personnel occupy professional positions and as such the public have high expectations of attitude and conduct of security personnel.

Qualities expected of security personnel include, but not limited to:	
Courteous	– must show consideration towards others
Alert	– Alertness in security is not just physical personnel should also be mentally responsive to vigilance
Tactful	– must think about how to act or speak without unnecessarily offending another.
Co-operative	– identify a common goal or mutual benefit with customers and employers.
Honest	– Security personnel work in a position of trust and therefore are expected to be honest.

Other qualities expected of security personnel are:

- Approachable
- dedicated
- Trustworthy
- Hospitable
- Inquisitive
- Effective
- Fair

Chapter 1

Community Policing

Security Infrastructure

Fig 3 Fencing and signages are territorial markings and provide surveillance opportunities. They indicate that the area is controlled

The starting point of a security plan is to identification targets, the associated risks and the steps to either remove the target from the risks or reduce the risks or both. This basic plan can be presented in documents such as policies, procedures and guidelines. The first step for a new security manager is to identify these documents and implement them with a view to increasing the risk of apprehension.

The situational approach to these plans must be to diminish the perception of certainty of success by a potential offender and enhance the risk of getting caught. Not every criminal would perceive the danger of getting caught. For this reason, there would have to be physical access control (barriers to stop unauthorised access or egress) to prevent unwanted persons from entering or leaving an area unless permitted. The correct implementation of these plans manifests as 'security' and it is what brings about the feeling of safety in individuals.

The feeling of safety is reassured through maintaining physical presence and routine patrols. From the offender's perspective, patrolling enhances the feeling (perception) of risk of getting caught. The perception of the risk of getting caught is the psychological deterrent of most crimes and other unacceptable behaviours. These concepts are the underlying foundation or basic framework through which security is provided and supported. These organisational policies, procedures, standards and guidelines forming the basic framework are referred to as 'security infrastructures'.

So, security means 'safety'. 'Safety' is a condition of mind. The condition is brought about by the (security) protection afforded to a given place at a time. The perception of protection is subjective and so varies from person to person. To address problems of safety, any security strategies must include both physical and psychological measures. The physical method is divided into two – the presence of a security personnel also known as 'manned guarding' and the 'physical guarding' which covers the use of physical barriers such as gates, grills, turnstiles, doors and so on. How the territory and its design, including signs interact with the manned guards and physical guards is what provides reassurance. This reassurance in an individual is regarded as the 'feeling of safety'. It is this feeling of safety that encourages protective behaviour from residents of a community. It enables individuals to claim ownership of their territory and control it. It improves crime reporting and helps victims to come forward to tell their stories.

Territoriality, access control and natural surveillance

Newman, (1972) used territoriality as the foundation for his theory of defensible space, encouraging residents to claim ownership of their surroundings and to spot and challenge strangers. Territoriality is the design of 'spaces and places' in a way that occupants feel responsible to defend and control the space whether they own it or not, (Schneider 2006:97). It involves using design to induce the feeling that the space belongs to the citizens and at the same time increases the perception that the citizens will intervene in a crime event, (Parnby, 2007:74). Apart from the obvious use of barriers and fences to mark territories, Newman, (1972: 3-9) also highlighted the ability of symbolic barriers like

Fig 4 Design facilitates natural surveillance & access control. Impression of a controlled territory

signage, colour, paving and surface changes to improve natural surveillance and convey the message that a place is not public and might be under watch.

Schneider, (2006:97) describes natural surveillance as the 'capacity of the physical environment to provide surveillance opportunities for residents', and in the case of commercial premises therefore; employees and passers-by should be able to see what is happening within a controlled space inside or outside. A space is not controlled unless access to that space is restricted. This is known as 'access control'.

Access control is the restriction of access to and from places; usually by creating a boundary between public and private spaces through physical means such as gates, grills, fences, paving, floor lighting. It can also be achieved by psychological means such as signage and environmental design. In any case, its aim is to deny access to at-risk targets and create a perception of risk of getting caught, (Crowe, 2000:36). It is an opportunity reduction measure aimed at increasing the perception of 'difficulty' by making the targets hard to reach and increasing the risk of apprehension, (Crawford 2007, as cited in Department of Criminology, 2009/2010).

The more difficult it is to attack a target the longer it will take the 'rational choice' offender to plan an attack. The perceived difficulty will also deter the offender. So, the situational challenge to security experts is to identify how to, not only create the perception of difficulty around a target but also to harden the target and make it difficult to attack.
Crowe, (2000) asserts that a design facilitating access control and natural surveillance would enhance the perception of 'difficulty' in terms of increasing the risk of apprehension.

This implies that an unused space will most likely lack the interaction with natural surveillance and access control. In rural communities, there may be more unused spaces than in urban communities. It may be argued that the closer the rural community is situated to the urban areas the more likely it will experience crime. This is because crime prevention interventions in urban areas are likely to displace crime to neighbouring vulnerable communities, due to availability of unused spaces. Routine patrol is one way of dealing with problems of unused spaces.

The holistic approach should be to protect the territorial 'space' with little or no emphasis on motivations for crime or who may be likely to commit it. It means that control measures should focus on the territory and the crime itself. However, understanding who may be likely to commit a crime will assist in understanding and investigating the crime itself. The principles to be derived from territoriality can be employed in the advisory and other security strategies as part of a holistic approach.

Victim Support Strategy

This requires identifying crime victims and supporting them to help them get through their ordeal. Victim support is needed to help the police understand specific crimes and criminal behaviour. With this understanding, it will be easy to prevent or investigate crimes. Further advantage of victim support is that it would improve community and police relationship.

The Advisory Strategy

In addition to 'victim support', police partnership building can be initiated through police advisory services to vulnerable persons, organisation, owners of property, controllers of territories or communities or the micro-security wards about the security risks faced in their communities (territories). In this way, a common policing goal can be identified for safer community and neighbourhoods. Working together towards this common goal is called police-community partnership.

The partnership may comprise of community representatives made up of; residents representatives, local business leaders, priests, pastors, local imams, councillors, independent people, the local police and local vigilante representatives. This partnership is expected to create the perception of territorial control. The situational impact on potential offenders is the perception that someone would report them and that eventually they would be caught. If this perception is achieved in more of the criminals, crime will stabilise in the area as less people make decision to join crime. Others may have to change the type of crime they commit or move elsewhere. This type of change is known as 'crime displacement'.

Policing Crime Hotspots

'Crime hotspot' is an area with a particularly high incidence of crime. Policing resources have not increased with increase in population and private property ownership. The situation is worse in developing economies that have yet to embrace private security and blend with the overall policing strategy.

In Nigeria for example, according to a former Information Minister, Professor Jerry Gana in his speech at the National Dialogue on "Effective Leadership and Good Governance", (2012), Nigeria as a nation has less than 500,000 police officers with a population of more than 180 million inhabitants. Comparatively, in Europe and other advanced economies the private security industry has blossomed to partner with the public police to meet the demand for security by occupying spaces that are difficult to reach by the public police.

The Internal/External Security Continuum in Europe (2009), citing De Waard (1999) estimated the number of security personnel in Europe to be around 592,050 in a population of 369 million people; representing 160 private security agents per 100,000 population in Europe. Overall in Europe, public police personnel are estimated to outnumber private police agents in a ratio of 2:1, which may vary from country to country. According to Internal/External Security Continuum in Europe (2009), in Britain for example the number of private security agents as at 2008 is 150,000; representing 251 private security agents per 100,000 of the population while that of the public police is 164,154; representing 275 per 100,000 of the population.

Compared to 1999 study for Britain, the number of private security agents was estimated to be around 160,000; representing 275 private security agents to 100,000 inhabitants, while the public police agents in the same year were estimated to be around 185,156; representing 318 public police personnel per 100,000 inhabitants. This figure shows a decrease in the number of public police agents between 1999 and 2008 and an increase in the number of private security agents in the same period. Another observation from these figures is the near equal number of private security agents and public police agents. Overall, this figure represents a disproportionate increase in the number of inhabitants requiring the services of the private and public police agents in the same period in Britain.

An increase in the level of civilisation (together with sophisticated modern technologies) has led to proactive and intelligence-led policing (Walsh and Conway, 2011). In a capitalist economy driven by the private sector, police funding has not increased in most developing economies to meet these new challenges for policing in the 21st century. That is why in Britain and America, private security has blossomed to fill the gaps and forge policing partnership with the public police. Thus, the private security industries in Europe and America have increased and in Britain the industry employs over 150 thousand personnel.

So, for this reason, it may be necessary for policing to adopt a scientific approach by focusing interventions in areas that experience most problems. In this way, it is possible to direct police patrols to those areas. Focusing crime prevention efforts on crime places would efficiently reduce crime. The mapping of crime and effective use of private security would assist policing priorities so that resources could be focused in areas where they are most needed.

Chapter 2

Access Control and Patrol

Fig5 Temporary physical Barriers to control access

This is a practical approach to managing security risks in buildings, offices, shops, car parks and so on. Unlike the "rational choice theory" the "routine activity theory" concentrates on preventing the criminal event and therefore protects the target, regardless of the kind of the potential offender. It assumes anybody to be a potential offender and the target can be attacked by anyone provided there is opportunity to do so. In the case of retail theft, resale value is key reason for attack.

Thus, items that fit CRAVED definition – Concealable, Removable, Available, Valuable, Enjoyable, and Disposable are predictably 'hot items' (Clarke, 1999) and vulnerable to offender's routine activities.

Rational choice theory assumes that physical and environmental factors play a significant role in the offender's choice of target. The offenders take into account the risk of apprehension in a quasi-cost-benefit assessment of the target. The presence of physical and psychological boundary fences and a capable guardian provide protection against 'routine activity' and 'rational choice' offenders.

Static and patrol means that the security personnel is located at a particular post or station (static) and expected to physically carryout checks at certain (patrol) locations within the assignment.

Assignment simply means the allocation of job or task to someone. In static and patrol duties, the area within which you are expected to carry out those tasks is also regarded as an 'assignment'. So 'assignment' is better understood as the allocation of duties to be performed in a given area or premises. Information is required by the security personnel on how to carry their duties effectively on the assignment. This is known as the 'assignment instruction'.

The assignment instructions cover the full operational instructions for the effective security of the client's/customer's premises. The document should be readily available to the relevant personnel whilst on duty. It is the security officer's responsibility to familiarise themselves with these instructions.

Assignment instructions are written by the company and agreed with the customer (client) for the following reasons:

- It can serve as evidence of agreement between the security company and the client on how the job should be carried out.
- The information enables the security personnel to understand and carry out their duties effectively
- It forms part of the contract between the security company and the client who usually is the owner of the assignment.

The personnel may be required to sign that they have read, understood and will follow the assignment instructions. Assignment instructions are restricted document. Unauthorised persons are not allowed access to the assignment instructions manual. Only authorised alterations and amendments are permitted.

Types of assignment

- Industrial
- Retail
- Maritime
- Aviation

Security personnel may be engaged at varying locations on short notice or temporary assignment. This can be due to operational requirements. It can also assist in removing the temptation to steal or commit other crimes. All assignments are different. For effective operation, it is essential for security personnel to have a clear understanding of the layout of the premises and knowledge of the local vicinity in which they are employed.

Confidentiality

A security officer has access to privileged information:

Examples:

- What is on site
- What security procedures exist, alarm codes, etc

If approached for information, what should the security officer do?

- Report to manager or keeper
- Make a note on your pocket book
- Describe the person
- Explain the circumstance in which the request was made
- Conspiracy charges could be brought if approaches are not reported

How might security personnel be approached?

- The person seeking information may pose as a colleague, manager or friend or relative of any authorised person
- May engage personnel in conversation about the personnel's job/task

Who should receive confidential information?

- control room personnel
- colleagues on duty only if they are sharing a task (ie have common duty objective in a given assignment)

Who should NOT receive confidential information?

- customers,
- family members
- friends
- other persons not specifically authorised to receive it

Access Control

Fig 5c

Fig 5d

Access control is defined as the prevention of unauthorised access or egress by persons or vehicles to premises and property. In security terms, the word 'access' means 'entry' and 'egress' means exit. In other to establish security in a given place and time, access and egress must be present and controlled. The word 'control' in this context means that entry or exit is prevented unless authorised. Basically, when personnel are on duty at premises, entry and exit to that premises are automatically prevented unless the person intending to gain access can show that they are authorised to do so.

Purpose of access control

- Safety
- Security

Safety: is of psychological importance. It is a mere perception by an outside or an internal observer. It should be looked at from two perspectives. The first perspective is that of the personnel in charge of security on that premises. Basically, the personnel will not feel safe if he does not know who is on the premises and whether they have the correct authorisation to be there. That is one of the reasons why the initial patrol is very important.

On the other hand, from the customer's perspective feeling of safety is reassured through physical patrols and customer care. So, the customer's safety perception depends on what they see the personnel do. It also depends on everything else they can see on the premises including the number of personnel, their alertness and fitness. It also includes what visible equipment the personnel have for the job. This includes, communication equipment, gates, touch and so on. All of this together provides some reassurance (safety) to customers and members of the public.

Security: the physical measures in place that have the capability to deal with a threat in a given space. In today's world security is a risk management practice intended to not only prevent crime but to also deal with its aftermaths. For example, security today should be able to prevent terror attacks and deal with any crisis resulting from it. The basics are to follow simple housekeeping, health and safety rules and procedures. The visible implementation of these rules and procedures aimed at addressing risks and concerns gives rise to 'security'.

The point of security is primarily to deter crime and unacceptable behaviours by increasing the perception of risk of getting caught.

This is achieved through:

1. Manned Service (presence of personnel)
2. Systems (electronic equipment; CCTV, scanners)
3. Physical Security (gates, barriers, shutters etc)

Good 'security' requires at least two of the above to be effective and support the objectives of 'access control'.

Access Control Areas

Access control is usually carried out at the most vulnerable areas of the premises, such as:

- Reception
- Gated houses
- Secure storage areas
- Important areas of the site

Persons subject to access control:

- Employees
- Visitors
- Contractors
- Cleaners
- Maintenance staff
- Delivery / courier personnel
- Visitors from Statutory Agencies
- everybody

Main features of access control

- Physical barriers – fencing, gates, grills shutters and ramps
- Signage – no access sign
- Presence of a capable guardian
- Mechanical systems – such as locks
- Electronic systems – such as electronic keypads, swipe cards, fob keys
- Biometric systems – finger print

Visitors log book

- Used log names of visitors and the purpose of their visit and date/time of access/egress
- It also indicates that a security 'pass' has been issued to the individual
- There may be separate logs for delivery personnel
- There may also be separate logs for engineers

Example of content of visitors' log book

- Date
- Visitor's name
- Visitors organisation
- Purpose of visit
- Person inviting and any letter of invitation
- Pass number issued

- Officer's signature
- Time pass returned
- Time of departure – should be the same as 'time pass returned'

Patrolling

Fig.5a Can you spot a terrrist or other potential offender

By checking identified vulnerable areas patrols serve to protect life, property and premises. It is during patrols that personnel may come across a burst water pipe or an exposed electricity cable and other hazards then take steps to prevent losses and wastes. It is also intended as physical a deterrent which is primarily achieved by way of maintaining physical presence at an assignment.

Assignment instructions manual should provide details of patrols requirements on a given site (assignment). The company's policy and procedures document may state general requirements for patrols. However, assignment instructions are specific to the site requirements.

Basic contents of the assignment instructions regarding patrols

- How many times during a shift he/she will patrol
- Patrol routes and times
- Routine duties to be performed during patrols
- Special duties for the shift
- What hazards may be encountered
- Emergency isolation points for emergency services (eg where to cut off supplies like electricity, water, gas etc)
- Incidents or occurrences from the previous shift
- Location of emergency equipment
- Location of telephones
- Emergency procedures
- Contact numbers (eg police, ambulance)
- Entry and exit points
- High profile areas (areas that may attract more wanted or unwanted interests or attention
- High risk areas (eg where incidents are more likely to occur)

How to meet these requirements are amenable to modifications by individual personnel as may be authorised in the assignment instructions or line managers or through own initiative.

What could affect the way some personnel may carry out a patrol?

- Handover notes from the off-going personnel
- Verbal information received from the personnel or any person
- Information from the control room
- Occurrences in and around the assignment

Types of patrol

Patrols may be required to take place inside or outside of the premises. This will depend on the assignment instructions. Patrols may be inside offices, factories, outside such premises' perimeter. Usually, in occupied business premises patrols take place inside (internal) and outside (external) of the premises at periods of little or no business activity.

There are four different types of patrols

- First or initial patrol
- Interim patrol
- Snap patrol
- Last patrol or final patrol

First patrol

- the first patrol is expected to take longer than subsequent patrols during a shift
- another name for first patrol is 'lockdown' patrol
- 'lockdown' because usually undertaken when business is closing activities for the day

This is the most important patrol because it:

- Helps set how subsequent patrols may be undertaken during the shift by being comprehensive
- Ensures the security officer's safety and the safety of the premises
- Allows the security officer to easily notice changes on subsequent patrols during the shift.

Interim patrols

These are patrols other than the last patrol. They are undertaken between the first and last patrols

Assignment instructions document will state:

- How many interim patrols must be completed during a shift
- How long they should be
- Regular or random times (altering frequency of patrols)
- What routes should be covered

Snap patrols

These are 'quick-check' patrols

Usually carried out at:

- high risk areas
- areas where a weakness has been discovered by the security officer, e.g. faulty exterior lighting, faulty camera system or alarm system failure
- doors or gates that cannot be locked

Last patrol

- the last or final patrol carried out on a shift
- also known as 'unlocking patrol'.
- usually carried out just before premises are opened up for the day's activities
- the final check before handing over to the next shift.

Patrol equipment

Equipment you may need for patrols

- Torch
- Keys and/or swipe card
- Pocketbook
- black ballpoint pen (ink can run if wet and blue ink is difficult to photocopy)
- Radio/mobile telephone
- Landline phones
- Pager
- High visibility clothing, if carrying out external patrols e.g. delivery bays
- Clocking device

Clocking device

It is also called 'diester'. It is hand-held electronic equipment which records each time the device makes contact with a point. The point is usually metal studs that come with the device, and then fixed firmly on a door, wall or any immovable object. These points are known as clocking points. It works like a bar-code reader

Fig 5b Patrol clocking point and its hand-held clocking device-diester

What is the need for clocking?

- Records time that each point was "swiped" or "clocked"
- Provides a time and date record that the security officer has been to each point
- Proves to the customer that the security officer is following the contract
- Provides a record of the last time the assignment was fully secure
- In the case of an incident, narrows down the time within which the incident occurred

Location of clocking points

Clocking points are usually situated at:

- Hazardous areas

- Location of valuable stock/equipment
- Other important areas around site

Steps before starting a patrol

Ensure the safety of the premises by following Fire and Health & Safety guidelines:

- Turn off any electrical appliances
- Put out cigarettes
- Check any equipment is in working order (Patrol Clocks, Torch etc)
- Carry out a test call to ensure the radio's correct operation
- If available heck CCTV to ensure its correct operation and position
- Inform the Control room or colleagues of the patrol
- Log the start time of the patrol in the occurrence book and pocket note book
- Lock the security base area
- Ensure that you know which areas are alarmed, and how to set any that need setting.

During the patrol

Internal Patrols

-   for security of life, contents and internal areas of buildings

What to check

- All internal areas as instructed
- Internal windows and doors
- That there are no fire hazards
- That any fire extinguishers are charged and ready for use
- That there is no slip, trip or fall hazards
- Surveillance equipment (like CCTV to ensure operation)
- Any machinery/equipment left running unnecessarily (apart from computers or faxes)
- The alarm status (active or disabled?)

External Patrols

-   for security of life and property with the perimeter or boundaries of assignment

What to check

- Doors and windows
- Ensure exterior lights are working
- Look for signs of intrusion
- For suspicious vehicles
- For breaches of Fire and Health and safety regulations (slip, trip and fall Hazards)
- For security of fences or boundaries and the perimeter

Action to take on patrols

- Clock all points
- Carry out checks; not just walk through
- Use pocketbooks to record anything unusual, suspicious, or hazardous

At the end of patrols

- On return to base, ensure that any required calls to control room are made, and write reports where necessary
- Inform control room and/or colleagues of the completion of the patrol
- Download the record on the patrol clock if used
- Record any findings in the occurrence book and, if necessary, complete the appropriate reports
- Continue with CCTV patrols, if available

What to do if there has been security breach on site

- Ensure your own safety and then follow the procedure defined in the assignment instructions and/or Policy and Procedures
- inform the management team and control room as soon as possible
- Preserve the evidence and secure the area
- Re-establish site security as soon as possible by first ensuring robust access control procedure is implemented immediately

Chapter 3

Electronic Security Systems

Principles of electronic systems

Detection:	What the equipment is programmed to sense
Control:	the internal processing of what has been detected and to do with the information
Action:	passing the information to human

Fig.6a RFID on contactless credit cards

Radio Frequency Identification (RFID) tags work in a similar way to Electronic Article Surveillance (EAS). It transmits signals using radio frequency. The tagged item emits radio signal. Attached to the security gate is the receiver. As the tagged item approaches and receiving signal it sounds alarm alerting everybody about the tagged item which should not near the security gate.

Electronic Article surveillance (EAS)

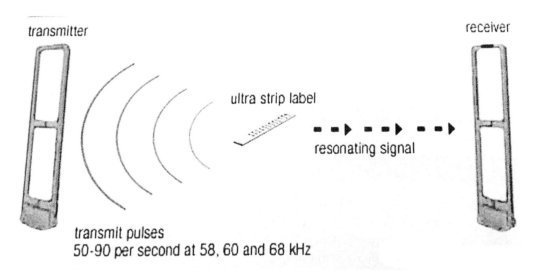

Fig 6 Electronic Article surveillance and how it works on tag or ultra strip label in shops

- Used by retail shops to tag high risk goods to prevent theft
- Tags are only removable by shop assistants
- If not removed, will set off alarm at exit/security gates

Fire alarms

Fig 7 Fire Alarm Testing

- Detect smoke or heat or both
- Process this
- Performs the 'action' by sounding alarm
- Can be linked to activate other things; like opening of fire doors and calling fire fighters
- When a system works together with other actions it is called an 'integrated system'.

CCTV

Fig 8 CCTV

- Stands for Closed Circuit Television
- An electronic surveillance equipment
- Receives images by way of data or signal
- This is then processed within the equipment
- The signal when processed becomes recognisable through a monitor or other device with screen
- Most effective crime prevention tool in shops, car parks and other enclosed areas
- Wired or wireless link to recorder and screen/monitor

CCTV Components

- Keyboards

- Cameras

- Monitor

- DVR recorder (digital)

- CVR recorder (analogue)

- Can be integrated to work with burglar/intruder alarms

Fig 8a

Operator controls and indicators

Fire Alarm panel - on activation, that is, on receiving information from the detectors

- Red light – means there is fire

- Yellow or amber light – means there is something else; possibly a fault

- Green light – means all is normal

- A small screen indicating location of source of information/danger

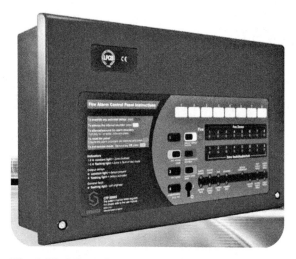

Fig 9 Mini fire alarm control panel 2 zones

Intruder alarm panels work in a similar way.

Fig 10 Intruder Alarm panel

Other things the control panel can do with the information from detector

- Message to security personnel, possibly on a pager

- Message to emergency services

- Activating CCTV cameras if they are linked to it

False Alarms

False alarms are erroneous reports produced by a system causing undue panic and security and emergency personnel to attend unnecessarily.

Impact of false alarms

- Can cause the system to be unreliable
- Can cause complacency in staff and visitors
- Can cause delays in response times
- Can be disruptive

Possible causes of false alarm

- Bad installation
- Extreme temperatures for heat detectors
- Wrong user operation
- Faulty equipment

How to prevent false alarms

- Regular maintenance checks
- Repair faults immediately
- Operators must be trained on how to operate it
- Any work on the system must be carried out by suitably qualified technicians

Response to Activation

Initial response

- Think of what instructions you were given regarding alarm activation. This applies to all electronic systems including metal detectors and other similar devices
- Then physically inspect the panel or device for indication lights or colours

Secondary response

- Proceed to investigate the subject or source of activation if authorised to do so in the assignment instructions
- Call for assistance

Record keeping

- Time and date of activation
- Location of activation
- Result of investigation
- Action taken

Chapter 4

Providing Security in the Hospitality Industry

The greatest challenge to any security personnel is how to blend security objectives with the business interests of their employer. There is no right or wrong approach; but any good Doorkeeper would adopt a customer focused approach to this problem.

Who are Doorkeepers?

Fig.11. Bodyguard

Doorkeepers perform manned guarding duties in hospitality premises, such as:

- Bars
- Restaurants
- Nightclubs
- Hotels
- Stadia
- Other outdoor events.

Primary roles of a Doorkeeper are:

- To decide who is suitable to be allowed onto licensed premises
- Search customers
- Maintain order and public safety
- Deal with overcrowding
- Help customers
- Provide trust and support to customers
- Provide security without spoiling customers' enjoyments
- Carryout orderly evacuations
- Opening and closing door at start and finish of events respectively

Remember that a Doorkeeper must prioritise these roles in the following order:

- Protection of life
- Protection of property and Premises
- Prevention of loss and waste
- Prevention and deterrence of crime

Control of Doors (points of entry)

Doorkeepers use their judgement to make decisions as to who may be allowed inside the venue. A Doorkeeper under the influence of drugs or alcohol is likely the get this decision wrong and create unsafe environment for themselves and other customers. This is why Doorkeepers must avoid alcohol and intoxicating substances.

Why would behaviour of a Doorkeeper at point of entry (PoE) affect safety of the entire venue?

This is because Doorkeepers decide who is suitable and what is suitable to be allowed inside the venue. Colleagues working inside are likely to rely on the decisions made by the Doorkeeper at points of entry. Unsuitable persons or items are likely to cause disruptions in the venue thereby requiring the attendance of other door staff in extreme cases. This can cause chaos and disturbance and the venue may need to be closed down by the police in order to deal with a problem in this scale.

Therefore, the job of door supervision is carried out at the 'doors' irrespective of where in the venue other personnel are located.

Admission of Suitable Persons and Objects

A Doorkeeper may refuse entry to the following unsuitable persons:

- Persons under the influence of alcohol or drugs
- Persons under age

- Troublemakers
- Persons already banned
- Persons not complying with any dress code in force

Unsuitable Items

- Knives and sharps
- Alcohol
- Any liquid
- Any weapon
- Any work tools
- Pepper spray
- CS gas
- Firearm

Reasons a Doorkeeper May Request a Customer to Leave

There is no guarantee that a customer that was assessed as suitable at the door would remain suitable throughout the event. At any time, a Doorkeeper can withdraw their permission to remain on the premises for the following reasons:

- Customer becomes drunk
- Customer becomes disorderly
- Customer breaks criminal law
- Customer spoils comfortable enjoyment of another
- Customer breaches health and safety rules
- Customer breaches any house rules
- Customer is seen with an unsuitable item

How may alcohol or drugs affect security of a venue?

The biggest challenge to policing is drunk or disorderly behaviour. It is not all disorderly behaviour that results from alcohol or drugs. However, disorderly behaviour in an alcohol venue is more likely to result from excessive alcohol consumption or drugs misuse.

Under the influence of alcohol or drugs, most people lose inhibition and become less worried about their environment. In some people, this can lead to disorderly or unacceptable behaviour. It therefore becomes difficult for people to maintain protective behaviour if they are drunk or disorderly or under the influence of drugs or alcohol. The environment becomes destabilised, thereby creating opportunity for other crimes to take place. The types of crime to be expected are 'violent crimes'.

Crimes

Majority of violent crimes require no prior planning or thought and the offender has little or no time to worry about any potential consequences. In around nightclubs or bars/pubs these crimes are more likely to result from influence of alcohol or drug.

Examples of crimes Doorkeepers may come across

Doorkeepers are more likely to come across crimes related to alcohol or drugs, such as:

- Criminal Damage
- Assault
- Breach of Peace
- Public order offences

The following offences RARELY occur in alcohol venues:

- Theft
- Fraud
- Robbery

To prevent these offences, Doorkeepers must continually observe all customers on the premises and monitor behaviours in order to assist customers and determine those unsuitable. Doorkeepers must play a lead role each time a customer requires help or support when injured or under the influence of drugs or alcohol. This will not only ensure that the Doorkeeper continues to meet their objective to protect life; but also, to prevent crime against those who may take advantage of the injured or vulnerable customer's condition to defraud them or rob or steal from them.

Doorkeeper - Customer Interaction

At the heart of any partnership relationship is 'trust'. Breakdown of 'trust' usually results in breakdown of partnership or relationship. When a Doorkeeper opens a door to let customers into the premises, the keeper lets customers in if they meet the conditions of entry and agree to abide by those conditions. This implies that the Doorkeeper has solicited the cooperation of the customer and made them aware of their responsibilities for adhering to venue's policies, maintaining order and public safety in the premises. At this point the Doorkeeper has entered a professional relationship with the customer and as a result, cooperation of the customer is needed for the Doorkeeper to achieve any of their objectives. Unlike in ordinary relationships where both parties have the responsibility of ensuring the relationship works, the Doorkeeper has the responsibility to ensure that the Doorkeeper – customer partnership or relationship works. This is done through the Doorkeeper exercising extra care to prevent break-down of customer trust. The Doorkeeper's image, attitude and behaviour are important to maintain the level of 'trust' required for the Doorkeepers sustain authority in the venue. 'Authority' is what the Doorkeeper requires to maintain order and public safety in a venue. The more the number of persons that feel there is order and public safety; the better the security of the premises and vice versa.

Role of trust and confidence in a team

Doorkeepers function better as a team. Each team must identify potential chal-lenges and problems in the venue; then decide on how best to approach each problem or potential problem. This approach has to be reviewed on shift-by-shift basis. A Doorkeeper can only be as good as their team. On the other hand, a team can only be as good as each member of the team wants it to be. At the centre of each team should be trust and confidence. Trust and confidence act as glue binding the team together. A 'together' team carries out particular task in a similar way at all time. This consis-tency then enhances customer's trust that Doorkeepers are following appropriate and approved procedures thereby minimising conflicts between Doorkeepers and between Doorkeepers and customers. As a result, an atmosphere of security is thereby created.

How does customer trust and confidence impact on security?

Any environment where customers have trust for Doorkeepers is not usually con-ducive for wrongdoers, rule breakers or criminals. This is because people tend to feel relaxed and safe in a comfortable environment. This may not happen if the Doorkeep-ers and those looking after the premises cannot be trusted. Trust can be achieved through honesty and good customer services such as helping customers and under-standing customers' viewpoints (empathy). Overall, this would enhance customers' feeling of safety and authority of the Doorkeeper to control and maintain order. If this is the case, customers are more likely to look after each other and the environment. This is what security psychologists refer to as, 'protective behaviour'. Therefore, a well looked after environment is a safe and protected environment.

The difference between safety and security

Safety is a subjective state of mind and can vary from person to person. This means that in individuals have different feelings as to whether their environment is safe. There may be different reasons for these individual feelings of safety. The reason(s) why an individual may feel safe or unsafe is referred to as 'security'.Therefore, one's ability to provide security in an environment depends on how safe people perceive that environment be. For example, the number of security guards patrolling the vicinity and customers' perception of their willingness to challenge or act upon suspicious behav-iours, together with availability of external back-up response and ease of offender's es-cape are factors that impact on ones feeling of safety in any environment.The greater the interaction of customers with these security measures, the higher the feeling of safety and the greater the perception of risks to a potential offender.

This perception of risk to offenders is one thing that deters offenders in that environment, provided the potential offender is a rational person. A child, a drug addict, an alcoholic and a person with mental disability may have difficulty perceiving risk or understanding legal consequences of their behaviours. Physical protection of targets such as use of padlocks, gates, secure safes, stab vests, are necessary to deal with offending risks presented by individuals in these groups.

Behavioural Standards

Reasons for Behavioural Standards

1. to increase public trust and confidence
2. to increase skills and professionalism and maintain national standards of behaviour for Doorkeepers

Maintaining safe environment, public trust and confidence are the most important tasks of a Doorkeeper. This is the main reason to set behavioural standards for Doorkeepers. Doorkeepers require no better tool than authority to be able to control their venues effectively. Without trust and confidence, Doorkeepers are likely to lose authority and the ability to fulfil their objectives.

Core Concepts in Security and Hospitality

In summary, the core security concepts are:	
• **Honesty**	Doorkeepers work in positions of <u>trust</u> and therefore are expected to be honest
• **Customer Care**	helping and looking after customers can enhance <u>trust</u>
• **Trust**	this is the glue that bonds the customer and security personnel
• **Safety**	customers may not feel safe if they do not <u>trust</u> the security
• **Authority**	of Doorkeeper is earned through honesty, helpfulness, <u>trust</u> and customer safety
• **Security**	is provided when customers can see and rely on the Doorkeeper's earned authority to control and maintain order; the strength of Doorkeepers back up response and ease of evacuation in emergency situations.

How can Doorkeepers Maintain Trust and Confidence in their Customers?

To achieve trust a Doorkeeper has to understand what the customer hopes to achieve. For most customers in leisure venues, they hope to have an enjoyable experience in a safe environment. In order for the Doorkeeper to succeed in getting the customer to cooperate and behave orderly, Doorkeepers must approach their tasks in a way that does not unnecessarily spoil the customer's enjoyment. This can be achieved through Doorkeepers positively looking out for customers to assist and following correct 'standards of behaviour'. By adhering to correct standards, it will be easier for Doorkeepers to control entry, maintain order; provide safe environment and carryout orderly evacuations.

Recommended Standards of Behaviour

Personal Appearance

A Doorkeeper should at all times:

- Wear clothing which is smart, presentable, easily identifies the individual as a Doorkeeper and is in accordance with the employer's guidelines
- Wear his/her licence (if required by regulators) on the outside of their clothing whilst on duty, displaying the photograph inside

Professional Attitude and Skills

A Doorkeeper should:

- Greet visitors to the licensed premises in a friendly and courteous manner
- Act fairly and not discriminate on the grounds of gender, sexual orientation, marital status, race, nationality, ethnicity, religion or beliefs, disability, or any other difference in individuals which is not relevant to the Doorkeeper's responsibility
- Carryout his/her duties in a professional and courteous manner with due regard and consideration to others
- Behave with personal integrity and understanding
- Use moderate language, which is not defamatory or abusive, when dealing with members of the public and colleagues
- Be fit to work and remain alert at all times
- Develop knowledge of local services and amenities appropriately

General Conduct

In carrying out his/her duty, a Doorkeeper should:

- Never solicit or accept any bribe or other consideration from any person

- Not drink alcohol or be under the influence alcohol or drugs
- Not display preferential treatment towards individuals
- Never abuse his/her position of authority
- Never carry any item which is or could be considered to be threatening
- Report all incidents to the management
- Co-operate fully with members of the police, Local Authority, Security Industry Authority, and other statutory agencies with an interest in the licensed premises or the way they are run

Organisation/Company Values and Standards

A Doorkeeper should:

- Adhere to the employing organisation/company standards
- Be perceptive of employing organisation/company culture and values
- Contribute to the goals and objectives of the employing organisation /company

(Security Industry Authority United Kingdom, 2005)

There are 3 types of behaviour which can be exhibited by different persons at different places and situations. These behaviours can be modified through training regardless of individual's personal values. They are:

- Assertive (positive)
- Aggressive (negative)
- Passive (negative)

Examples of Assertive Behaviour (Positive Behaviour)

- Making eye contact
- Being very clear with what you expect or want
- Ability to reach decisions
- Understanding other person's point of view
- Taking responsibility for decisions
- Being firm
- Being fair
- Relaxed posture and facial expression
- Able to speak clearly
- Eager to provide solution to problems
- Being polite, positive and professional
- Eye contact (without glaring)

Aggressive Behaviour (Negative Behaviour)

- Shouting
- Glaring (intense eye contact)
- Threatening behaviour
- Being sarcastic
- Interrupting others
- Blaming others
- Putting others down
- Stating opinions and treating them as facts

Passive Behaviour (Negative Behaviour)

- Non-eye contact
- Apologising even when not responsible or when not in a position to have changed the outcome
- Lengthy communication without going straight to the point
- Making promises or agreeing to do things you do not want to do or unable to do
- Backing down
- Speaking with a low and strained voice

Chapter 5

Communication and Customer Care Skills

Effective Communication Tools

Fig 12 Verbal Communication

- Be conscious of facial expressions and postures when interacting with customers
- Greet customers first, and then say your name and position.
- Remain open minded and do not get emotionally involved with customers, whether they are complaining about your work or making funny jokes.
- Ensure options are offered whenever a customer's exact needs cannot be met

Elements of Communication

Communication is sending and receiving messages. Messages can be in the form of written, verbal and non-verbal signals. Therefore **'message'** is at the centre of all communication with the **'sender'** and **'receiver'** at the extremes. The first thing every good communicator does is to compose the 'message' then consider the receiver **'understanding'** of the receiver. The sender then sends (**encodes**) the message in the simplest possible way for the receiver to understand. This would require the receiver to breakdown the received communication in order to (**decode**) the message in their own way. Because there is no standard way of encoding and decoding thoughts or message, **it is vital that both the sender and receiver check understanding with each other.**

Types of Communication

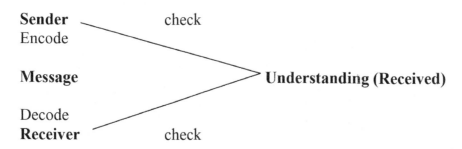

Sender — check
Encode

Message → Understanding (Received)

Decode
Receiver — check

Fig.13. Elements of communication

Verbal Communication: message is understood mainly from (7%) spoken words and (38%) tone. Examples of verbal communication are; radio, face-to-face and phone communication. During face-to-face communication, messages received from person other than spoken words are called non-verbal communication messages.

Non-verbal Communication: A persons positioning, what they are wearing, eye contact; all make up non-verbal communication. The difficulty for the sender with this type of communication is that messages derived from body language are not usually encoded as the sender may be unaware the communication. This means the receiver decodes body language communication; which may reflect negatively on the security personnel without the opportunity to check receiver's impression. This can result in an unfair situation as body language signals alone cannot be completely re-lied upon. For this reason, security personnel must be conscious of what body signals they may be sending.

Written Communication

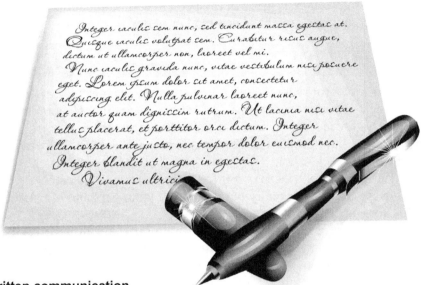

Fig 14 written communication

Time	Description of Activities
1636	I INFORMED STORE MANAGER CONCERNING FEMALE EMPLOYEE COMPLAINT IN REGARDS TO HOMELESS WMA. REFER TO DAR ENTRY AT 15:14 HOURS
1651	ALARM ON IN A 2002 DODGE I WENT TO INVESTIGATE. OWNER HAVING TROUBLE WITH SYSTEM.
1700	I AM PATROLLING IN FRONT OF STORE AND MONITORING ALL EXTERIOR ACTIVITY. ALL IS WELL AND SAFE AT THIS TIME
1710	STORE MANAGER SPEAKS WITH HOMELESS WMA CONCERNING COMPLAINT BY FEMALE EMPLOYEE
1802	LUNCH PAGE 3
1832	LUNCH OVER.
1840	I OBSERVE A BMA PAN HANDLING IN FRONT OF STORE. COMPLIES WITH REQUEST TO LEAVE
1900	I AM MONITORING ALL EXTERIOR ACTIVITY AND GUARDING BOTH FRONT ENTRANCES. ALL SEEMS NORMAL AND SAFE AT THIS TIME. LOT 'S FULL
1914	POLICE CAR PATROLLING IN FRONT OF THE STORE
1922	I AM CONFERRING WITH PLAZA SECURITY OFFICER

Fig 15 Daily Occurrence Report Example

Messages transmitted on paper or email, are examples of written communication. In the private security industry security personnel are expected to keep written records of occurrences and incidents in the workplace. They may also be required to write witness statements. One advantage of written communication is that content can be used a proof of work occurrence or incident and will help the writer give accurate accounts at a later date. One disadvantage is the lack of speed in communication. It is difficult to know if a written communication has been read or understood.

The following documents may be available to the security personnel:

- Search Registers – for recording findings and refusals during search
- Incident Logs – for brief recording of incidents' dates/times/ /actions taken
- Time Sheets – for recording start and finish times of shift
- Handover notes – for preparing messages to be passed on to the personnel taking over shift
- Daily Occurrence Book (DOB) – for recording all occurrences
- Key Register – Keys are usually tagged with ID numbers and registered in this book for easy retrieval
- Accident Books – for reporting accidents and injuries resulting from it
- Pocket Books – personal book for on-the-spot information taken immediately at location
- Incident Report – for detailed recording of incidents' dates/times/action taken/background information
- Statements – Usually written for incident's requiring police investigation

Difference between 'Occurrence' and 'Incident'

- Occurrence is known ordinary event which is part of security personnel's day-to-day activity, presenting no threat to life, property or business. Examples are taking over and handing over shifts, routine patrols, routine checks, phone or radio calls etc.
- Incident is a known or unknown occurrence disrupting security personnel's day-to-day activities and presenting threat to life, property or business. Examples are spillage, accidents, flood, fire, power failure. These are also considered emergences because immediate action is needed to deal with the problem.
- All incidents are occurrences; but NOT all occurrences are incidents.

Written communication must be:

- Legible
- In black pen

All corrections must be made by drawing a line through the word or sentence to be corrected. The correction must then be initialled.

Avoid:

- Use of pencil
- Use of correcting fluid
- Tearing pages
- Using pocket book as a personal diary

Importance of good communication skill in security

- Helps security personnel understand needs of customers
- Helps personnel to successfully negotiate with customers thereby minimizes need for use of force or police attendance on civil or trivial matters
- Raises security personnel's moral through understanding customers' needs and taking steps in advance to meet them in order to avoid conflict
- Helps in notifying customers of any changes in advance

Importance of good communication skill in a team

- Helps create a friendly environment
- Helps build rapport, trust and relationship with members of a team
- Creates open and supportive environment in order to encourage sharing of ideas amongst team members

Remember to be:

A - Accurate
B - Brief
C - Clear

Customer Service and Customer Care

The basic expectations of a customer are: greeting, eye contact, finding out what customer's needs are and satisfying those needs. These are basic skills we need in order to sell our services. Also, these are basic expectations of customers. Determination to meet these basic expectations is what we refer to as 'customer service'. Below these expectations would create a problematic situation giving rise to poor image of the organization and reduction in business.

However, the standard of service expected from security personnel is usually higher than the basic customer service. This is because security personnel occupy positions of trust and are more likely to control behaviours of people on their premises without impacting negatively on the business objectives of the service employer. In delivering this level of service expectation, greater 'customer care' is required to meet both the security and client's business objectives equally.

Customer care therefore means:

- Being professional with every customer
- Showing concern with customer's needs
- Being clear with customer about what service the can expect
- Looking after customers as you would wish to be looked after yourself
- Being helpful where possible, even if it is out of job description
- Use the customer's name if known
- Be polite, positive and professional
- Make eye contact when you greet the customer
- Explain your reasons when you have to say no to a customer's request
- Be approachable, show your interest in the customers' needs
- Always offer other alternatives ways to help solve customer's problems
- Avoid open criticism of your colleagues or company
- Smile
- EMPATHISE (understand customer's point of view even if you may not agree with it

Poor Customer Care includes

- Lack of good communication skills
- Lack of commitment and confidence
- Lack of positive attitude towards customers
- Lack of listening skills and inability to give feedback to customer
- Lack of training and inability to follow instructions
- Showing lack of concern
- Making jokes
- Ignoring or failing to acknowledge customers
- Appearing bored or impatient
- Failing to do what you have promised

The Steps to Follow for Good First Impressions

Firstly
- Initial good impression, such as smiling, greeting, eye contact and so on.
- This would show that you are ready and willing to help

Secondly
- The customer expects the security personnel to establish what the customer actually needs
- Then followed explaining to the customer how the security personnel intend to approach the request. This is necessary to ensure that the customer is directly involved in the solution from the beginning.
- Then proceed with the agreed approach to deal with the customer's request.

Finally
- Even if the outcome is not one expected by the customer, the approach is expected to leave a good impression of the security personnel and good impression of the security organization with the customer

Radio Communication
Introduction to Radio Systems and Procedures

Fig 16 Radio Commnication **Fig 17 Radio equipment & accessories**

There are different radio systems. Emergency services including the police may receive communication support from different radio systems. All radio equipment may have the same or similar features. What makes it a system is that each radio is part of a net or network managed or controlled centrally. Modern radios have the ability to be programmed using a computer. This allows the information management officer or controller to manage communication security and frequencies.

Radio Check procedure

- Set-up radio by loading battery component if not on charger
- Check antenna for damage
- Power on the radio (wait for a beep sound and amber light)
- Set the volume
- Rotate channel knob to select the right channel number (channels are usually pre-programmed on a computer and can be re-programmed if needed)
- A non-stop tone indicates that the radio has no pre-programmed channels (for some radio types)
- Check frequency setting
- Check for any communication security
- Check location
- Connect headset if available
- Make a test call
- Firmly press the push-to-talk (PTT) button and wait one second before speaking
- Release the PTT button to listen

The copying of one radio program to another is known as 'cloning'. Security personnel may not be expected to do this as they should receive pre-programmed radios.

Inter and Intra-Team Radios

These types of radios can be found in control rooms and are used for communicating to external agencies as well as internal teams. Local authority operated control rooms and similar agencies may have one channel pre-assigned by the police and other partners for inter-team communication. These channels can be assigned to more than one group; i.e. ambulance, fire and CCTV control rooms. For example, four radios can be cloned (programmed together with same channel receiving same signals) and used at the respective control rooms for inter-team communication. For external teams to join a net, they may require permission from a net controller or control room of the team they wish to contact.

Advantages of Radio Use

- It enables speedy communication
- It enables quick deployment of personnel; especially in events management
- It enables proper co-ordination of emergency and other responses
- It provides the quickest means to call for back-ups during patrols and conflict management
- It can be used to send other signals during close protection activities or door supervision in high risk venues

Radio Discipline

Opening up of net

Net opening is required to allow net controllers to give permission to join the net or team communication. Follow assignment instructions for the correct net opening procedure. For example:

- Each radio operating on the net is a station
- Each station must seek permission from net controller before joining the net
- Net Control Station must give permission to authenticate request from each station
- Only one station can speak at a time
- Must listen out before speaking to ensure that the radio frequency is clear
- Must not cut in on other transmissions, unless urgent
- Must leave a short pause at the end of each transmission
- Short pauses are also necessary to allow another operator with a more urgent message to cut in
- All calls must be answered immediately and in correct order; usually alpha betical order
- Speak clearly and slowly as your call may need to be written down by controller and other operators/stations

Example:

Net, this is Control, authenticate …... over
Control, this is Alpha B, I authenticate … over
Net, this is Alpha C, I authenticate …….over
Net, this is Alpha D, I authenticate …….over
Net, this is Control, out

In the above example, there is one controller coordinating activities of three team members; Alpha B, Alpha C and Alpha D. There are four radios (stations) in the net. The first person to speak; usually the controller, speaks to the net. The first person to respond - responds directly to the controller. Subsequent persons respond to the net in alphabetical order. Finally, the controller acknowledges by responding to the net and 'out'. 'Out' means no reply is necessary. The station is now open.

Anyone wishing to join the station later will have to follow a similar procedure.

For example:

Control, this is Alpha E reporting into net, over
Alpha E, this is Control, authenticate, over
Control, this is Alpha E, I authenticate, over
Alpha E, this is Control, I authenticate, over
Control, this is Alpha E, roger out
'Roger' means 'received last transmission satisfactorily'

Closing down of net

Net, this is control, close down, over
Control, this is Alpha B, authenticate, over
Net, this is control, I authenticate, over
Control, this is Alpha B, roger, out
Control, this is Alpha C, roger, out
Control, this is Alpha D, roger, out
Control, this is Alpha E, roger, out

It is easy to see that there is a slight difference between net opening up and net closing down procedures. In the 'opening up of the net' the Control said the last word and 'out'. In the 'closing down of the net' the last word was said by the last station to respond alphabetically. It was not necessary for the control to say the last word because by this time all the stations on the net have closed. There is no longer available station to receive communication from control until a new shift starts again.

Radio Checks or Check Calls

It is the responsibility of the Control Room Operators (CRO) to ensure that security personnel (radio operators) are alert on the net. Using a list of all security personnel operating a radio on the net, CRO's can tick names of those that have completed a radio check call. Assignment instructions should dictate how often radio check calls should be made from security personnel to CRO. However, in busy communication traffic, it might not be necessary to make check calls to CRO as they are already monitoring all communications. At less busy communication traffic, CROs should carryout radio check calls as follows:

Net, this is Control, Radio Check, over
Control, this is Alpha B, Roger, out

Again, all security personnel should respond in alphabetical order with 'Roger out'.

Advantages of Check Call

- Check calls ensure that all operators on the net are safe
- Check calls ensure that all operators on the net are alert

Lost Contact Drill

Control Room Operators (CROs) have the following options in the event that security personnel fail to respond to check call:

- Make mobile phone call
- Send text message to their mobile or pager
- In outdoor/event management or open field, contact nearest personnel to

make physical contact with the non-responsive personnel

- In corporate or indoor operation contact mobile patrol unit to make physical contact
- Report to operations manager
- Contact the police in an emergency situation

Table 1. Pro - Words

OVER	This is the end of my transmission to you and a response is necessary
RECEIVED or ROGER	Received and understood your last transmission satisfactorily
OUT	This is the end of my transmission to you and no reply is required or necessary
SAY AGAIN	Repeat your last transmission
WAIT	I have to pause for a few seconds
WAIT OUT	I have to pause for longer than a few seconds
STANDBY	reply immediately and is normally followed by an indication of time, e.g. WAIT one, meaning WAIT one minute
ETA	Estimated time of arrival
ETD	Estimated time of departure
AUTHENTICATE	Requested to say your password or code word to prove you are genuine
I AUTHENTICATE	I am responding to your request to prove I am genuine and here is my code word

Call Signs

- Call signs are needed to identify the sender and receiver
- Call signs are used to establish connection between a sender and a receiver. For example, 'Net, this is Control, Authenticate ……over'. The call sign here shows that the call is initiated by the 'Control' directed at the 'Net'.
- Call signs can be alphabets; A, B, C or Alpha B, Alpha C etc.
- Call signs can also be alphanumeric; A1, B1, C1 or Alpha A1, Alpha A2
- Response to calls directed to the net must follow alphabetical order
- If a station fails to answer, the next in order answers after a pause of 5 or more seconds as the assignment instructions may dictate
- If there are 2 stations with the same alphabets, for example; Alpha A1, Alpha A2, Alpha A1 should respond before Alpha A2 and so on.

Person's Description

Radio communication is a good example of verbal communication. Non-verbal communication (NVC), also known as body language is missing. Therefore, there is the potential that vital communication could be lost.

> ## To avoid misunderstandings or breakdown in communication, radio communicators must:
>
> - Speak slowly
> - Avoid using long sentences
> - Avoid using two words where one could do
> - Avoid non-work-related conversations
> - Pause between words

For example, when describing a person, the security personnel has to give brief description of incident the communication relates to, then give description of person(s) involved as follows:

- Height
- Gender
- Approximate age
- Ethnicity, race
- Hair colour and style
- Head wear
- Build/size/weight
- Upper clothing
- Lower clothing
- Footwear
- Other features (Scars, tattoos, badges or marks on clothing)
- Direction of travel

For Vehicle description, the following order must be followed:

- Make
- Colour
- Vehicle Registration number (VRN)
- Direction of travel

The Phonetic Alphabets

Phonetic Alphabets can be used for spellings to make sure the person listening does not confuse different letters that may have similar sound, like letters 'D' and 'B'. In the security industry only approved phonetic alphabets may be used; such as NATO phonetic alphabets below.

A	Alpha	J	Juliet	S	Sierra
B	Bravo	K	Kilo	T	Tango
C	Charlie	L	Lima	U	Uniform
D	Delta	M	Mike	V	Victor
E	Echo	N	November	W	Whisky
F	Foxtrot	O	Oscar	X	X-ray
G	Golf	P	Papa	Y	Yankee
H	Hotel	Q	Quebec	Z	Zulu
I	India	R	Romeo		

Communication must be (ABC):

- Accurate
- Brief, and
- Clear

Chapter 6

Awareness of the Law
in the Private Security Industry

Fig 18. The Law

Common Law

The 'common law' is the law, which has been created by judicial decisions, as opposed to 'statute law' which is created by legislation passed by parliament. Common Laws are also known as 'case laws' or 'precedents'. Common Laws are made by Judges.

Statute Laws

Statute laws are created by the legislature. Statute law can be passed to supersede a common law

The Civil Law

Civil Law Characteristics

- Deals disputes between citizens
- Case is usually brought by one person, group or organization against another organization or group or individual.
- Usually actions arise following disagreements
- The person or organization taking action is referred to as 'claimant'.
- The other part sued is referred to as 'defendant'.
- There is no power of arrest to the police or private security personnel

Areas of Civil Law

- Contracts (such as employment contracts)
- Divorce (family and custody issues)
- Torts and negligence (such as Health and safety law breaches)
- Property and land law (such as law of trespass)
- Trust and Equity
- Libel - written defamation of one's character that cannot be proven to be true
- Slander – verbal defamation of one's character that cannot be proven to be true

The areas of civil law most relevant to security personnel are:

- defamation
- Libel
- Slander
- Property and land laws

Libel

This is described as defamation by written words. Security personnel should avoid making allegations without describing the facts or evidence in support of such allegations. There must be reliable witnesses and/or CCTV/video footage to support any allegation the word 'suspect' or 'alleged' must be used throughout when describing a suspect.

Slander

This is defamation by oral communication of false or malicious statement or report injurious to a person's or organization's reputation. Security operatives must not make verbal statements to third parties unless they are authorized to do so in their assignment instructions. If authorized any statements must be factual and not opinion.

Compensation in Civil Cases

Restitution is the act of compensating for losses or making good or ensuring the claimant is placed where he/she would have been had the wrong not been committed. For example, if the claimant wins the defendant may be ordered:

- to refund money to claimant
- perform specific tasks such as, apologise to the claimant
- repeat performance of the failed obligation where this is practicable

The court may also award damages in certain circumstances. Damages are aimed at ensuring that the innocent party is placed where he should have been had the guilty party performed his obligation. This is usually the remedy for breach of agreement.

Property Laws

Trespass

Trespass is the act of being on another's property without permission from the owner or authorized person. Law of trespass is broken when the trespasser refuses to leave when requested to do so by the owner of the property or authorized persons such as security personnel.

How to deal with Trespass

As a civil matter, there is no power of arrest. Powers of private security operatives are limited to dealing with trespass on private lands. For example, private security personnel may be requested (in writing) by the police to prevent unauthorized access to police cordons in investigation scenes on public land or premises.

Steps to follow

- Ensure that the individual is actually trespassing and not lost or confused
- Inform them of the persons authorized to access the premises
- Politely ask them to leave
- Explain the reason for the request to leave
- If they refuse to leave, then they are certainly trespassing
- Warn them that reasonable force may be used, indicating that you would rather they leave peacefully
- Escort them from the premises
- There is no requirement for use of force, unless necessary
- Involve the police, if the situation does not resolve itself or if there is risk of injury to anyone involved, including members of the public
- Should the trespasser leave before police arrival, make a note in pocketbook of the incident, including direction of exit.
- Note a brief description of the individual, such as what they are wearing to ensure identification in case they attempt further entry.

The Criminal Law

Criminal laws prohibit behaviours harmful to the society, usually against people or property enforced by the police and within criminal courts. Punishment can include imprisonment and fines.

Unlike in civil offences, arrests can be made by the police in all cases of criminal offences. In certain circumstances, security personnel may be able to arrest a suspect of a criminal offence. Security personnel can arrest in circumstances where the crime committed is a serious one (indictable) and it is necessary to arrest the suspect.

Common Crimes

Assault

Assault is the threat of violence. For example, if a person threatens to cause injury to another person and intends to carry out that threat unless prevented; an assault has taken place even if there is no physical contact. If physical contact is made, an offence of battery can be suspected

Battery

Battery means that a person has intentionally or wilfully touched or made physical contact with another person without that other person's consent.

Assault and battery attract the same punishment. It is usually considered 'common assault if assault or battery results in no injury. However, if the other person suffers injury, the offence becomes more serious as explained below.

Types of Assault

Common Assault – Where assault has taken place; but there is no injury as a result.

Examples of Common Assault:

- Pushing
- Slapping

These incidents do not usually result in an injury.

Actual Bodily Harm (ABH) – Where any injuries sustained are minor and may not be life threatening or lead to any disability or require hospital treatment or any treatment for longer than 6 months. Common

Examples of Actual Bodily Harm:

- Black eye
- Minor scratches

Grievous Bodily Harm (GBH) – Where the injury is serious or life threatening.

Examples of Grievous Bodily Harm (GBH):

- Substantial amount of blood loss
- Permanent disablement
- Sustained or repeated attack on one victim
- Assault on vulnerable person

Theft

The offence is committed by a person who dishonestly appropriates property belonging to another with the intention of permanently depriving the other of it.

Key aspects of this law important to security personnel are:

- Dishonest appropriation – here appropriation means obtaining or removal. Evidence of dishonesty could be in the form of concealment of goods
- Intention to permanently deprive the owner – here the security personnel must be satisfied that the suspect have no reasonable excuse for removing or taking the good away. This could be that the suspect has left the shop or has the intention of doing so without paying for the good and at the same time has refused to pay for the good when reminded to do so

Robbery

The offence is committed by a person when he steals, and immediately before, or at the time of doing so, and in order to steal, uses force on any person or puts any person, or seeks to put any person, in fear of being then and there subjected to force.

Burglary

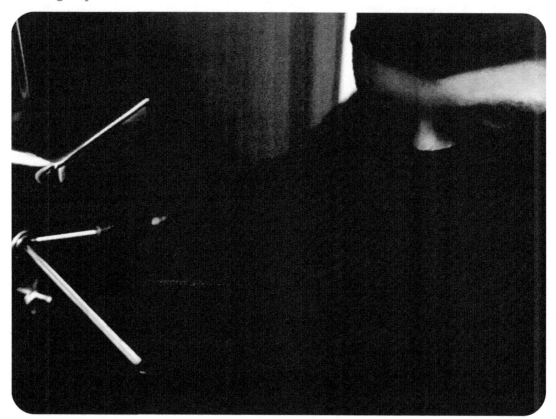

Fig 19 Burglary

The offence is committed by a person who enters a building, or part of a building, as a trespasser with intent to steal, inflict grievous bodily harm, rape or cause unlawful damage, or having entered as a trespasser, steals, inflicts, or attempts to inflict grievous bodily harm

Aggravated Burglary

The offence of aggravated burglary is committed when a person commits burglary and at the time has with him: any firearm, imitation firearm, any weapon of offence or any explosive.

Criminal Damage

Fig20 Criminal damage

Someone without lawful excuse destroys or damages property belonging to another, intending to damage or destroy the property or is reckless as to whether such property would be destroyed or damaged.

Other Criminal Offences Doorkeepers may come across

- Possession of a firearm
- Supply of drugs
- Possession of drugs
- Possession with intent to supply
- Possession of an offensive weapon
- Possession of bladed or sharply pointed articles
- Theft
- Fraud
- Robbery
- Murder
- Sexual offences
- Threat to damage
- Damage with intent to endanger life

Theft

It is theft if he dishonestly appropriates property belonging to another with the intention of permanently depriving the other of it…..' (OPSI archive).

Security personnel working in shops are more likely to come across theft incidents. Theft in retail shops is usually referred to as 'shoplifting' or 'shop-theft'.

Who is a shoplifter?

A shoplifter is described as one who comes into the shop during normal trading hours; while pretending to be a legitimate customer, steals from the owner.

The main problem for security managers when it comes to theft is that the law allows for opportunities for suspected offenders to make excuses, even after they have been caught. Going by this law a suspected shoplifter seen concealing an item in-store will not have committed theft as there is a chance that they might change their mind within the store. This often makes it difficult to prove that he/she had the 'intention to permanently deprive the other of it'.

It is also important to point that not all shoplifters conceal items before removing them from store. If arrested, they could easily argue that they simply forgot to pay. This is known as 'neutralising behaviour'.

What security personnel can do to prevent theft

Security personnel working in the private security industry have limited powers to deal with crime. However, they are better equipped to prevent crime than to deal with crime after it has been committed. When a crime is suspected to have already occurred, security personnel can work in partnership with the police by at first instance reporting the crime to the police.

If the offence relates to minor property theft or damage security personnel can utilise company's internal civil procedures to prevent the continuance of the offence as opposed to arrest. For example, security personnel may seek to recover the property from a suspect through negotiation if safe to do so.

On the other hand, security personnel can also arrest the suspect if they consider the offence to be serious. Theft may be deemed serious if the suspected thief refuses to cooperate with the personnel. In this case, the personnel can easily establish evidence of 'intention to deprive the owner' of the property. Even if it turns out eventually that the customer was not a thief, the personnel would have been right to arrest the person regardless of whether the arrest took place inside or outside the premises.

But to ensure the police would have a better chance of convicting the person of theft; it is recommended that any arrest takes place outside the premises if the personnel have reasonable belief that theft had occurred. There must be evidence of what had been stolen.

- Continuous surveillance to identify unusual behaviour (CCTV and/or foot patrol)
- Determine possible reason for unusual behaviour
- Check if something has been appropriated (taken)
- Check for dishonesty (concealment)
- Find out if the item belongs to another person (other shop)
- Find out if the customer has paid for the property or forgotten to pay
- Get the customer to pay for the property or recover the item
- Be polite, positive and professional

Once the property has been recovered it may never be known whether the intention was to deprive the owner of it unless the suspect confesses. It is not for the security personnel to enquire about the person's intention so long as the property has been recovered.

Breach of the Peace

Fig 21. Note the existing peaceful nature of this environment.

Breach of the peace takes place when an act or violence has been threatened or done which either harms a person or likely to cause harm, (UK Court of Appeal; R V Howell; 1982). Going by the Court of Appeal definition above, the key words in 'breach of the peace' are 'threats of violence'. In this case, anyone with reasonable and honest belief that another's behaviour is likely to be threatening or result in harm can carry out an arrest for breach of the peace. There is no need to show that violence or harm actually took place before a police officer or anyone can make an arrest. For example, 'any threat, disorder or disruption to the peace in public or private that results in violence or the threat of violence may constitute breach of the peace.

Though, trial usually takes place in magistrates' courts and proceedings are civil in nature, breach of the peace is not a criminal offence. However, there is a common law power of arrest to anyone including security personnel. However, arrest is usually and better carried out by the police.

In breach of the peace cases, any person can make a complaint to the magistrate, including the police. The police or people making the complaint are treated as complainants in the proceedings. Although the trial is civil in nature, the court must apply the criminal standard of proof. This means that the police most prove their case beyond reasonable doubt as opposed to the standard of proof in civil trial (balance of probability). The test of 'Balance of probability' means that the accused is more likely to be guilty (little doubt) than not. The test of 'Beyond reasonable doubt' means there is 'no doubt' at all that the accused is guilty.

If found guilty, the magistrates usually issue a 'binding over' order that requires the defendant to agree to be of good behaviour for a period of time set by the magistrate. For this reason, convictions would not be recorded and there will be no punishment.

What options are available to security personnel if breach of the peace is suspected?

- Firmly inform the person that their behaviour is unacceptable and that they should stop
- Request the person to leave the premises should they repeat
- Request the person to leave the premises should the personnel have reasonable belief that the person is likely to repeat the breach
- Seek assistance from colleague or police if there is imminent threat of harm or actual harm
- Make complaint to the magistrate
- There is also a common law power of arrest. Security personnel should not arrest unless there is no option or it is 'necessary' to arrest in order to stop the person inflicting harm or running away after such harm had been inflicted.

Use of Force

Arresting a person will almost certainly involve use of force as the person is no longer free to do anything without the approval of the security personnel carrying out the arrest. In reality, it is usually difficult to achieve cooperation of the suspect under arrest. This is because the arrested person is usually confined to a space and the psychological implication of this loss of liberty is the tendency for an arrested person to become violent; thereby resulting in inevitable use of force.

Common Law

A person may use such force as is reasonable in the circumstances for the purposes of:

- Self defence
- Defence of another person
- Defence of property

Fig 22 Fight is forbidden

In order for use of force to be legal, it must satisfy the following tests:

- Necessity (can you justify why you had to use force?)
- Reasonableness (Can a neutral person accept your justifications for use of force?)

A neutral person is any third party that has not taken side. This could be a passer-by or innocent bystanders. This test is applied in a court where a neutral jury will decide whether you have justified your actions and if the accept your justifications in the circumstance.

For example, it will be difficult for security personnel to justify striking a customer in the chest which has resulted in an injury following a slap on the security personnel by the customer. The test of 'necessity' here in terms of self-defence is whether the strike on the customer's chest was necessary to prevent the slap or any further imminent attack and if there were other options; including less forceful interventions available to the personnel in the circumstance to prevent the slap or a repeat. It is important to note that one of the options to be considered by security personnel in all circumstances is the option to remove self from the situation.

Relevant Articles of the Human Rights

Activity note - teachers and students may refer to relevant parts of the country's constitution in this area.

Qualified Rights – are rights which may be interfered with by state authorities in order to investigate or deal with crime

Absolute Rights – are rights that nobody can interfere with in any circumstance; for example, Article 6 - Right to a Fair Trial'

Basic Elements of Article 6

- Everyone is entitled to a fair and public hearing within a reasonable time by an independent and impartial tribunal established by law
- Judgment shall be pronounced publicly but the press and public may be excluded from all or part of the trial in the interests of morals, public order or national security in a democratic society
- Everyone charged with a criminal offence shall be presumed innocent until proved guilty according to law
- Everyone charged with a criminal offence has the following minimum rights:

(a) to be informed promptly, in a language which he understands and in detail, of the nature and cause of the accusation against him;

(b) to have adequate time and facilities for the preparation of his defence

(c) to defend himself in person or through legal assistance of his own choosing or, if he has not sufficient means to pay for legal assistance, to be given it free when the interests of justice so require;

(d) to examine or have examined witnesses against him and to obtain the attendance and examination of witnesses on his behalf under the same conditions as witnesses against him;

(e) to have the free assistance of an interpreter, if he cannot understand or speak the language used in court.

Other relevant Articles to Security Personnel

Article 2 – Right to life (absolute)
Article 3 – Prohibition of torture (absolute)
Article 4 – Prohibition of slavery and forced labour (absolute)
Article 5 – Right to liberty (qualified)
Article 6 – Right to fair trial (absolute)
Article 7 – No punishment without law (absolute)
Article 8 – Right to respect for private and family life (qualified)
Article 9 - Right to freedom of thought, conscience and religion (absolute)
Article 10 – Right to freedom of expression (qualified)
Article 11 – Right to freedom of assembly (qualified)
Article 14 – Prohibition of discrimination (qualified)

CHAPTER 7

Arrest

Fig 23 Only the state police can use hand restraint (Handcuffs)

'Arrest' is serious. It is defined as 'the taking away or depriving a person of his liberty'

Even where security personnel consider it necessary to arrest, it is only carried out as a last resort.

Reasons why arrest should be considered as a last resort:

- Allegations of assault can be made against the security personnel
- Allegations of false imprisonment can be made against the security personnel
- There is increased risk of harm to all involved
- Security personnel may be prosecuted for excessive use of force
- It could eventually result to loss of employment, loss of licence, fine or im prisonment with criminal records

Arrest Procedures

While the police have special powers the security personnel have ordinary powers and therefore have same powers of arrest as an ordinary citizen.

For a lawful arrest, the security personnel should tell the arrested person:

- Who he/she is
- That he/she is arresting them
- The reason the person is being arrested (e.g. suspicion of theft)
- why he/she believes the arrest is necessary
- call the police immediately

Responsibilities of security personnel following arrest

- Safety of the arrested person
- Observation of the arrested person
- duty of care
- medical assistance; for example, contacting the ambulance where needed

Duty of Care and Arrest

The keeper has legal duty of care following arrest. This is because an arrested person has lost their freedom and therefore not responsible for anything that happens to them whilst in custody. The Doorkeeper would be responsible if the person in their custody suffers harm which would not have been suffered had the person not been in custody; especially if the harm suffered results directly from the arrest or detention. Therefore, a Doorkeeper must ensure arrested persons are continually observed.

Other Reasons for Continual Observation of an arrested person

- To prevent escape
- To prevent disposal of evidence
- To prevent assault
- To prevent self-harm

Questioning of Suspects

Private security personnel have no power to question arrested suspect. However, private personnel can question anyone suspected of committing a criminal offence only for the purpose of establishing whether an arrest or police involvement is necessary.

In dangerous situations where weapon is involved or attack is ongoing security personnel must contact the police immediately.

- If there is conflict and weapon is involved – it may be necessary to arrest and call the police (take due consideration for your safety & others).
- If there is no conflict or disturbance, but there is weapon present or threat of weapon, – It may be necessary to begin negotiations for exit or removal and a written report completed, (take due consideration for your safety).
- If there is the presence of firearm, CS Gas; regardless of whether there is conflict – police should be contacted immediately, (take due consideration for your safety).

Power of Arrest

There is no power of arrest for private citizens or security personnel for summary offences. However, there is power of arrest for private citizens and security personnel for Indictable Offences. There is also citizen's power of arrest for either-way offences.

Classification of Offences

Summary only offences

These are minor matters, which are tried only in a Magistrates courts. To begin the criminal justice, process a defendant may be ordered to attend a magistrate court by summons or arrested with or without a warrant by a police officer. Such offences include most motoring offences and other relatively minor matters such as drunkenness, common assault and prostitution offences. They can be tried only in a magistrates' court.

Indictable Only Offences

These are most serious of crimes and must be tried before a jury in a crown court and receive sentence in the crown court. These include, murder, rape, robbery, causing death by dangerous driving, arson with intent to endanger life, firearm with intent to endanger life, GBH and criminal damage.

Either-way offences

Not all offences are summary or indictable. There are offences that can be tried either way (i.e. at either a Magistrates or Crown Court), such as theft and burglary. In certain cases, a defendant can opt for trial by jury or a Magistrate can send them to the Crown Court, if they feel the offence deserves it or they have insufficient sentencing powers to deal with the matter.

ARREST

Circumstances under which security personnel may be able to make an arrest

- If one is suspected or have committed an indictable offence
- It must be necessary to make the arrest in order to stop the offence or prevent escape of suspect

Arrest can be made by anyone without a warrant regardless of the seriousness of the criminal offence so long as the individual can justify that it is necessary to arrest the person in question.

Examples of 'necessity' of arrests without warrant

- In order prevent one causing physical injury to himself or any other person
- In order to prevent one suffering injury
- In order to prevent loss or damage to property
- In order to prevent one making off before a police officer can assume responsibility for him

When an arrest without a warrant may be considered

- There must be actual, suspected or attempted involvement in the commission of a criminal offence
- There must be reasonable grounds for believing that the person's arrest is necessary (see examples above).
- The arresting officer must have witnessed a crime being committed or attempted or violence being threatened or have credible information that a serious crime has recently been committed.

Reporting Arrests and Crime

First, security personnel must report in writing why they believe an arrest was necessary. It must be based on fact and this will be in some form of evidence, either in the form of a statement or in goods, for example, in the event of a theft. From the moment an arrest is made, this evidence must be gathered and protected; in other words, controlled.

Reporting

Primarily any report in the workplace is completed for the employer and not the police. However, the report may be requested by the police to investigate a crime. Therefore, it must be reported factually without expression of opinion.

Reports must be:

- Factual
- Security personnel should have their pocketbook with them at the time of the event and should use it immediately as soon after the incident as possible

General Reporting Format

- Your name, role and company you work for
- Your security experience and expertise
- The day, date, time and place of what you were doing
- Details of the incident in chronological order
- Exact details of finding of evidence and any statements made by the suspect
- What occurred when police arrived (i.e. I informed the police officer)
- Witnesses present; including colleagues present at the time of incident

There are a number of people likely to require a report following an incident, a crime or an arrest:

- Employer
- Customer
- Control room
- Police
- Health and safety Executives
- Environmental Health Department of Local Authority

Control of Evidence

Security personnel are likely to come in contact with evidence or crime scene. A scene of a crime can be a break in, a suspect package or the scene of an assault.

To avoid contamination of evidence the following guidelines must be adhered to:

- Act calmly and think how they should approach this task in a rational manner
- Inform control room
- Do not enter buildings or rooms, unless it is essential to do so
- Do not touch or disturb anything at the scene
- Use local knowledge to identify what has been disturbed, removed or indeed, left behind
- Secure the scene
- Restrict and control access, until the Police have completed their investigation

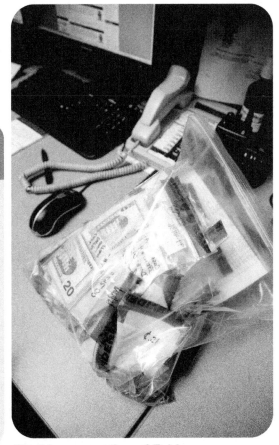

Fig 24 preservation of Evidence

Chapter 8

Searching

In security context, searching is a process of examining a person or property in order to find something lost or concealed. Security personnel routinely carryout searches to ensure substances or objects are not brought into certain premises or removed from certain premises without permission. The authority to carry out searches must come from the premises management, usually in writing as a separate document or stipulated in assignment instructions document.

Security personnel usually carry out searches as a routing work activity; mainly as a precautionary measure. For this reason, security personnel have ordinary powers and therefore cannot carryout searches based on suspicion of crime without permission of the member of public or customer to be searched. Security personnel such as Doorkeepers cannot use force to carryout searches.

The police have special powers and can carry out searches as a routing and also on suspicion of an offence. The police have the power to use reasonable force to do so in limited cases as outlined in the police and criminal evidence act 1984 (Home Office, 2011).

Generally, a person's consent must be sought and received before a search could be carried out. For the Doorkeeper, there are three laws relevant to their search role:

- Article 6 of Human Rights (right to be presumed innocent until found guilty following a fair trial in a court of law
- Article 8 of Human Rights (right to privacy)
- Article 14 of Human Rights (right not to be discriminated against)

Reference to 'Human Rights' is a reference to the *European Convention for the Protection of Human Rights and Fundamental Freedoms (Rome, 4 November 1950).*

Conditions that Must be in place Before 'Searching' could Commence

Search only if it is a condition of entry

Search must be authorised by management or employer. If Doorkeeper has been authorised to carryout searches they must adhere to search policies and procedures of the premises management. Doorkeepers have no search powers. However, they can search persons entering certain premises with their full and informed consent. As a condition of entry, refusal to be searched can result to the Doorkeeper denying access to the customer.

Admissions or entry Policy

People must be made aware of any search policy and procedure as soon as they have made contact with any staff of the premises responsible for access or exit on the premises. In the manner approved by management, Doorkeeper must make people aware of items or substances not permitted in the premises or that cannot be removed from the premises.

Permission

Doorkeeper has to receive informed consent from person to be searched before searching could begin. Doorkeeper must be able to explain their actions including why the search was necessary.

Conduct of Searches

Fig 25 Woman SEARCH Woman

Polite – searches must be carried out with respect and courtesy. Great care must be taken to minimise humiliation, embarrassment and inconvenience to persons to be searched. Under no circumstance must force be used. Length of time for search must be kept to minimum. Search must be targeted at those places where prohibited items could possibly be concealed. For example, it is not necessary to ask a person to take off their shoes if you are looking for a concealed Can of Beer. Persons should not be required to remove clothing in public, except outer wears like coat, jacket or gloves. By being polite Doorkeeper can gain more cooperation at every state of the search.

Positive – Doorkeepers routinely carry out searches as a precaution, to ensure prohibited items are not brought into certain premises. For this reason consent to search becomes a condition of entry. Consequently, positive attitude must be exhibited to ensure public confidence. Unlike the police, Doorkeepers have no special powers of search and therefore should not carryout searches based on suspicion about individuals. Please refer to the 'specific search' section of this book for best practice in dealing with 'suspicion' within search procedure.

Professional

Doorkeepers must be able to demonstrate great skill. This assures the customer that procedures are being followed and improves trust and confidence in the process.

- Hands must not be placed in bags or pockets during searches
- Feeling around inside collars, belts and socks are best carried out by the person being searched
- Pocket searches should also be carried out by the person being searched
- All body searches must be carried out by a Doorkeeper of the same sex. However, anyone can search bag or belonging of another person of the opposite sex.
- Searches must be non-discriminatory on grounds or race, nationality, age, ethnicity, disability, gender or sexual orientation
- Any search that goes beyond removal of outer clothing such as; coat, jacket, gloves, headgear and footwear must take place away from public view
- Searches involving exposure of intimate body parts must be avoided completely; instead metal detectors should be used.
- Searches must be in accordance to policy of premises. Specifically, aviation security operatives must adhere strictly to the procedures set by their employers for conducting searches as this book does not cover aviation security practice. However, the principles highlighted here will be required in order to interpret and enforce aviation search policies without compromising the core objective of SIA licensing; which is 'to enhance public trust and confidence in those providing security services'.

In short:

- So long as personnel is carrying out searches as a condition of entry with full and informed consent of the individual involved there should be no problem about safety and law
- Suspicious behaviour inside premises requiring that a person inside the premises is searched should be carried out as if the person is making a fresh request to enter the premises; in which case the search should be carried out near or at point of entry.

How to Search

Fig 26 Use Metal Detectors in combination with hand searches

Step 1

- Ensure premises is safe
- Search premises for dangerous or prohibited items
- Ensure fire exit doors are in order and not obstructed on the outside
- Ensure CCTV equipment is running and cameras are positioned correctly
- Ensure radio and other communication equipment are in order

Step 2

- Ensure conditions of entry are clearly displayed highlighting prohibited items

- Ensure there is another person, usually a colleague present as a witness or back-up for safety
- Position of the back-up person must be such that both are able to see each other's back without blocking the entry
- Ensure there is a conveniently raised and safe platform such as a chair or table to place personal belongings and must not block entrance or exit

Step 3

- Stand to the side, place feet a part to achieve stability and keep palm in open view
- Make eye contact with the person to be search
- Greet the person
- Ensure the customer is as relaxed as possible
- Confirm that the person is aware of prohibited items
- Seek consent
- Request the customer to disclose any prohibited item in their possession (verbal disclosure)
- Request the customer to empty their pockets (self-search technique)
- Seek consent to check the personal belongings
- Seek another consent to conduct a full body search on the customer
- Start from outer wears like jackets, coats, head covering or headgear
- It may be easier to search jackets and coats while they are still on the person
- With the customer facing you, draw an imaginary line running vertically from the middle of chest to belt waist line
- Draw another imaginary line horizontally across the middle of the imaginary vertical line.
- There are now 4 squares in front
- With elbows tucked in, search each square by placing two palms together on one front shoulder then pat-down while spreading palms from centre of abdomen to side of rib-cage; then pat-down to the belt area of the waist.
- Repeat for the other side of the front
- Use palm for non-sensitive areas and back of hand for sensitive areas like armpit region; between the middle thigh and belly-button around the back.
- To search the back area, repeat by standing to the side at the back of the customer and placing two palms together on one back shoulder then pat-down and spread palms from centre of back to side of rib-cage; pat-down to the belt area of the waist.
- Repeat for the other side of the back
- To search upper arms (hand), place one hand under arm (half-way between armpit and elbow) and the other above it and pat-down to the wrist.
- Repeat with the other hand
- To search lower arm (leg), place one hand inside leg and the other outside leg; then pat-down from the middle of thigh to the ankle
- Repeat for the other leg

- Use metal detector to search sensitive areas like armpit region, breast area and area between middle of thigh and belly-button.
- Where there are no metal detectors, same sex Doorkeeper will be required to use back of palm to search identified sensitive areas with full consent
- Ensure search position is comfortable throughout

Step 4

- Say thank you
- Ensure the customer has not left any of their belongings behind
- Quickly tidy up the table or chair before commencing another search to en sure evidence can be accounted (audit trail). The best way to avoid mix-ups is to use shallow baskets or trays.

Avoid the following bad practices:

- placing hand in customer's pockets
- using hands to feel underneath belts
- feeling collars
- feeling sensitive areas with palm
- grabbing, groping or applying unnecessary pressure on the searched person's body
- embarrassing comments
- requiring individual to expose private areas

The reasons why bad practices must be avoided are:

- allegations of theft,
- allegations of sexual assault
- allegations of planting evidence
- Health and safety risks (injury etc.)
- Can impact negatively on public trust and confidence

If the sensitive areas have to be searched with hand, it is good practice to wear rubber gloves or needle proof gloves depending on the circumstance surrounding the search.

Protective gloves:

- provide barrier between the person' body and Doorkeeper's skin and minimises risk of allegations of sexual contact
- ensures health and safety of both Doorkeeper and the person searched
- needle-proof gloves protect against sharps and should be worn if sharps are identified risks

Types of Search

Doorkeepers may be authorised to carry out all or any of the following types of searches:

- General searches – everyone gets searched. This type of search is preferred to take place at the point of entry
- Random searches – selecting persons at random for searching. Selection method used must be approved by management or employer and must be non-discriminatory. For example; bag of balls of different colours may be used. A person picking a particular colour could mean that a search would have to take place.
- Specific Searches – means that particular individuals may be selected for a search. The selection must be non-discriminatory and cannot be based on any personal or physical characteristics; such as type of clothing or distinctive skin or facial features. Furthermore, it is not good practice to base selection on previous wrong doing or past records of a particular customer. When it comes to search requirements pursuant to the Human Rights laws as highlighted above, a person is either suitable to enter a premises or unsuitable and the decision is best made at point of entry. Once a person is inside premises, they must be under the same search policy as everyone else. This is necessary to ensure safety of Doorkeepers and others in the venue. Doorkeepers should therefore minimise the need for specific searches.

How can Doorkeepers minimise the need for specific searches inside premises?

- Properly explain searching as a condition of entry
- Properly explain what the searching is expected to achieve (objectives) at point of entry
- Properly explain possible sanctions for breaches searching objectives; for example, removal from premises or ban
- Search properly at point of entry
- Continual observation in the premises

Why is continual observation necessary prior to specific searches?

1. It ensures Doorkeeper can explain reasons for suspicion to the person
2. The reasons for suspicion on their own must breach one or more conditions of entry to warrant an approach. For example; a customer in a nightclub opens a fire exit without authorisation. This single act on its own requires a Doorkeeper's attendance to find out why the fire door has been opened. The answers given by the person that opened the door may lead the Doorkeeper to suspect that the person was either involved in drugs activity or giving access to unauthorised persons or objects. It may not be necessary for the Doorkeeper to request to search this individual and the Doorkeeper may simply ask the individual to leave the premises straight away. If the individual offers to be searched by the Doorkeeper to prove innocence; the Doorkeeper may consider carrying out spe-

cific search and issue further conditions in this circumstance. It this is the case, the search should only be conducted as a condition of entry. This implies that the suspected offender would be informed that they are no longer allowed to remain on the premises and therefore would have to be re-admitted into the premises.If consent is given, the specific search should now take place at or near point of entry. A Doorkeeper must not conduct a search if they have already reached a decision to refuse entry.

This approach ensures that Doorkeepers only ever carry out specific searches with full consent of the persons to be searched. It is expected that searches that take place inside premises are more likely to result to violence than those taking place at point of entry. It is also assumed that it would be a lot easier to refuse entry than to request a person to leave premises.

Possible reasons why customer may refuse to give consent for search:

- Humiliation – this is felt more inside the premises than outside it
- Embarrassment – again felt more inside the premises than outside
- Inconvenience – this is experienced more inside than outside premises

Importance of following professional search principles

- Trust - it ensures public trust of Doorkeepers is maintained
- Fairness - it is a fair way to carryout search with respect for the individual's rights
- Effectiveness - it is an effective way to maintain order and safety without unnecessary allegations

Recording

Doorkeepers should remember at all times that it is good practice to carryout searches as a condition of entry. Indiscriminate search operations that take place outside points of entry may result in poor image, cause rowdy situation, conflict and loss of public trust. This implies that should a person refuse to give clear consent the Doorkeeper may refuse entry.

What should be recorded?

- Date and time of search
- Details of Doorkeepers conducting search
- Details of the person being searched; including ethnicity
- Indicate whether consent was given
- Description of items found
- Indication as to whether item was seized
- Reason why item was seized
- Time and date item was handed over to police or management

- Indication as to whether the person was given access or refused entry

It is recommended that premises wishing to confiscate illegal substances from customers obtain written authorisation from the police. If authorisation is given, the police must ensure there are evidence bags and other equipment required for collecting, transporting and storing the seized items. In the absence of police authorisation document and necessary equipment; confiscation of illegal items by Doorkeepers is not encouraged.

> ### There is no requirement for Doorkeepers to record searches unless the search has resulted in:
>
> - Finding illegal or prohibited items
> - Police arrest

Arrest of Persons found in Possession of Illegal or Prohibited Items

Generally, Doorkeepers have ordinary (citizen's) power of arrest and can arrest for serious (indictable) criminal offences or criminal offences that are likely (either-way) to be serious.

Doorkeepers are not police officers and are employed by private organisations to carryout specified duties. It is recommended in this book that Doorkeepers report criminal activities to the police if taking place outside the premises. If the criminal activity takes place inside the premises, the Doorkeeper may consider arrest or ejection of the suspect and inform the police.

As stated in the arrest module of this book, Doorkeepers must assess whether it is 'necessary', to carry out an arrest in all circumstances. If arrest is found to be 'NOT' necessary, Doorkeeper might be prosecuted in a civil court for false imprisonment or wrongful arrest and in a criminal court for assault.

In this case, if a Doorkeeper has any other option than arrest, the Doorkeeper may be accused of wrongful arrest or false imprisonment unless they can show that it was necessary to arrest the person in order to prevent a serious criminal offence or prevent the suspect from running away. For example, if a customer is found in possession of drugs or knife, a serious criminal offence has already been committed. It is no longer necessary to prevent an offence that has already been committed unless the Doorkeeper has reasons to believe that another criminal offence is likely to be committed with the knife or drug and the offence is imminent. Furthermore, it may also be necessary to contact the police and arrest the suspect without suspicion of another imminent offence, if the person making the arrest has reasons to believe that the suspect will run away before the police arrive. Therefore, the decision to arrest is entirely that of the Doorkeeper.

But Doorkeepers can carry out their duties without an arrest. This is because Doorkeepers' main role is to decide on suitability of persons to be allowed on licensed premises by enforcing conditions of entry. The Doorkeeper's primary responsibility therefore, is to refuse entry to unsuitable persons or items. 'Arrest' is a secondary responsibility and does not have to be carried out. The Doorkeeper can simply report the crime, with description of suspected offender to the police.

Offensive Weapons

'Offensive weapon is defined as any article made or adapted for use for causing injury to the person, or intended by the person having it with him for such use or by someone else'.

Made Weapons

These are articles manufacture for the purpose of causing injury.

Fig 27 All legal or illegal firearms must be refused entry

Fig 28 Bayonet

Fig 29 Knuckle Duster

Examples of weapons made for causing injury:

- Firearm
- Knuckle-duster
- Flick knife
- Bayonet
- Extendable baton
- CS gas

Adapted Weapons

These are articles adapted for the purpose of causing injury.

Examples of weapons adapted for causing injury:

- Wood with a nail in embedded in it
- Plastic pen with sharps at the tip

Intended Weapons

These are weapons that are not made or adapted, but in possession with the intention of causing injury to the person.

Examples are:

- Bottles
- Kitchen knives
- Penknives
- Razor

Note that penknives with blade longer than 3 inches are illegal. It is a serious (indictable) offence to carry an offensive weapon in public without lawful authority or reasonable excuse.

Defence

Lawful Authority

A person arrested by the police for possession of offensive weapon may be released without charge if they can convince the police or court that they have lawful authority to carry the weapon.

Example of lawful authority

- Legal permission to carry firearm in public (police office on duty; etc)

Reasonable Excuse

There are people whose work or duties require them to carry offensive weapons for legitimate purposes. These persons are entitled to claim 'reasonable excuse' defence.

Examples of 'reasonable excuse' are:

- for use at work
- for religious reasons
- as part of national costume

Possession of Blades or Pointed Articles

The law prohibits carrying article which has blade or is sharply pointed, in a public place. This includes folding pocket knife if the cutting edge of its blade exceeds 7.62cm (3 inches). The prohibition extends the offence to school premises.

Public Places

Public places are places where the public have paid or unpaid access. This includes nightclubs, shops, streets, roads churches, cinemas, stadiums, etc. Doorkeepers and management have legal responsibility to prevent crime and disorder in licensed premises. This implies that offensive weapons are automatically prohibited at the premises. However, it is for Doorkeepers to make a decision, in guidance by their employers as to whether an item can be brought into the premises, even if the item is legal. For example, it is not illegal to be found in possession of blades or points less than 3 inches in length. But as an outcome of risk assessment, the management and Doorkeepers can prohibit such items from entering their premises even though it may be legal to carry the item.

Options available to Doorkeepers on finding offensive Weapon on a Suspect

Security is not pure science. There is no one solution to any one problem. In fact, when security personnel come across a problem there is definitely more than one way of solving that problem. That is why assignment instruction documents are required to give the person necessary information, policies and procedures needed for the security personnel to carry out their duties effectively; and could vary from location to location. Even at that, the assignment instruction cannot answer in detail, all questions or solve all problems security personnel may encounter at work. This is why the most important quality of any security personnel is 'judgement'. With good judgement skills, the security personnel is able to quickly assess situations and identify possible consequences of the options available to him/her before reaching a decision as to which option is the best. This ability can be impaired severely if the security personnel is involved in abnormal consumption of alcohol or abuse of drugs.

If a Doorkeeper comes across a person carrying an offences weapon, such as a knife or a firearm (gun), the following options are available to him or her:

- seize the weapon and arrest the suspect
- seize the weapon, retain it, refuse entry and inform the police

As stated earlier, Doorkeepers must remind themselves of their objectives and priorities at all times. The number one objective of a Doorkeeper is 'protection of life' followed by protection of property and premises. Prevention of loss and prevention of crime are third and fourth objectives respectively. When it comes to 'crime fighting' security personnel are only equipped enough to prevent crime than to deal with crime, which is the precept of the public police, (Kinsella and McGarry, 2011).

For example, a person is found in possession of an offensive weapon. A Doorkeeper's crime prevention skills are not relevant to prevent the possession of offensive weapon which has already taken place long before the Doorkeeper became aware of it. The Doorkeeper is therefore not obliged to make an arrest on the basis of crime prevention. However, if the Doorkeeper honestly believes that the weapon is about to be used to attack a person or property, an arrest may be considered. In this case, the keeper can justify the arrest on the ground that it was 'necessary' to arrest the person in order to prevent that crime. In the absence of such honest belief, the Doorkeeper can simply report the crime to the police without arrest.

The seriousness of the offence will determine how urgent police contact should be made. For example, if a person is found with a firearm, the person should be refused entry and police should be contacted immediately and the company's incident report document completed.

If a person is found with a small amount of illegal drug; the person must be refused entry and reports completed. The Doorkeeper is not obliged to make an arrest, but must complete reports. Although, the Doorkeeper has decided it was not necessary to make an arrest; the Doorkeeper may decide to inform the police about the offence. If the police are on their way to come and arrest the suspect and the Doorkeeper has reasons to believe that the suspect is likely to run away before the police arrives, it may be necessary for the Doorkeeper to make an arrest in order to prevent the person from running away.

Table.2 Possible Actions When Specific Items are found

Offences	Possible Actions
Possession of firearm	Refuse entry; contact police immediately; avoid arrest and seizure; complete reports documents
Possession of firearm with intent to endanger life	Refuse entry; contact police immediately, consider arrest and seizure; take reasonable care of own and other's safety; complete reports documents
Possession of firearm or imitation with intent to cause fear or violence	Refuse entry; contact police immediately; consider arrest and seizure; take care of own and other's safety; complete reports documents
Possession of drugs	Refuse entry; avoid seizure; avoid arrest; complete reports documents
Possession of drugs with intent to supply	Refuse entry; consider arrest and seizure; take care of own and other's safety; complete reports documents
Supplying drugs	Refuse entry; consider arrest and seizure; take care of own and other's safety; complete reports documents
Possession of other offensive weapons	Refuse entry; avoid arrest and seizure; complete reports documents
Possession of other offensive weapons with threat to life or property	Refuse entry; contact police; consider arrest and seizure; take care of own and other's safety; complete reports documents

Chapter 9

Health and safety at Work

Aim: To introduce students to the legal framework within health and safety in the workplace to promote, stimulate and encourage high standards of occupational health and safety within the workplace.

In 2008/2009, the rate of work related injuries in the United Kingdom was recorded to be 1.2 million per year, costing the country 29 million days of work lost due to work related injuries and ill-health. Health and safety law aims to prevent accident and ill-health arising from workplace.

Health and safety covers:

- Employers, Employees and Self Employed
- Casual Employees, (including part-time) and Trainees
- Sub-contractors
- Anyone who uses the workplace (premises)
- Anyone using equipment
- Visitors and customers
- Suppliers
- Users of the end product
- Anyone on the premises
- Anyone on the premises unlawfully

Responsibilities for Health and safety

Employer's responsibilities

Duty of Care – are legal responsibilities of employers for safety of others and they are as follows:

- **Safe premises, plant and Machinery** – duty to provide safe premises, plant and machinery and duty to maintain
- **Safe place of work** – duty to take reasonable steps to minimize danger in the workplace
- **Safe systems of work** – duty to ensure that work methods and system of supervision are in line with the objectives of the health and safety law
- **Competent employee** – duty to hire competent employee and give them proper instructions

In fulfilment of these duties, employers are expected to provide:

- Safe access and egress (entry and exit)
- Training for employees
- A written safety policy as an instruction document

Employee's Responsibilities

Duty of Care – are legal responsibilities of employees for safety of themselves and others and they are as follows:

- Take reasonable care to avoid injury to themselves or to others (including visitors and customers) by their work activities, obey all regulations
- Co-operate with employers and others, so that they may discharge their legal responsibilities concerning the health, safety and welfare of employees and others (including visitors and customers)
- If safety equipment is issued, security personnel must comply with any specific rules or instructions regarding its use. Refusal to do so could lead to a breach of duty, which to criminal prosecution or dismissal or both.

In fulfilment of these responsibilities, private security personnel have the following health and safety responsibilities at work:

- Take reasonable care of their own health and safety
- Ensure their actions or omissions do not adversely affect health and safety of others
- Follow health and safety procedures
- Follow health and safety rules and instruction provided by their employer
- Use Personal Protective Equipment (PPE) provided by their employer
- Report damage on PPE
- Be aware of emergency procedures

Responsibilities for the Self-employed

Duty of Care – are legal responsibilities of self-employed for safety of themselves and others. Self-employed persons have the same duty of care as an employee. They differ from employees in that they are responsible for their own training. They are also required to provide their own equipment; where needed.

In fulfilment of these duties, employees and self-employees are expected to:

- Take reasonable care of their own health and safety
- Ensure that their acts or omissions do not adversely affect the health and safety of others
- Follow health and safety policies provided by the employer and keep up to date with any revisions, new requirements or regulations

- Obey all safety rules
- Use protective equipment and clothing properly, reporting any damage to it
- Be aware of emergency procedures and ensure that they are followed when needed

Vicarious Liability

This means that an employer is liable for the actions of his employees in the course of the employment. This implies that the employee can also be held responsible for their actions.

Provision and use of Equipment

Equipment provided by employers for use at work must be:
- Suitable for the intended use
- Safe
- Maintained and inspected to ensure safety
- Used by trained individuals or by people who have received instruction or information on its use
- Has protective devices, markings and warnings on the equipment

Manual Handling Operations

Fig 30 Manual Handling

Manual handling is:

- The supporting and transporting of a load by hand or body

Manual handling as a risk

- Manual handling accounts for one-third of all reported injuries (lasting over 3 days) each year.
- Manual handling can cause musculoskeletal disorders. This is injury or damage to joints or other tissues in the back or upper part of the legs (between the knee and the hip)

Options available to employers for dealing with the risks of manual handling

- **Avoid** dangerous manual handling where possible
- **Assess** the risks
- **Reduce** the risks

Manual Handling Risks

- Fractures
- Spinal disk injuries
- Burns
- Damage to muscles
- Cuts and abrasions
- Damaged ligament
- Damaged tendons
- Back injuries
- Trapped nerves

How to assess, avoid and reduce manual handling risks

The following points must be considered before reaching a decision to lift or move an object:

- If it is necessary to lift or move the object; for example, if the object is secure or is the object blocking an exit
- The weight of the object
- Stability of the object
- Ease of grip
- Any Handholds
- Surface texture
- What potentially could go wrong with the manual handling

- What to do to prevent any identified problem
- If Personal Protective Equipment (PPE) or clothing may be required
- If lifting equipment is provided and can be used

Risk Assessment

Aim:

To identify hazards and take action to either:

- Eliminate the risk
- Adapt/Accept/Reduce the risk
- Provide protection from the risk

Risk assessment simply means knowing what problems (hazards) are likely to be encountered and how best to avoid or solve them.

A procedure for avoiding or solving the problem in order to minimize risks posed by the hazard is therefore designed by the employer.

Hazards and Risks
The initial steps in any risk assessment would involve identifying things that have the potential to cause harm (hazards) and assessment of the chance (risk) that harm would occur and the severity of harm.

Hazard - Anything that has the potential to cause harm.

Risk - The chance, great or small, that harm could happen in certain circumstances.

Steps in Risk Assessment

Risk assessment is employer's responsibility and usually follows the following format:

1. Identify the hazards
2. Quantify the risks (severity of possible injury)
3. Consider options available hire a security guard to man access to dangerous areas or close the dangerous area entirely depending on 1 and 2 above
4. Record findings in case it may be needed another time to avoid having to repeat entire assessment
5. Information and employee training would be necessary for awareness of risk and control measures

Examples of hazards

- Wet floor
- obstructions
- Noise pollution
- Violence and assault
- Locked fire exit doors
- Lifting a load
- Storage of dangerous liquids
- Blocked passages or doors
- Poor lighting
- Spillage
- Overcrowding
- Work equipment handling
- Lone working

Fig 30 Yellow Triange Wet Floor sign

Examples of Risk

- Slip and trip from wet floor
- Injuries from poor lighting
- Diseases
- Fires
- Floods

Note the difference between hazards and risks

Workplace Violence

In the United Kingdom, the Health and safety Executive's (HSE) definition of workplace violence is 'any incident in which a person is abused, threatened or assaulted by anyone in circumstances relating to their work'.

The keywords here are:

- Abuse
- Threat
- Assault
- Work

Lone Workers

Lone workers are individuals working without another person, colleague or close supervision. Lone workers are most at risk of abuse, threat or assault in the work place from members of the public or customers.

Employers must carry out risk assessment of tasks by:

- identifying the problems
- decide what action to take
- take action; such as use of 'check calls'
- training on violence prevention and personal safety; such as conflict management training
- review action and check progress

Equipment and measures to protect lone workers:

- Mobile phone/radio calls – this can be used to for help and make to check calls to let others know they are safe.
- Personal alarms – can enhance feeling of safety and reassures staff
- Installed panic alarms and CCTV in work locations can also be of help

Effects of workplace violence

- Stress, anxiety, fear and depression
- Employees may blame self for violent incident
- Low morale
- Loss of confidence
- Physical harm or injury
- Disability
- death
- Job may become less attractive leading to staff retention problems
- Sick Absence
- Low output due to increased sick leave
- Increase in sick pay and possible compensation pay-outs

Role of Security Personnel in Minimizing Risks from Workplace Violence

- Understand employer's policies on risks of workplace violence
- Learn how to recognize the risks
- Know your roles and responsibilities
- Find out what support your employer has in place for victims of workplace violence
- Refer to assignment instructions or other policy documents
- Report and record all incidents of workplace violence
- Obey safety signs

Procedure for Dealing with Spillage

**All spillage is potentially dangerous regardless of the form.
Most commonly, spillage occurs with liquids. The steps to follow are:**

- inform anyone who may affected
- inform colleague or keeper or controller
- evacuate the area
- isolate the area to prevent spreading
- follow employer's procedure on how to deal with the particular substance spillage

Reporting Accidents

Reporting of Injuries, Diseases and Dangerous
Occurrences (RIDDO)

This requires that employers, self-employed and people in control of work premises to report:

- serious workplace accidents
- occupational diseases
- dangerous occurrences; including near misses

Any death or serious injuries must be reported immediately to authorities. All other injury reports must be kept within the organization except for injuries incapacitating the injured person beyond certain number of days.

Precautions against Infectious Diseases

Bodily fluids may carry infections that can be transmitted from person to person during:

- Body searches of infected persons; vomit urine etc
- Contact with dirty needles
- Contact with blood or other body fluids during an arrest
- First aid treatments (bleeding injuries)

Appropriate precautions

- Wear disposable plastic, latex or vinyl gloves if risk is present
- Use waterproof plaster to cover cuts, bruises
- Contaminated clothing should be rinsed in hot running water and dried
- Hand washing

Personal Protective Equipment (PPE)

These are examples of Personal Protective Equipment's that security personnel may require depending on the nature of work environment:

- Helmet

- Ear defenders

- Eye protection

- Safety boots

- Hi-visibility vest or jacket

- Cold weather clothing

Fig 31 Hi-Visibility Jacket

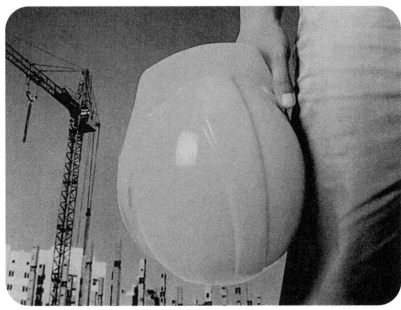

Fig 32 Helmet

First Aid Awareness

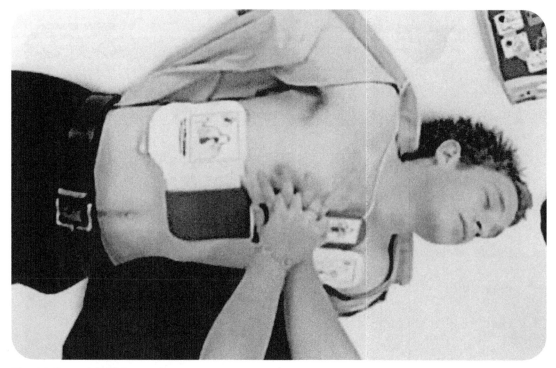

Fig 33 first-aid CPR

All workplaces should have a first aid box and an appointed person in charge of first aid and where necessary calling emergency services. An employer has a common law duty of care to ensure that their actions or omissions do not cause or worsen injury to another person.

Definition of First Aid

First aid is defined as emergency treatment given to an injured person or a person taken ill until full medical treatment is available.

Aims of First Aid

- Make casualty comfortable

- Prevent condition from worsening

- Promote recovery

Actions to take

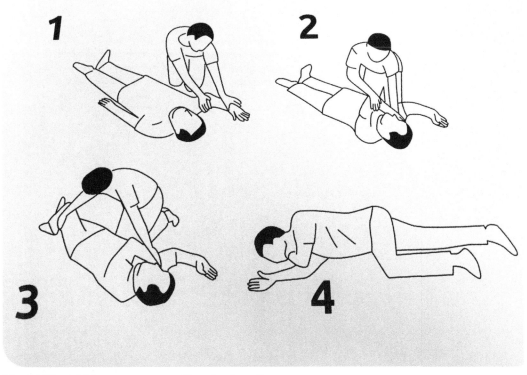

Fig 34 First Aid recovery position instructions

- Assess the situation
- Ensure your own safety
- Make the surrounding area safe
- Shout for help
- Open air way
- Check for normal breathing
- Contact emergency services for assistance

Before providing first aid you must first check that:

- You have an up-to-date first aid qualification
- You have been appointed or authorized to give first aid

In all other cases and if in any doubt, call the ambulance by dialling an emergency number on your phone.

Chapter 10

Fire Awareness

Fire kills and destroys property and livelihoods. Fire can be prevented by keeping as far as possible, from each other, the three elements that have to come together before fire can star.

The Three Elements of Fire are:

- Oxygen
- Fuel
- Source of Heat (source of ignition)

Examples of Sources of Heat

- Heaters
- Lighting
- Naked flames
- Electrical equipment
- Cigarettes and matches
- Anything that can get very hot, such as sun or anything that can cause sparks

Example of Source of Oxygen

- Air we breathe (21% of air is oxygen).

Examples of Fuel

Fuel is anything that can burn:

- wood
- paper
- plastic
- rubber/foam
- loose packaging materials
- waste rubbish
- furniture

Basic Fire Prevention Measures

Employers' responsibilities

- Employers must carry out fire risk assessment (what could start fire? What could burn? Who might be at risk?)
- Provide fire detection and warning systems (smoke alarms, fire alarms or bell)
- Ensure regular Portable Appliance Test (PAT) on electrical appliances
- Have appropriate firefighting equipment
- Provide safe fire exit doors
- Provide safe evacuation routes from premises
- Ensure appropriate training is received by staff on procedures and fire drills
- Review and update fire risk assessment on regular basis

Security Personnel's responsibilities

- Keep sources fuel and ignition as far apart as possible
- Ensure heaters cannot be knocked over to avoid accidental fires
- Ensure electrical equipment and lights are switched off when not in use
- Report faults in electrical equipment
- Avoid running wire under carpets or pressed down by objects, like furniture
- Electrical equipment must be kept away from sources of heat

There is requirement that:

- Companies carryout fire risk assessment
- Companies nominate competent person to assist them to carryout fire risk assessment
- Companies must implement appropriate safety measures to minimize fire risk to life
- Companies provide information, instruction and training on fire safety to staff

There must be:

- Risk assessment
- Means of escape
- Means of giving warning
- Means of fighting fire

Fig.34a Smoking is a fire hazard

Risk assessment must:

1. Identify potential fire hazards
2. Identify people likely to be at risk
3. Evaluate and take action to remove and reduce risks to persons and property
4. Review risk assessment continuously to meet changes on site

Table.3. Types of Fire Extinguishers and Classes of Fire

Type / Extinguisher	CLASS A Combustible materials (e.g. paper & wood)	CLASS B Flammable liquids (e.g. paint & petrol)	CLASS C Flammable gases (e.g. butane and methane)	CLASS D Flammable metals (e.g. lithium & potassium)	Electrical Electrical equipment (e.g. computers & generators)	CLASS F Deep fat fryers (e.g. chip pans)	Comments
Water	✓	✗	✗	✗	✗	✗	Do not use on liquid or electric fires
Foam	✓	✓	✗	✗	✗	✗	Not suited to domestic use
Dry Powder	✓	✓	✓	✓	✓	✗	Can be used safely up to 1000 volts
CO2	✗	✓	✗	✗	✓	✗	Safe on both high and low voltage
Wet Chemical	✓	✗	✗	✗	✗	✓	Use on extremely high temperatures

Fire Extinguishers

There are six types of extinguishers. Fire extinguishers serve
to eliminate one or more of the elements of fire. All extinguishers
manufactured since January 1st,
1997 must meet the BS EN3 standard. Fire extinguishers in the UK
are now colour coded covering between 5-10% the extinguisher's
surface. The aim of the colour cod-
ing is to make it easier to identify
fire extinguishers and their contents.

The best extinguisher for electrical fires is carbon dioxide extinguisher. Water is the best
extinguisher for textiles. Foam is
the best extinguisher for flammable
liquids.

Fig 35 Fire extinguisher and stand

How to use fire extinguishers

1. **Water based extinguishers**
will conduct electricity. Avoid using it
on electrical equipment, including
cookers, computers, sockets etc. In
all cases, pull safety pin to break
tamper seal. Aim at base of fire moving jet sideways for fires spreading
horizontally. For fires spreading verti-

Fig 35a Types Fire Extinguisher

cally, move jet upwards slowly in the direction of fire. Squeeze lever slowly to star
discharging the extinguisher.

2. **Foam extinguishers** lay a blanket of foam over the burning liquid.

   ▪ Flammable liquids – aim hose at far side of fire to smother the fire.
   Do not aim the hose directly on the fire to avoid spreading. Squeeze lever
   slowly to star discharging the extinguisher.

3. **Powder extinguisher** – aim the hose at base of the flame if fire is on a solid or textile. If the fires is on electrical equipment simply aim hose directly on fire. It will be best to switch of power beforehand if safe to do so. Dry powder can cause environmental pollution. In an enclosed space, use of dry powder can affect health.

4. **Carbon Dioxide (CO2) extinguishers** – Avoid holding the horn because when activated CO2 extinguishers produce extremely cold CO2 which can lead to severe frost burns.

- On flammable liquids aim the hose at base of fire and swing hose or horn sideways across fire.
- On Electrical equipment switch off appliance if safe to do so, then point the hose directly at the fire and slowly discharge the extinguisher.

5. **Wet chemical extinguisher** – It is important to turn off heat source if safe to do so. Spray slowly in a circular motion well above the fire so as to allow the chemical to fall gently on the burning oil avoiding splashing.

6. **Fire Blankets** – pull the tapes to release blanket. Hold blanket in a position that shields the fire away and covers the hand; the place blanket gently on pan to smother the fire.

Security personnel do not have to fight fire. It is safer to evacuate and call fire fighters than fight fire. The above methods can only work well with small fires with known fuels. Basically, a small fire should not require more than one extinguisher. If security personnel's initial assessment indicates that more than one fire extinguisher may be needed or the fuel culprit is unknown or fuel is likely to be gas or metal, fire fighters must be called immediately and evacuation commenced straight away.

In assessing if it is safe to fight fire the following questions must be asked:

- What has started the fire?
- Is the fire less likely to spread fast?
- Am I likely to get hurt?
- Can one extinguisher put out the fire?
- What can I do (to stop the fire or to be safe)?
- Do I know where the extinguishers are?
- Do I know how to operate the extinguisher?
- Is my exit clear?

If answer to any of the above questions is 'no' security personnel must sound alarm, call fire fighters and evacuate the area.

Fire Extinguisher checks

Fig 36 Fire Extinguisher-FULL CHARGE

During patrols, security personnel must check:

- location of extinguishers
- that extinguishers are fully charged and not discharged or damaged
- that the pins are in the correct position and not bent

A fully charged extinguisher should have the green indicator vertical the scale or a pointer on the green indicator. Any damage must be reported to site manager and recorded in the daily occurrence book or fault report book. Assignment instructions must be checked to ensure correct reporting procedure is followed.

Other Fire Fighting Equipment

It is important that all business premises should provide means of fighting fire. Premises may be required by authorities to install certain firefighting equipment as an outcome of risk assessment.

- Primary action is to use pressurized CO2 to produce a cooling effect thereby removing heat.
- Designed for computers, laboratories and electrical equipment
- It is a high-pressure CO2 system.
- It discharges automatically to remove oxygen and heat

Dry and Wet Risers

Fig 37 Dry Riser outlet

- Designed for fighting fire in large buildings
- Buildings may have in-built riser system
- Riser system has empty pipes rising vertically with an outlet on each floor secured in a riser cupboard.
- Fire fighter can deliver water from the in-let pipe outside the building on the ground floor to any floor level without the need to lay hosepipes from ground floor to multi-storey floors.
- While dry risers are usually empty pipe networks, wet risers are already primed with water

Sprinklers

Fig 38 Fire Sprinkler System

There are other types of sprinklers; but for the scope of this book we shall describe wet pipe sprinkler systems that operate with equidistantly spaced valves or sprinklers which opens automatically in the presence of heat to release water.

- This type of sprinkler system contains pressurised water
- Activates automatically within 1-4 minutes of sensing the predetermined heat level
- Each sprinkler activates independently at a predetermined temperature
- Only valves or sprinklers near the heat will activate thereby making efficient use of water and minimizing unnecessary water damage.
- The pipe-work is fitted overhead, and spaced, equidistant along the pipe-work, are special valves; sometimes called fuses.
- Has to be shot down manually.
- Sprinkler systems can be found in places where 'class A' fire risk is suspected.

Foam Flooding System

Fig 39 Foam flooding system

In general, foams work by filling spaces and preventing air and oxygen from reaching the base of fire. The heat generates steam with the foam. This steam mixes with surrounding air. As this steam/air mixture cools, it produces wetness that is more capable of penetrating any class 'A' object than water. As a result the burning class 'A' material cools below its ignition point; and the fire stops.

- Foam flooding system allows foam to be pumped from outside without the need to enter the room
- There is usually an inlet valve from outside the building for fire fighter use in pumping foam
- Foam flooding can be found in places, such as paint stores, boiler rooms and anywhere where a large volume of flammable liquid is stored like petrol stations.
- The inlet valve should be covered in a panel with clear indicator notice
- Just like that of dry riser's, access to foam inlets must be kept clear.

Fire Doors

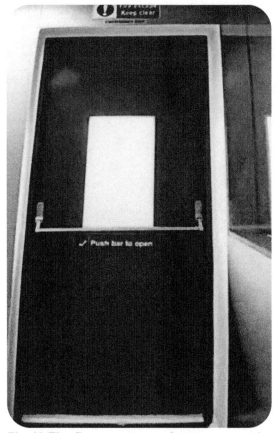

Fig 40 Fire Door - means of escape must be kept clear

Fig 40a Fire door must be kept closed

- Used to reduce spread of smoke or flame from one room to another or from one house/flat to the other
- Must be closed at all times unless electronically controlled
- Must be kept available for use and unobstructed at all times.
- Must have clearly visible safe escape signage (green background with white symbol)

Practical Steps to Follow on Discovering a Fire

There are two main ways security personnel may become aware of fire:

- Discovering a fire before automatic fire alarm activation
- Automatic fire alarm activation upon detecting heat or smoke alerting security personnel

Actions to take upon receiving automatic fire alarm signal

1. Check the fire panel to confirm location of fire incident
2. Inform Fire Brigade
3. Inform control room and management about the incident
4. Restrict access to the property
5. Evacuate
6. Extinguish fire if safe to do so

Fig 40b Fire Alarm

Fig.41 Fire alarm manual call point

Upon discovering a fire without the help of automatic fire alarm activation:

1. Sound the alarm by breaking the glass on the wall fitted alarm control point or use air horn or whistle as the site assignment instructions may indicate.
2. Call Fire Brigade
3. Inform control room and management
4. Evacuate
5. Extinguish if safe to do so
6. Even after the fire has been extinguished by security personnel, fire fighters must still be called to ensure the fire does not re-ignite.

Assignment knowledge

Security personnel must have good knowledge of their assignment, potential dangers, who is likely to be harmed in certain dangerous situations and how to prevent or minimize harm. Assignment Instructions document should provide this information aimed at informing and educating security personnel about potential dangerous incidents and how and what to communicate while dealing with the problem.

Guided by the assignment instructions, security personnel should be able to communicate the following with the Fire Brigade upon arrival

- Account for missing persons following evacuation
- Class of fire
- Fire location
- Hazards and risks in the property
- Location of foam or water inlets
- Access and escape routes
- Fire alarm control panels
- Report timings in pocketbook immediately followed by a full report in the incident book as soon after the incident as possible

Fig 42 Green Background-Fire Exit direction

How to Evacuate

- Using verbal and non-verbal techniques encourage people to use fire exits and wait at assembly points
- Security personnel must position at or near each exit door in the direction of assembly point in order to guide people unfamiliar with the escape routes clearly
- Security personnel must stay calm to avoid causing panic
- Security personnel must not allow anyone back into the property
- People must be warned not to take lifts and all lifts must be locked on the ground floor where possible
- Carry out a headcount of all in assembly point and check the names against access control logs
- Follow assignment instructions to report unaccounted persons immediately

Chapter 11

Counter-terrorism and Anti-terrorism

Most of deaths from terrorism have been recorded in five countries. In 2012 and 2013, Iraq, Nigeria, Afghanistan, Pakistan and Syria were the five countries most affected by terrorism. Globally, these countries account for 78% of total deaths from terrorism. In 2014, Iraq and Nigeria, were responsible for 53 per cent of all deaths from terrorism. These two countries host the most dangerous terrorist groups. Boko Haram and ISIL (also known as ISIS) were blamed for 50% of global terror deaths in 2014. Boko Haram was responsible for 6,644 deaths while ISIS was responsible for 6,073 deaths.

While terror deaths were said to had declined in some countries, it has risen in others. The country with the biggest increase is Nigeria, with 5,662 more people killed from terrorism in 2014 than in 2013, representing 306 per cent increase. Iraq is second to Nigeria, with an increment of 3532 in terror deaths compared to the previous year. This yearly increase alone is more than the number of people who were killed from terrorism around the world in 2005, (Global Terrorism Index, 2015).

Counter terrorism refers to offensive measures taken by military intelligence and national law. Anti-terrorism implies defensive strategies including a wide range of activities undertaken by public and private groups to prevent acts of terrorism and mitigate the consequences. Much of this book is concerned with the mitigation and prevention efforts.

Mitigation

- Minimising damage to targets
- Displacing it to other targets that are less vulnerable and less desirable to the perpetrators from the perpetrator's point of view

Practical examples of mitigation efforts:

- Engineering and scientific understanding of Bomb-blast on structures
- Target hardening of vulnerable structures
- Plan on fire and security evacuation routes
- Improving material affected by blasts
- Efforts to bring communities into renewed existence after attack

Target hardening

Fig 43 Fortified to resist vehiclar intrusion. Good protection against bomb loaded vehicles

Prevention

- Usual crime prevention strategies
- Risk and vulnerability assessments
- Situational crime prevention measures

Why terrorism prevention is more challenging than other crime incidents

- Terror incidents are relatively too small
- Conversely, potential terror targets are so huge
- Hence, difficult to predict next target
- Difficult to protect all potential targets

Physical measures

- Separate vehicular traffic from building and some other infrastructure
- Private security
- Natural (human) surveillance
- Local police and citizen partnership
- Community-based policing
- Crime maps uploaded onto public internets

Fig 44

Electronic measures

Refined electronic control devices that reads:

- Identification cards

- Code numbers
- Biometric information (eg hand shape, eye characteristics
- CCTV
- Lighting

Risk assessment

Types:
- Qualitative or Heuristic (ad hoc) – once risk identified, no need to measure magnitude (how big or small). Action must be taken to either eliminate it, reduce it or provide protection from the risk. This method is routinely applied in vast majority of premises. See the health and safety chapter for details on qualitative risk assessment.
- Quantitative – requires measurable data and weighing cost of prevention versus cost of protection in relation to consequence of attack. Here, magnitude of consequence determines how much to invest in its prevention. This is the method employed in high risk places such as construction, train and air transport and leisure companies; like roller coaster operators. Due to the less frequent nature of terrorism this method also guides decision making in places considered to be at high risk of terror attack.

Approaches:

- Inductive or event tree
- Deductive or fault tree

Event tree

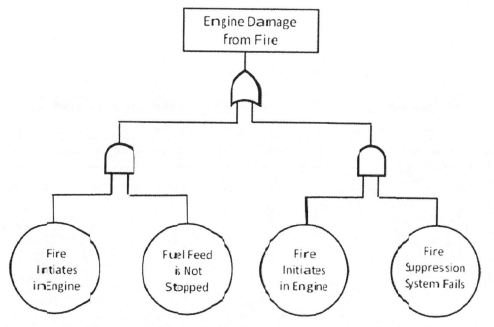

Fig 45 Event Tree Risk Assessment-starts from minor scenarios that may lead to the bigger event engine damage

- Starts with considering scenarios or events that may lead to occurrence of a bigger undesired event
- Traces an initiating event through a sequence with different possible outcomes
- Uses inductive logic to infer results

Fault tree

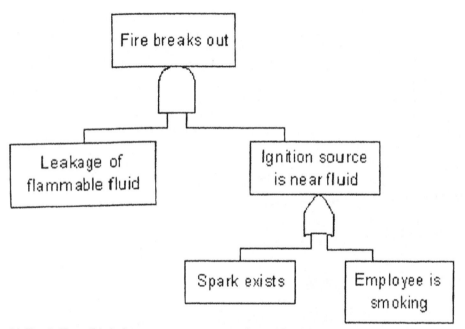

Fig 46 Fault Tree Risk Assessment - starts from the big event eg. Big fire deducing to the possibility that employee might be smoking or presence of spark

- Starts with possible occurrence of a big undesirable event
- Uses logic diagrams to represent deductive reasoning
- To determine how the event may occur

Fig 47 This fire can be traced back to a number of possible causes

Risk Management

- Addresses the outcome of a successful adversary
- The likelihood it will occur
- The attack scenario
- The population affected

The three important questions

- What can go wrong?
- What is the likelihood that it would go wrong?
- What are the consequences? Also, add population size throughout the analysis

Threat Definition

- Collects specific information about adversary

Classes of adversaries

- Outsiders
- Insiders
- Outsiders in collusion with insiders

Full range of tactics

Define:

- Deceit
- force
- stealth
- number of adversaries

Deceit - attempted defeat of security system by using false authorisation and identification
Force – overt forcible attempt to overcome a security system
Stealth – any attempt to defeat the detection system and enter the facility covertly
Number – number of adversaries (small group? 2-4 individuals? etc.)

Threat characteristics - Capabilities

- Weapons
- Tools
- Explosives
- Motivation (ideology, financial or personal reasons)

A highly-motivated adversary who is willing to die for a cause is much more different from a burglar who will flee when discovered.

Summary of Risk Assessment Process	
Planning	*purpose, objective*
Threat definition	*characterise threat* *Likelihood of attack*
Asset Identification	*Prioritise assets*
Vulnerability assessment	*Effectiveness of protection system*
Analyse Risk	*analyse potential adversary paths and scenarios to asset and exploitable vulnerabilities in the physical security system*
Decide whether risk is acceptable	*consider options: avoidance, reduction, spreading, transfer and acceptance*

Vulnerability Assessment

A vulnerability assessment answers the first question in risk assessment - What can go wrong?

- Determine security system effectiveness (is it consistently able to do what it is expected to do – the objectives)
- High value assets? – *threat of greater capability and motivation will attack*
- Low value asset? – *less capable and motivated threat will attack*
- Determine if security equipment is *installed, operated and maintained*
- Determine if procedures are followed
- Determine if personnel are appropriately trained

Hostile Reconnaissance

This refers to the form of military style surveillance operations likely to be undertaken by terrorists before carrying out an attack.

They may do it in the following ways:

- In vehicles
- On foot
- Recording target locations
- Documenting target locations

To assess whether certain activity may be suspicious, assess the following:

- The likelihood of the subject location being a target
- Any difficulty in identifying the person carrying out the suspicious activity

- Any effort to conceal identity
- The type of suspicious activity

Examples of suspicious activity

- People in stationary vehicles watching a building or structure for no visible reason
- Slow moving vehicles near public buildings, structures, bridges
- Parked vehicles in unusual places
- Using recording equipment, camera phones or making notes or sketches for no reason apparent to any person
- Unusual interest in specific access/egress areas, stairwells, hallways and fire escapes for no reason apparent to any person
- Loitering at or near premises for long periods, watching customers for no apparent reason
- Asking detailed or unusual questions about buildings and business operations, facilities (such as room layouts), security or parking for no apparent reason
- A member of the public in offices and 'out of bounds' areas, plant rooms and similar locations.

Potential Terror targets

- Crowded places
- Economic, government and transport systems
- Military and iconic sites
- Especially those in major city locations

Fig.48 A crowded place in a city

What security personnel CAN do

- Security personnel should report any incidents or suspicious activity to the police.
- Approach the person acting suspicious and request them to explain what they are doing

What security personnel CANNOT do

- Stop or detain that person or stop them leaving if they refuse to answer
- NO power to stop a person from taking a photograph of anything or any person in a public place
- NO power to request for any images taken to be deleted
- NO power to request to view images taken
- NO power to seize any camera or phone used to take any image
- These powers are ONLY available to a police officer following certain stringent rules.

Chapter 12

Emergency Procedures

Emergency can be defined as any occurrence at any time with or without warning, potentially dangerous to life, property and business that it must be dealt with immediately.

Types of Emergency

- Fires
- Pollution
- Flood
- Power failure
- Bomb threat
- Explosions
- Burglary
- Accident
- Gas leak
- Spillage
- Suspect packages (unattended belongings)

Although the definition of emergency here encompasses property and business losses, security personnel's priority must be to save life.

Security personnel must remember their main functions and follow them in the order below:

1. The protection of life
2. The protection of property and premises
3. The prevention of loss and waste
4. The prevention and deterrence of crime

Planning

As discussed earlier, assignment instructions manual will detail:

- Potential threats to life and property
- Who and what may be affected
- The severity of threat

- The chance of occurrence
- Actions to take to avoid, reduce or eliminate potential threat

Readiness

Readiness requires planning. It is the responsibility of security personnel to demonstrate preparedness by ensuring that they are:

- Familiar with assignment instructions and its emergency procedures
- Familiar with warning systems (fire alarm, burglar alarm etc)
- Familiar with communication systems, such as radio and emergency phone procedures
- Familiar with control teams and control room communication procedures
- Familiar with location of fire extinguishers
- Familiar with water, electricity and gas isolation points
- Familiar with contact numbers of the relevant persons to contact in time of emergency
- Familiar with evacuation points (also known as muster points)
- Familiar with site map
- Familiar with alarm manual activation points
- Familiar with details of nominated or appointed first aid persons
- Familiar with any previous relevant training or induction on dealing with emergency (most businesses would carry out emergency response drills to help personnel with planning preparations.

Remember, that the aim of:

- **P**lanning and
- **P**reparation is to
- **P**revent
- **P**oor
- **P**erformance

(Highfield publications)

Response

Security personnel will normally be expected to respond to most emergencies with the aim of carrying out a safe evacuation. Drawing from prior training and assignment instructions, it is for the security personnel to respond with speed to any emergency and make appropriate and vital decisions with the same speed.

Basically, security personnel will be confronted with the following questions in dealing with any of the emergencies listed above:

- Is there an imminent threat to life or property?
- What is the nature of threat or danger (confirm if it is liquid fire or gas fire, flood, etc.)?

- Who and what is in danger? (the vulnerable)
- Is it safer to isolate (cordon off) danger from the vulnerable or
- To simply prevent unauthorized access to the danger area? or
- To remove (evacuate) the vulnerable from the danger area?
- Who should be contacted to help and how long will it take for the help to arrive?
- Can the threat or danger be safely attacked while help is on the way?

If security personnel are in any doubt about answers to the above questions, sounding the alarm, evacuating the site and calling emergency services by dialling an emergency number should be the appropriate response.

Emergency and Disaster Management

It is important for security personnel to be able to distinguish between 'disaster' and 'serious incident or emergency' as quickly as possible. This is because security personnel are not well trained or equipped to deal with disasters as opposed to ordinary emergencies. In order to save lives, security personnel need to know immediately when to involve external agencies. For this reason an immediate assessment is required to ascertain as to whether an incident should be treated as an ordinary serious emergency or a disaster. The quicker the security personnel can involve external agencies the quicker they can respond and save lives.

Example of a disaster is a terror event killing at least one person and causing disruptions to normal daily activities of those living and working or commuting in the vicinity. Assignment instructions should detail any potential risk of serious incident or disaster and provide a separate emergency procedure to follow in respect of any identified disaster or serious emergency.

Disasters would have the following characteristics:

- Disasters are likely to affect wider community and cause disruptions to the community around site of main attack or incident
- Due to the scale, disasters cannot be dealt with by local authorities and emergency services in the same manner they deal with other day-to-day incidents
- In addition, disasters would definitely involve serious injuries or death of dozens of people and must cause major disruptions to community or section of community.

If the incident does not meet the above test, it is probably an ordinary emergency in which case emergency services and local authorities can deal with it as part of their day-to-day activities.

In all cases of disaster and emergency, security personnel will have to:

1. **Confirm** – there is an incident and decide whether the incident is an emergency or disaster; then contact emergency services and/or other external agencies if needed

2. **Clear** – use all available warning systems to alert and evacuate everyone by sounding alarm and opening all exit doors in the direction of escape routes

3. **Cordon** – Prevent unauthorised access to danger areas or access/egress (exit) routes

4. **Control** – Incident control point must be established by security personnel and all responders. A control point is simply a coordination point. For example, security manager must appoint people immediately and charge them with the responsibility to implement emergency procedures; ensure that all security personnel know who to take instructions from; and are doing what they should be doing, such as opening exit doors and using emergency equipment (alarm sounders) appropriately. The police, ambulance and fire fighters may have their separate incident control points. It is important that security control points identify various other incident control points and liaise (establish line of contact) with each identified control point.

Procedure for making emergency calls

> **Get the correct emergency number from the assignment instructions. Dial the emergency number to contact emergency services and expect to be asked the following:**

- What service is required (police, fire, ambulance)?
- Phone number for the emergency team to call back?
- Location of the security personnel and location of incident (address/postcode)?
- Type of incident (fire, accident, crime)?
- Any casualties? Give details

Emergency contact team may give further instructions. If unsure as to whether instructions have been understood; stay calm and wait for the emergency services to arrive.

The emergency services (call centre) should immediately analyse and assess the information to determine scale of the incident and response. If the emergency services decide it is a major emergency, this will be declared and all security personnel will be expected to work under the instructions of the emergency services. Security personnel must seek assistance immediately if in doubt of how to carry out any instructions or activities for which they have not received prior training. Security personnel must make note in their pocket book of any instructions or briefings by their controller. Particularly, security personnel must write down in their pocket book details of whom they have been instructed to take orders or further instructions from.

Summary procedures

- In the event of fire – shut doors and windows and leave belongings behind
- In the event of bomb threat evacuations – doors and windows should be kept open and people should be encouraged to take their belongings with them
- In the event of gas leak – electrical switches and other electrical equipment should be left untouched and doors opened to allow gases to diffuse out
- If unsure – still evacuate and call 999 immediately
- Be vigilant
- Take note of anything unusual
- Assist the emergency services
- Answer all calls and make a note of threatening phone calls
- Take reasonable care of own safety
- Always involve someone else when dealing with emergencies
- Do not touch suspicious items or substances
- Exit doors must be opened in all emergencies – if security is a concern, then the exit doors should be manned

Dealing with suspicious calls

- Remain calm
- Make notes
- Note date and time of call
- Treat call as genuine
- Do not interrupt caller
- Inform controller
- Report to the police

Dealing with suspicious items

- Do not touch or smell
- Confirm that it has been left unattended
- Identify the owner
- Evacuate the area
- Secure and cordon off the area
- Inform control
- Inform the police

Chapter 13

Business Continuity Management

Business continuity management aims to reduce the impact of disasters or emergencies in organisations. In its planning, it may be appropriate 'to think the unthinkable'. It is a question as to how the organisation could survive the aftermath of a disaster or crisis or emergency.

Business continuity planning concerns how to achieve a balance between preparing for situations in which business continuity plans will have to be used, while at the same time doing everything possible to prevent use of the plans.

Identifying and assessing known risk

Identifying

- List and review every type of risk that the organisation might face
- Repeat for each level of organisational hierarchy
- Involve more junior staff in the risk and security problem

Assessing

- Thorough security survey of personnel, physical assets, information, areas of liability and business interruption
- A Security Survey is a thorough physical examination of a facility and its operations with respect to personnel and company assets. Examine the risks these assets are exposed to, and review the measures that are in place to protect them and to mitigate liability.
- Physical assets survey should take account of the environment of the organisation and how to defend the space
- Find a socially acceptable balance giving access to people and defending the space.
- Does the environment make criminal perceive fear of getting caught? Good lighting, no obstructions to surveillance of crime targets; understand the designated use of an area.
- Pay attention to doors, windows, lighting, security glazing, roofs.
- Alarms, CCTV and access control systems

Aim of physical security

- Deter
- Delay
- Detect

It is important to understand how these can hinder urgent escapes in event of emergency. So, in business continuity planning, there is need to unify both security and risk management to *resolve conflict between prevention of unauthorised access and allowing people leave in urgent situations.*

What to assess

- Type of activity
- Frequency of activity
- Importance of activity

Assess each against associated risks in terms of:

- Impact (horizontal line graph) – low, med, high
- Frequency (vertical line graph) – low, med, high
- Each with numerical value 1=low, 2=med, 3=high

Table 4 – quantitative subjective risk scores

	1	2	3	4
high				3
medium				2
low				1
	low	medium	high	Totals

Impact

Borodzicz E.P. (2005)

Risk can also be calculated by multiplying 'likelihood' score with 'impact' to give a 'risk score'.

Four Risk Management strategies

Risk avoidance

This might not be an option where the organisation's business, for example is chemical production. The dangers of chemical cannot be completely avoided.

Risk transfer

Instead the chemical company might consider transferring the risk by obtaining insurance or subcontracting.

Risk retention

This is where insurance cover was not obtained. Risk must be assessed in terms of likelihood and impact on the organisation's activities.

Risk reduction

1. Target hardening techniques to reduce likelihood
2. Deal with the impact of the risk

Target hardening refers to physical measures taken to prevent access to a target or to make such access difficult. For example, locking expensive items away in cupboards or placing concrete barriers around important buildings to prevent vehicular terror attack.

The first approach would require cost-benefit analysis. Money spent doesn't always equate protection achieved. There is need to complement systems with human security or manned guarding.

Chapter 14

Recording Incidents and Crime Scene Preservation

Fig 49 Crime Scene Cordons

Reporting and recording incidents have for many years been an integral part of security personnel's role. In the past the bulk of security training and roles was focused on observation and recording or reporting. Over the decades, security roles have expanded beyond, observation, reporting and recording; but still form core responsibilities of security personnel.

Reasons why Reporting and Recording are important

- Written records are necessary to ensure the management and organisation are able to monitor procedures in the frontline and improve them where necessary
- Helps organisation identify areas that require further staff training
- Written records and reports can be used as evidence in court

- They can also be used to ensure security personnel is protected against malicious allegation
- Written reports will help security personnel give accurate account of incident in days or months following the incident

Types of Records

- Pocket book – used for brief or skeletal reports of occurrences as they happen to ensure easy-to-forget essential facts are not forgotten during the subsequent detailed report in an incident report book or daily occurrence book. This book may be provided by the employer. If not provided, it is recommended that security personnel use their own pocket book; but that pocket book cannot be used for non-work related records.
- Incident log-book – is used to log date and time of incident and its brief description, usually in a tabular form
- Incident report – is used for detailed report of an incident
- Daily Occurrence Book (DOB) – this takes the form of a log book. Most log books are tabular forms (forms in the form of tables) used to provide a snapshot of all incidents and occurrences on a particular work shift. In security an occurrence is anything that occurs or the security personnel does on site; for example, start and end times of patrol, official phone calls or received calls and son on, are most common occurrences. Other things that should appear in a Daily Occurrences Book (DOB) include accidents, emergencies, and fights and so on. In security these are referred to as 'incidents' for which incident reports must be completed. But they can appear in the DOB in the form of incident log; or some company procedures may require a separate log, for which an incident log book has to be provided.
- Formal police statement form – In the United Kingdom official police statements are usually recorded in a form called 'MG11' form for presentation as evidence in court.

Details of an incident report

What – this is where the incident is identified. For example, 'fight between two persons' or 'Fire in the building' or 'damaged property' or 'suspicion of stealing'. Avoid using words that may also have other meanings. Use the simplest words to describe what happened.

When – It is also important to state date and time it happened or you became aware of the incident

Who – it is important to describe persons involved or at risk

How – this is where to explain in facts how it started and how it ended. It is important to explain here what you did from the start to the finish.
Response - This should include time police or ambulance or fire fighter or any response team were contacted and time they arrived the scene. It should include details of attending officers and any witnesses present.

Basic guidelines for reporting

- Be simple and plain in language
- Be Accurate
- Be Brief
- Be Clear
- Avoid abbreviations
- Avoid use of correction fluids
- Avoid tearing papers
- Always sign and date your report
- If error is made, draw a single line across it, initial it and write the correct word or sentence next to the deleted word
- Ensure deleted words are still legible
- Each shift should begin with a fresh page
- Entries should be made at the time of incident or as soon after the incident as possible
- All entries should be made in pen
- Check all your entries regularly

Use of force statements

Following any incident where security personnel has used force on a person, written report must be completed immediately after the incident as soon after the incident as possible. This is because use of force is not a requirement of security job and therefore any use of force has to justified by the person who has used force as to why they believed it was 'necessary' to use force and that it was the only option or all other options would have failed to achieve the objective.

Facts which must be included in reports following use of force are:

- Description of behaviour of the other party
- Your responses to it including description of force and level of force used
- Description of any injuries
- First aid and medical support provided
- Was the person taken to hospital? Which hospital?
- Details of why you had to use force in terms of necessity, reasonableness and proportionality in your own personal thought

Necessity – means your opinion as to why you thought force had to be used
Reasonableness – means how a neutral person would view your action
Proportionality – means, whether the force used was too much compared to the resistance or threat. For example, if you use a hammer to kill a crawling insect, say cockroach; the force used is not proportionate and it may be difficult to justify its necessity. If this is the case a neutral right thinking person would think you did not act reasonably.

Summary

Remember to be

A: Accurate
B: Brief
C: Clear

Evidence

Evidence is anything that can help to reveal or determine the truth. This includes records of what the security operative knows, has done or seen in relation to the incident. The security personnel may later be required in court to give account (evidence) of what they know or have done or have seen. This is one of the reasons security personnel must document everything they see, know and do, in relation to an incident.

Balance of Probability

In civil proceedings, the court would weigh the evidence for and against an individual. If the evidence is heavier for one side, the judge would decide for that party, which may also be a decision against the other party. This is called 'balance of probability'. Balance of probability means that, for example; there is more evidence that Mr. A breach his agreement with the other party than not. This implies there is very little doubt that Mr. A breached the agreement.

Beyond Reasonable Doubt

In a **criminal case**, the test is different. The evidence has to show 'beyond reasonable doubt' that a person committed an offence as charged. If there is any doubt as in the case of Mr. A, the prosecution would fail. For this reason, evidence must be handled carefully by security personnel so as to avoid any doubt as to the truth of the evidence.

Types of Evidence

Direct Evidence

What the security personnel actually saw or what happened to him/her.

Circumstantial Evidence

These are facts that may point to one or more conclusions. These are usually facts that have little or no direct connection with the matter under inquiry. For example; Mr. A sees a person running away with an object that looks like a lap top computer. This person was later identified as Mr. C. A few seconds later he came across a person who complained that he had been robbed of his lap top computer and other items.

Mr. A calls the police. Mr. A's evidence would be circumstantial evidence because he did not see Mr. C robbing the victim or stealing from the victim. If he had seen the theft or robbery it would be classed as direct evidence. Circumstantial evidence would need to be supported with direct evidence.

Primary Evidence or Best Evidence

This is the original object or document involved in the case. Original entries on incident logs, statements, DOB, pocket books and reports would normally form part of primary evidence. Objects can also be primary evidence if they are the actual objects involved in the case.

Secondary Evidence

This refers to copy of the original documents. Mostly, police can only request and be given a copy of any evidence.

Documentary Evidence

This refers to any documents produced in court. This includes incident reports, CCTV tapes, DVD, audio CDs or tapes, etc.

Oral Evidence

This is given when a person speaks in court without reading from a written statement.

Real Evidence

This includes any evidence, produced in court in its material or physical form to demonstrate the truth. For example, attack weapon or the actual computer robbed from a victim; if found and produced in court, would be 'real evidence'.

Forensic Evidence

Finger Prints, DNA and blood are very useful in forensic investigation.

Finger Prints

No two persons have the same finger prints pattern. Finger prints are easily left on smooth surfaces. Therefore, latex or rubber gloves can be used if handling objects involved in an incident. Security personnel must avoid handling any object in a crime scene, unless it is necessary to save life. The personnel must not forget to give account of his/her actions immediately to the police and ambulance team on attendance.
DNA

It is only identical twins that have the same DNA profile. Each person has unique DNA profile except identical twins. DNA samples from a crime scene are analysed in a laboratory to identify offender and eliminate suspects from inquiry. Possible samples include hairs, saliva, blood, skin, sweat, urine, semen and so on. Samples can also be extracted from cigarette ends, hankies, drink cans or bottles.

Blood

Blood stain on surfaces like weapon can carry finger prints. Blood spattering pattern can also give glues as to how the crime took place. DNA is present in blood.

Preservation of Evidence

There is need to preserve all evidence from crime scene to the point it reaches the courtroom to preserve integrity. Evidence is handled in a similar may to that of a retailer receiving new stock, identifying them by their origin and labelling them to ensure customer have the correct information about the product they are about to buy. If the labelling is poorly made, then the customer would begin to worry about the integrity of the product.

Security personnel are not required to handle evidence. However, they may have access to media containing evidence like CCTV DVD or tapes, which the security personnel must handle in such a way that the evidence does not lose integrity. For the sake of integrity, custody of evidence must be controlled and documented by security personnel at all times.

Crime Scene Evidence

This approach also applies to evidence security personnel are not allowed to touch or handle – Crime Scene evidence. Crime Scene simply means the actual location of crime event. It is believed that evidence is usually left at a crime scene following a crime event. For example, when a suspected thief is arrested by private security personnel, the location of arrest is the crime scene. This is because private security personnel are only legally allowed to arrest suspects at or not too remote from the crime scene. If anyone is seriously injured at the scene, the scene of attack (crime scene) must be protected by first using tapes or tables/chairs, or any objects capable of ensuring that access control (prevention of unauthorised access) to the scene is maintained. The same principle of preservation applies for all crimes requiring police investigation. It is important to note that the security personnel have initial custody of evidence on a crime scene until police arrive. For this reason, must document all access to the crime scene and reasons for access and if such access was authorised. On police arrival security personnel should await further instructions from the police and act accordingly.

Reasons for Crime Scene Preservation

1.   To ensure chain of custody is maintained – Following a crime event, the crime scene becomes gated territory housing evidence. Access control to the territory is necessary to ensure only authorised persons could enter and record of what they did on entry must be made on pocket book immediately.

2.   To prevent damage/destruction of evidence – if fingerprints are left on surfaces, they may be damaged with someone else's fingerprints thereby affecting its integrity.

3.   To prevent evidence from being moved – apart from contamination, moving evidence from its original location or rearranging it, would affect its integrity.

4.   To prevent contamination of evidence – a person's hair strand or particles from their clothing could affect results of DNA samples collected from the scene.

General Conduct of Security Personnel

- Security personnel must remain calm at all times
- Security personnel must inform other colleagues and not dealing with a crime scene on alone
- Where possible, security personnel may identify any potential evidence left at scene in their pocket book.
- Security personnel must control access until police arrive
- Security personnel must not touch anything at the scene
- Security personnel must at all times take reasonable care of their own safety and safety of others
- On police arrival, security personnel must give account of who might have accessed the crime scene and what they did at the scene to the police.

Chapter 15

Starting the Business

Incorporated and Unincorporated Business

Business may be run as incorporated or unincorporated. Unincorporated businesses require no registration with the government. However, you may be required to register with the Inland Revenue for tax purposes. On the other hand, incorporated businesses will require formal registration with the appropriate bodies authorised by law for that purpose. For this type of business, they would usually have suffixes such as, private limited company (Ltd), public liability company (Plc), limited liability partnership (LLP) etc.

The difference

Unincorporated businesses are usually treated as being the same as their owners whereas incorporated businesses have separate legal personality from their owners. For example, if an incorporated company such as a 'Ltd' company owes money, the owners of the company will not be liable to repay that debt. The owners' liability is limited to the number of shares they purchased in the business. Creditors cannot go after the owner of an incorporated business to recover debt except where such owner has personally guaranteed the loan.

Sole Trading

This is an unincorporated business medium. Sole traders are also known as 'sole proprietors'. This is a person who runs a business on his own as a self-employed person. There is no formal administrative step to set up this type of business. All that is needed is to contact the Inland Revenue to let them know you have started a business. This is to enable the Inland Revenue send tax bills and collect taxes from trading profit. A sole trader is personally liable for all the debts of his business. A sole trader has unlimited liability.

Partnership

This occurs where two or more persons run and own a business together. The partnership is run on the basis of an agreement. The agreement does not have to be in writing. It may be written or oral agreement. No formal registrations with public body is required. In this case each partner will have the responsibility of registering with the Inland Revenue for tax purposes. Each partner pays his own tax from their share of the business profit. The partners have unlimited liability. They have no separate legal status from that of their business. So, creditors can sue them as individuals and as partners and pursue not just the business assets but also personal assets of the partners themselves. 'Joint and Several' liability means that a creditor can pursue one of the partners for the full amount of the debt.

Contractual Co-operation

An agreement for two or more parties to run a business together. It is usually for the purpose of a particular business objective:

- To explore and develop oil and gas fields
- In property development
- To conduct research and development with a view to developing new products

These agreements are sometimes called 'joint ventures'. Once the objective has been achieved the contractual co-operation agreement may come to an end.

Company

A company in the UK is formed by registering certain documents with a public official. In the United Kingdom, the public official charged with the responsibility of registering and overseeing company administrations is the Registrar of Companies at the Companies House.Other countries may have a corporate affairs department for this purpose. A company has a separate legal personality. It can do anything a natural person can do.It is separate from its owners.Companies are not subject to income tax as in sole trading and partnerships. They are subject to a different tax regime – corporation tax. Companies will register with the Inland Revenue as employers for Pay As You Earn (PAYE) and National Insurance purposes for companies in the United Kingdom.

Limited Company

Liability of its members a limited by its constitution. The constitution governs how the company should be run. It will allow directors to limit liability for debts of the company.

Limited by guarantee

- Usually for organisation that are not seeking to make a profit such as charities and professional sports clubs
- The members guarantee that they will pay a specified sum, usually £1 to creditors regardless of the amount of the debt of the company
- No need for members to contribute large amount of money

Limited by shares

They take the form of private company limited by shares and public company limited by shares.

- Private limited company can raise money from restricted circle of owners by way of issuing securities in the form of shares.
- Private limited company is prohibited by law from raising money from the public at large
- Public limited company can raise money from public by issuing securities in the form of shares
- The number of share owned by a member is the extent of their liability to the company.

Chapter 16

Common Terminologies

Contract and In-house security

A 'contract' staff is one employed by a contract security firm, supplied under contract to a client of the private security firm. This is different from 'in-house' staff where the security staff is directly employed by the company at which premises work is carried out.

Assignment Instructions

Assignment means 'area of responsibility'. It is also called a 'Site'. Assignment Instructions are instructions written and provided by the employer and given to the security personnel to ensure duties are carried out effectively on a given Assignment or 'Site'. Assignment instruction can be used as guidance documents aimed at informing and regulating activities of the security personnel. Instructions can also be verbal; but a written instruction can be used as reliable evidence in court to determine liability in legal law suits. Therefore, it is in the security personnel's interest to use pocket book to report verbal instructions that may not be clearly expressed in assignment instructions document.

In the private security industry, security personnel is usually employed to protect assets of individuals or organizations under a contract of service between their employer and the client, on premises usually away from that of their employer. Assignment instructions are usually necessary to specify operational responsibilities of parties and forms part of the contract between the employer and the client (service employer). It is the responsibility of security personnel to familiarize themselves with contents of assignment instructions.

Contents of Assignment instructions

- Emergency contacts
- Emergency procedures
- Details of premises
- Duty objectives
- Reporting procedures
- Shift patterns

COMMON TERMINOLOGIES
- Reporting for duty
- Patrol details
- Responses to alarms
- Health and safety policies/risk assessment
- Search procedures
- Access control requirements
- Equipment
- Radio procedures

Confidential information

Confidential information is defined in security operations as work related information or instructions which security personnel may come across within or outside work premises intended to; inform, instruct, or educate employees in confidence. Confidential information cannot be disclosed to unauthorized persons, including families or friends. Assignment instructions document is an example of confidential document. Conspiracy charges may be made against anyone that discloses confidential information to unauthorized persons if found to assist in the planning or execution of a crime event.

Manned Services

Manned Services is the use of personnel such as uniformed or plain clothed officer in protecting commercial, industrial and retail premises, transporting cash and valuable.

In this book, the terms 'security personnel', 'security officer', 'Doorkeeper' will be used interchangeably. Doorkeepers perform manned guarding duties in hospitality premises, such as hotels, clubs, games and sport events, etc. Security officers perform manned guarding duties in non-hospitality premises. The term 'security personnel' is a general term used to refer to both security officers and Doorkeepers.

Manned Services sector comprises of:
- *Doorkeepers;* responsible for deciding on the suitability of patrons to be allowed on to a licensed/leisure premises. In the United Kingdom, licensed premises are premises approved by law to carry out licensable activities such as supply of alcohol by retail, provision of public entertainment and late night refreshments (hot food or hot drinks between the hours of 11pm and 5am; UK Licensing Act 2003)
- *Security Guards;* responsible for protecting non-licensed premises such as shops, office buildings, construction sites, aviation and maritime assignments. A security guard may be employed in a reception, caretaking or customer service role but differs from a caretaker or customer service officer or receptionist in many ways. One of the main distinctions is the link between security guarding and loss prevention. Loss can be in the form of damage, injury, theft, crime and

wastes. In addition to customer service, a security guard is expected to antici-pate and prevent the occurrence of these incidents as a matter of duty. This re-sponsibility is observed in all sectors within manned services. The regulatory authority for private security industry (SIA) allows holders of Door Supervi-sion licence to work as Security Guards.

- **Keyholding;** Keyholding is simply holding keys. Keys can be electronic or physical. A keyholder may be needed for emergency access to buildings or for snap patrol checks of secure areas. Anyone with a security licence can legally perform keyholding duties in the UK.
- *Cash and Valuables in Transit* (CVIT); responsible for secure transportation of cash and other valuables from and to locations, including banks retail shops and cash depots or warehouses
- **Vehicle Immobilising;** responsible for wheel clamping
- **Private Investigation;** responsible for investigation of civil and criminal of-fences as may be authorised by a party or parties to civil cases or may be ap-pointed as authorised agents of investigatory authorities. Private investigators come under a different regulatory arrangement and are not currently regulated by the Security Industry Authority.
- *CCTV Operations (Public Space Surveillance)*; responsible for observing, recording and processing images obtained through surveillance of public spaces
- *Close Protection;* responsible for the protection of persons or groups against assault or physical harassment

• **Systems** – These are also referred to as, technologies of control and the sec-tor comprises of intruder alarms, CCTV, fire systems, Biometrics, Radio Frequency Identification (RFID) technology; often referred to as 'bar code or Electronic Price Code', swipe cards and other access control systems. In security, systems are ex-pected to perform two or more roles and can be manipulated to work well or interact with other security measures at play. In turn those other security measures able to work well with a system to produce an expected result or output becomes part of the security system. These include the security guards, gates, barriers padlocks, policies and procedures and so on.

• **Physical Security** – These can also be referred to as mechanical security and include locks, grills, gates and barriers. It can also include certain aspects of the de-sign of the property aimed at making unauthorized access difficult; for example, locking away high value goods in shops.

Routine activity offender

Routine activity' offender attacks a target where the space at the 'time' provides opportunity to attack the target. There is usually no prior planning of the crime event.

Rational choice offender

Rational choice offenders would first identify a target and evaluate the protection around the target before making the conscious decision to approach the target.

Control Rooms

A control room is simply a coordination centre for security operations. Coordination centres do not have to be a room. They can be in the form of mobile vehicles or even non-sheltered. The principle behind the working of a control room is to bring all duty posts or operations under one imaginary territory with a single communication link between a controller and each operation or duty post.

Functions of Control Rooms

- Provide back-up and evidence
- Provide answers to questions from customers and members of the public
- Monitoring security personnel's safety through 'check calls'
- Plan how the site may be covered
- Harmonise activities of security personnel with service employer's requirements

Types of Control Room

- Remote monitoring centre for alarm
- Remote monitoring Centre for CCTV for Security
- Control rooms for telephone answering and check calls

Basic Equipment

Security personnel would require the following equipment in all sites:

- Assignment instructions
- Daily occurrence book – to report each task carried out by personnel in a shift
- Keys
- Torch

Specialist equipment

Nature of the site and duties to be carried out may require use of specialised equipment. Equipment that may be required are:

- Clocking device (for proof of patrol checks)
- Swipe card
- Radio
- Phone
- Pocket book
- Pager

CHAPTER 17

A Summary of Skills and Functions expected of A Security personnel in Various Roles and Assignments

Functions security personnel are expected to perform towards protection of life

	Store Detective	General Security Role	Leisure Venues	Retail Security Personnel	Skills Requirement/ Competence
Housekeeping	Dealing with fire hazards such as litters	assignment instructions	Keeping access roads clear; taking down displays	Ensuring empty boxes packed flat	Health & Safety at work
Customer Care		Dealing with emergencies; flood, assignment instructions etc.	Administering first aid		Customer Care & Social Skills
	Dealing with those emotionally unstable	Dealing with violence	Evacuations		Emergencies & Conflict Management

Functions security personnel are expected to perform towards protection of property and premises objective

	Store Detective	General Security Role	Leisure Venues	Retail Security Personnel	Skills Requirement/ Competence
Housekeeping	Fire prevention, assignment instructions	fire hazard checks	patrols	Packing empty boxes	
Preventing Crime & anti-social behaviour	Preventing shoplifting, assignment instructions	Access control, CCTV, searching, patrols	Locking and unlocking of premises, alarm setting & unsetting	Patrol shop, open & visible presence, Guarding entrances and exits	Patrolling Access control, searching & Security Systems

Functions security personnel are expected to perform towards prevention of loss objective

	Store Detective	General Security Role	Leisure Venues	Retail Security Personnel	Skills Requirement/ Competence
Housekeeping	Preventing losses due to carelessness	assignment instructions	Control of keys, turning off lights to save energy	Checking rubbish bins for misplaced goods	Health and safety skills
Customer Care	assignment instructions	Recording of safekeeping of lost and found property, assignment instructions	Manning entrances and exits, assignment instructions	assignment instructions	Customer Care & Social Skills

Functions a security personnel are expected to perform towards prevention of crime objective

	Store Detective	General Security Role	Leisure Venues	Retail Security Personnel	Skills Requirement/ Competence
Preventing crime & anti-social behaviour	Surveillance, Vigilance, assignment instructions	Foot patrol, access control, CCTV, assignment instructions	Visible presence, access control, searches locking & unlocking premises, assignment instructions	Patrols, guarding entrances and exits, searches, matching goods with receipts, perimeter checks, assignment instructions	Patrolling; Access Control; Searching; Security systems
Information gathering & sharing	Seizing & storing evidence, report writing, police liaison and court attendances, assignment instructions	Reporting offences to police, assignment instructions	CCTV monitoring, filling forms and liaising with police, assignment instructions	Detection of unusual behaviour and investigation of behaviour, assignment instructions	Communications and reporting

Schneider, R.H. (2006)

References

Armitage, R., and Pease K. (2007) 'Design and Crime: Proofing Electronic Products and Services against *Theft' European Journal on Criminal Policy and Research* 14 (1): 2-7.

Beck, A., Peackock, C. (2009) *New Loss Prevention: Redefining Shrinkage Management,* New York: Palgrave Macmillan

Beck, A., Peackock, C. (2009) *New Loss Prevention: Redefining Shrinkage Management,* New York: Palgrave Macmillan

Beck, A., Willis, A (1998) 'Sales and Security: Striking the Balance' in M. Gill (eds) *Increasing The Risk for Offenders: Volume ii,* New York: Palgrave Macmillan, 95

Brega, A.A., (2007) 'Policing Crime Hot Spots' in Walsh B.C., Farrington, D.P. (eds) *Preventing Crime: What Works for Children, Offenders, Victims, and Places,* 179-192, Springer.

CALL, (2010) 'Handbook Radio Operator' *Tactics, Techniques and Procedures* US Unclassified: No. 10-33

Chemguard, (2007) 'High Expansion Foam Systems' http://www.chemguard.com (accessed: 6/01/13)

Cote, S. (2002) 'Crime as Rational Choice in Criminological Theories: Bridging the CPS, (2011) 'Wounding and Inflicting Grievous Bodily Harm with Intent: Offences against the person', www.cps.gov.uk/legal/s_to_u/sentencing, (accessed: 5/11/12)

Crowe, T.D. (2000) *CPTED Concepts and Strategies in Crime Prevention Through Environmental Design: Applications of Architectural Design and Space Management Concepts (2nd Edition),* Butterworth-Heinemann: National Crime Prevention Institute, an imprint of Elsevier.

Crown Prosecution Service (CPS), *Offensive Weapons, Knives, Bladed and pointed Articles,* www.cps.gov.uk/legal/l_to_o/offensive_weapons_knives_bladed_and_pointed_articles/, (accessed: 19/01/2013)

Department of Criminology (2009/2010) *Module 1: Leicester: Department of Criminology, University of Leceicester*

Department of Criminology (2009/2010) *Module 1: Leicester: Department of Criminology, University of Leceicester*

Department of Criminology (2009/2010) *Risk Communication Unit*, Leicester: Department of Criminology, University of Leicester

Dyson, J. and Walker, A., (2011) 'Door Supervision Handbook', in J. Dyson, and A. EF Johnson Technologies, (2009) Atlas System Solutions, www.efjohnson.com (accessed: 15/12/2012)

Fielding, N and Thomas, H (2008) 'Qualitative Interviewing' in N Gilbert (ed) *Researching Social Life*, London: Sage, 245-266

Fire Advisor, 'Gas Based Flooding System' www.fireadvisor.com (accessed: 6/01/2013)

Global Terrorism Index (2015) 'Measuring and Understanding the Impact of Terrorism' Maryland: Institute for Economics and Peace

Health and safety Executives, (2009) *The Health and safety (Safety Signs and Signal): Guidance on Regulations,* London: HSE.

Health and safety Executives, (2011) 'Health and safety Policy' www.hse.gov. uk/risk/fivesteps.htm (accessed: 6/01/2013)

Hind, S., (Australian Institute of Criminology) *'Private Policy and Policing: Does private enterprise have a role in delivering the output of public safety and security'?* http://www.aic.gov.au/publications/previous%20series/proceedings/1-27/~/media/publications/proceedings/23/hinds.ashx, (accessed 15th November 2011).

Home Office, (2003) *Licensing Act* 2003, www.homeoffice.gov.uk/drugs/alcohol/licensing-act-next-steps/, (accessed: 14/02/2013).

Home Office, (2011) *Police and Criminal Evidence Act, 1984: PACE Code A: Police Officers of Statutory Powers of Stop and Search,* London: HO

Home Office, (2012) *Amended Guidance Issued under Section 182 of the Licensing Act 2003*, London: Stationery Office: HO

Internal/External Security Continuum in Europe (2009) *A report on the ethical issues raised by the increasing role of private security professionals in security analysis and provision*, Amsterdam: INEX

Johnston, L., (1999) 'PRIVATE POLICING IN CONTEXT' *European Journal on Criminal Policy and Research 7*: 175-196

Kinsella, C., McGarry, J., (2011) 'computer says no: technology and accountability in policing traffic stops' *Law and Soc Change* 55: 167-184

Kinsella, C., McGarry, J., (2011) 'computer says no: technology and accountability in policing traffic stops' *Law and Soc Change* 55: 167-184

M.Gill (ed) *The Handbook of Security*, New York: Palgrave Macmillan, 90-111.

MI5, (2011) *Other Issues (Former Threats)* www.mi5.gov.uk/output/other-issues-former-threats (accessed 10 April 2012).

National Counter Terrorism Security Office, *NaCTSO Guidance Note 3* (2015)

Newman, O. (1972) *Defensible Space*, London: Architectural Press

NICE & NTA, (2007) *Misuse of Drugs and other substances: Implementing NICE Guidance:* NICE

Office of Public Sector Information (OPSI) *Theft Act*, 1968, http://www.opsi.gov.uk/ RevisedStatutes/Acts/ukpga/1968/cukpga_19680060_en_1#pb2-l1g7, [accessed 10th September 2010].

Ogbonna, E. and Harris, L.C., (2006) 'Managing organisational culture: Insights from the hospitality industry' *Human Resource Management Journal 12* (1), 33-50

Parnaby, P. (2007) 'Crime prevention through environmental design: financial hardship, the dynamics of power, and the prospects of governance' *Crime Law and Social Change* 48 (3): 73-168.

Past to the Future' in S. Cote (ed) *The Reasoning Criminal: Rational Choice perspectives on offending,* London: Sage Publications, 291-296.

Schneider, R.H. (2006) 'Contributions of Environmental Studies to Security' in Skills for Security (2011) 'basic job training programme' *Skills for Security*: version 1-2011.

Stenning, P.C., (2000) 'POWERS AND ACCOUNTABILITY OF PRIVATE POLICE' *European Journal on Criminal Policy and Research 8*: 325-352

The Crown Prosecution Service, *Binding Over Orders,* www.cps.gov.uk/legal/a_ to_ c/binding_over_orders/, (accessed: 13/January 2013)

The Nation Online, (2012) 'Okorocha Gana call for state police' http://www.thenationonlineng.net/2011/news/56987-okorocha-gana-call-for-state-police.html (accessed 9th Aug 2012)

The National Archives, (1986) *Public Order Act* 1986, www.legislation.gov.uk/ukpga/1986/64, (accessed: 13/01/2013)

The National Archives, (2002) *Police Reform Act,* 2002, http://www.legislation.gov.uk/ukpga/2002/30/section/39, (accessed 14th November 2011)

The National Archives, *Offences against a Person Act 1861,* www.legislation.gov.uk/ukpga/vict/24-25/100/contents, (accessed: 13/01/2013)

Wakefield, A. (2006) 'The Security Officer' in M.Gill (ed) *The Handbook of Security,* New York: Palgrave Macmillan, 383-405.

Walker, A. (2015) *Working as a Door Supervisor: Course Book (3rd Edition),* Highfield International Ltd

Walker, A. (2015) *Working as a Security Officer: Course Book (2nd Edition),* Highfield International Ltd

Walsh, D.P.J. and Conway, V., (2011) 'Police governance and accountability: overview of current issues' *Crime Law Soc Change 55*: 61-86

Wortley, R., & Mazerolle, L. (2008) 'Pattern Theory' in Environmental Criminology and Crime Analysis' in R. Wortley and L. Mazerolle (eds) *Crime Pattern Theory,* London: Willan Publishing, 78-93.

Your Rights, *Arrest at Common Law for Breach of the Peace: The Liberty Guide to Human Rights,* www.yourrights.org.uk/yourrights/the-rights-of-suspects/police-power-of-arrest/arrest-at-common-law-for-breach-of-the-peace.html, (accessed: 13th January 2013)

Printed in Great Britain
by Amazon

26967835R00090

THE
CANCER
ROLLER
COASTER

How to manage the emotional and mental impact

JULIETTE CHAN

C000068467

Copyright 2019 by Juliette Chan

All rights reserved. This book or any portion thereof may not be reproduced or used in any manner whatsoever without the express written permission of the author except for the use of brief quotations in a book review.

Printed in the United Kingdom
First Printing January 2019

First Edition

ISBN: 978-1-9164894-6-2 (Print)
ISBN: 978-1-9164894-7-9 (eBook)

Librotas Books
Portsmouth
Hampshire
PO2 9NT

Contents

INTRODUCTION

We cannot direct the wind but we can adjust the sails.

– Author Unknown

'D on't underestimate the psychological impact,' Helen, my cancer nurse specialist, reminded me with a warm smile. I was glad to see her at my bedside and felt reassured as I came round from my operation to remove the cancer in my colon. 'Sure, OK,' I said and drifted back to sleep.

It wasn't until many months later that I realised I wasn't sure what she meant. What are the signs? What should I be looking out for? How do I know that I have a problem? Am I going to have a breakdown? Will I develop a mental health issue?

Five months on, I looked back to the time of my diagnosis and it was like someone had pressed the 'Pause' button on my life. On a practical level, I'd found myself on the cancer conveyor belt of tests, consultations and decision-making. Mentally and emotionally, it felt like more of a roller coaster ride.

My energy levels were low and I was always tired. I couldn't focus on work for more than half an hour and I struggled to motivate myself. I'd lost my mojo and I had 'washing machine brain' – full of inane thoughts that just went round and round. Questions preoccupied my brain: Why am I still tired months later? When will I feel normal again? Will I ever feel normal again or is this how I'll be for the rest of my life – a fragile imitation of myself? Will the cancer come back?

It all started one Tuesday, two days after my 50th birthday, when I had a colonoscopy to investigate why my irritable bowel symptoms had worsened over the last year. When they found a tumour in my colon, I wasn't concerned as I figured it wouldn't be cancerous, just a benign lump that could be removed. After all, I was the fittest I'd been for years. I was running, swimming and cycling six times a week and eating a healthy diet, with occasional treats here and there. I'd completed my first sprint triathlon in 2015 and was training to do four more in 2016.

A few days after the colonoscopy, I was home alone and received a letter for a follow-up appointment the following Tuesday. It was with a consultant I'd never seen before so, naturally, I looked him up online; 'Cancer Team' came up. My first reaction was 'Huh? How can that be? Cancer?' I was convinced they'd got my biopsy results mixed up with someone else! I'm active, fit and healthy; surely cancer doesn't happen to people like me? Obviously, it did, and you can read more of my story in Part 2 of this book.

Along the way, with some help, I recognised that going through cancer is about dealing with a series of losses, and the initial psychological impact is grief. This was an 'aha' moment for me because handling grief is something that I have expertise in. However, having met and connected with many cancer patients, I've noticed that there isn't much knowledge or understanding of grief arising from the cancer experience.

What's more, much of the advice given about handling emotions stops at 'talk about it'. But sometimes, talking isn't enough; cancer can trigger a significant emotional and mental response in some people and without the right understanding and proper support, they often struggle to function, or bury their pain and act as if everything is OK. That breaks my heart because it doesn't have to be like this.

And that's why I was compelled to write this book – to raise awareness of cancer grief and to guide those affected by cancer towards greater peace of mind and heart.

One Size Doesn't Fit All

Cancer is a unique experience for each person. There are hundreds of different types of cancer and they are caught at different stages, and require a number of tests and individualised treatments. There isn't a one-size-fits-all cure and on top of that, your treatment experience and your response to the treatments can range from 'dreadful' to 'excellent'.

To start with, there are the three words no-one wants to be told – 'You have CANCER'. As you absorb the news and what it means to you and those around you, you then have to cope with the cancer conveyor belt – a series of tests, consultations, decision-making and treatments. Add to that the strain of breaking the news to your family, friends and work, of having to handle their reactions, opinions and advice, and of keeping them up to date. It's a lot to cope with.

If the odds are in your favour, you survive the cancer conveyor belt, but the regular check-ups and tests to monitor you for the next few years can bring back some uncertainty and anxiety. Or maybe you are still living with cancer. Perhaps it comes back or it spreads and you need further treatment, so you feel like you're back at square one. It might be that the cancer is incurable and although ongoing treatment keeps it under control, you're living as best you can with the uncertainty. Or maybe you have limited time left. Whatever your circumstances, you are facing a different reality to what you had previously, one which is unique to you.

Whilst our experiences of cancer cannot be compared like-for-like, there are common physical, emotional and mental responses that most people can relate to and need to adjust to.

In my survey of cancer patients aged between 30 and 60, at different stages of their cancer experience:

- Almost 90% experienced fatigue and low energy levels.
- Three-quarters had physical side-effects.
- About a third said that they felt more emotional and had concerns over their mental health.
- About one in five struggled to function at work or had problems with eating.
- One in ten reported feeling differently about their relationships.

Regardless of where you are on the cancer conveyor belt, the mental and emotional impact of cancer is a psychological roller coaster.

Psychological Impact

Having cancer is a life-changing experience and it leaves its mark on you physically and psychologically.

The Oxford Dictionary defines the word 'psychological' as:

'Of, affecting, or arising in the mind; related to
the mental and emotional state of a person.'

In my experience, and that of others I've interviewed for this book, cancer patients are generally better informed and prepared for the physical side-effects once the treatment is over. It is recognised that there may be ongoing pain, fatigue, nausea and so on; it is understood that you need to rest frequently and that your physical capabilities may be limited for a while; and it is accepted that time will help your body to heal.

However, it's a different story when it comes to dealing with the psychological after-effects – the mental and emotional impact of the experience. Whether done consciously or unintentionally, the most widespread response is to ignore, bury or avoid uncomfortable or unfamiliar feelings and thoughts. But in the quiet moments, if you pay attention and listen to yourself, you are likely to find that your mind and your emotional heart are not at peace.

Commonly, thoughts about the cancer go round and round. You may be asking yourself questions similar to those raised by respondents to a survey I did for this book:

- When do I feel normal again?
- When will this go away?
- Will I get past all this?
- How do I stop thinking about the cancer coming back?
- How do I move forward with life without the fear of reoccurrence?
- Why do I wonder where and when cancer will come back? Is that a normal thought process?

- How do I recover from the trauma of a shock diagnosis and how do I improve mentally down the track from cancer?
- When can I overcome the stress?
- How do I cope with terminal diagnosis?
- Why did my ribs break? Will they always be weak? Will they break again?
- Why hasn't anyone got any answers?
- Why did some friends find it hard to interact normally with me when they found out I have cancer?
- How can I cope with feeling more emotional than before getting cancer in everyday situations?
- Is it normal to think about what has happened on a daily basis, sometimes even dreaming of it all?
- Will I ever stop thinking: 'Is it going to come back?'
- How do I get my adult children to understand that I need their practical support a bit more? They are so used to me coping well.
- How can I move forward positively, being vigilant but not focusing on whether it will come back?
- Is there ever going to be a normal day again?
- Will I ever forget this in time? Will I feel normal again?
- How do I deal with thoughts about dying?
- Why did I survive?
- Why am I still here when others died?

At every stage of the cancer experience, even after treatment is over, you will encounter psychological reactions. Everyone does because it's how humans process significant change. If you're not prepared, ready or willing to admit to having an emotional or mental response, just know that it's happening inside you regardless.

Dealing with the Psychological Impact

From my research and my own cancer experience, there is a lot of useful advice to help cancer patients look after themselves physically, nutritionally and financially. However, I found that the advice on dealing with emotional and mental side-effects is patchy and usually stops at 'talk about it'.

Talking is, of course, helpful and gives you immediate comfort. It also helps you to discover and understand what's going on. However, in order to be fully at peace with your cancer experience, you also need to take action to address and release your emotional pain, not just talk about it. Whether you are living with cancer or have been given the all clear, performing an emotional clear-out will give you freedom to live life on your own terms without any unresolved emotions weighing you down.

Those who are fortunate to get therapy find it useful, but not everyone is able to or willing to access these services. It could be that you don't have the money or there is a long waiting list. Perhaps you simply 'don't do counselling/therapy'.

However, you have an innate ability to deal with the traumatic events you face. We all do. But over time, with the 'busy-ness' of life and striving to succeed or survive in the modern world, you may have lost the connection with this ability. This could leave you struggling psychologically or putting up barriers so you don't have to feel pain. Either way, your potential to live and function fully becomes restricted.

The objective of this book is to help you address the questions above, and give you and your close friends and family a better understanding of the emotional and mental impact of cancer. It will also equip you with the know-how to help yourself (and others if relevant) to let go of any emotional pain caused by the cancer. It is possible for you to take care of the psychological impact and to live well.

How to Use this Book

This book will show you how you can help yourself and it will equip you with tools and ideas that you need to handle the psychological impact of your cancer experience. It will be of value to you no matter where you or your nearest and dearest are on the cancer conveyor belt. It will help you to reconnect with yourself and figure out a way forward that works for you, whatever your current circumstances.

If it's not you who has or had cancer, you will still experience emotional and mental reactions. Although your own life may not have been threatened, it will have been changed and much of it beyond your control. This book will also help you to come to terms with the psychological impact of what's happened and to deal with it.

The book is split into three parts so that you can access the section that will be most useful to you at this point in time. For instance, if you have just been diagnosed, it is unlikely that Part 3 will be relevant to you now but Parts 1 and 2 will provide you with a lot of valuable insight as to how to tackle the psychological effects as you experience them.

Since each part is designed to be stand-alone, you may find that there is some repetition. This is intentional.

Part 1: Psychological Response to Cancer
This section outlines the mental and emotional responses to the transformative experience that is cancer. It will deepen your understanding of the psychological side-effects.

Part 2: Stories of 'Normal'
Here, there are real-life personal stories from eight people to illustrate the range of emotional and mental responses that people have to cancer. In doing

so, I recognise fully that your experience will not be the same; parts may resonate with you but others may not. There is no one-size-fits-all.

Part 3: The Workbook
This contains a series of exercises, split into four stages:

- Stage 1 – Mapping Your Cancer Experience
- Stage 2 – Discovering Your Guide to Life
- Stage 3 – Taking Stock
- Stage 4 – Letting Go

I am not a medical professional but the workbook is based on my experience of helping over 400 emotionally vulnerable people who struggled after being hit by a significant life-changing event. It is also the process that I personally used to work through the psychological effects of my bowel cancer.

The exercises are organised to help you discover and work through the mental and emotional impact of your cancer experience and to let go of any associated emotional pain that may be limiting you. It also guides you to figuring out what you now want in your life, because whether you like it or not, things are not exactly as they were.

Note of Caution
The workbook is therefore not intended for anyone who has a history of medically recognised depression or other psychological conditions that mean you are considered to be at risk of harming yourself or others. If this is you, then you must share and discuss the exercises with your medical team and take their advice as to whether or not you should do them.

The workbook is designed to help readers face hidden and buried emotional pain from their cancer experience but in your case, it could mean you facing too much in one go. You will need extra support and guidance, so always work with your medical or mental health team.

PART 1

_____

PSYCHOLOGICAL RESPONSE TO CANCER

Grief is like the ocean, it comes in waves ebbing and flowing. Sometimes the water is calm, and sometimes it is overwhelming. All we can do is learn to swim.

– Vicki Harrison

As mentioned above, the psychological impact involves both your mental and emotional states. What's more, your body, mind and emotions are interconnected; each affects the other. Human mental, physical and emotional interactions are obviously complex and the purpose of this part is not to provide some deep scientific explanation, but to give you the key information so that you can begin to understand what is happening to you and why.

The Psychological Roller Coaster

It is natural that when your physical wellbeing is under threat from cancer, you will experience a range of unpredictable thoughts and emotions – random in nature, intensity, timing and duration. The most common analogy that cancer patients use to describe this experience is: 'It's like an emotional roller coaster.' There are really low moments, times that feel scary or insecure, and also instances of relief, exhilaration and joy.

The side-effects vary from person to person and not all of these will apply to you, but here are the emotions that cancer patients commonly report:

- Moody
- Brain-fogged
- Fatigued
- 'Depressed'
- Lost
- Lonely
- Angry
- Resentful
- Vulnerable
- Confused
- Unsettled
- Empty
- Numb
- Grateful
- Relieved
- Happy

Additionally, there's often increased angst over returning to work and mounting financial stress, or perhaps you're just generally more anxious altogether. This can be compounded by reduced confidence and a diminished ability to concentrate, two symptoms often suffered by those affected by cancer. Half of the 40 people who responded to my survey for this book said that they felt more intolerant. There may also be the worry of the cancer returning. Or if you're living with cancer, the mental and emotional pressure can be constant and overwhelming.

The psychological impact of your cancer experience can leave you unable to fully function at home or at work. Your relationships may be strained as your cancer will undoubtedly affect those around you, so you find yourself out of kilter with your family and friends. Things they care about might seem trivial to you or you might find that you can no longer feel joy fully.

Perhaps you find it difficult to focus or to communicate how you feel because you're not sure how you feel. You may be tired of talking about your cancer and want to think about other things in life, but your ongoing treatment or check-ups are constant reminders that all is not 'normal'.

Cancer is unquestionably a life-changing experience. Even if, like I did, you take the attitude that the cancer will not affect how you live, and decide that you're going to live life to the fullest and not 'wallow', you are a human being and are therefore not immune from the emotional and mental consequences of cancer.

However, it is true that no two people will feel exactly the same; what one person considers to be a minor incident could be a significant cause of emotional pain for another. It is pointless and unhelpful therefore to compare yourself against others. There is no right or wrong approach, only what feels right for you.

Let's start by considering the mental and emotional impacts separately.

Mental Response to Cancer

This all boils down to survival. Faced with a potentially life-threatening illness like cancer, your brain's primal function is to guard you and keep you safe. The 'fight/flight/freeze' response kicks in. This is inbuilt and you may not even be aware that you're hyperalert.

Besides the potential dangers of the physical cancer itself, your mind will also perceive and act in response to other threats such as physical pain, uncomfortable thoughts and emotional heartache. It is also threatened by unfamiliar or unpleasant situations such as chemotherapy, radiotherapy, a major operation, etc.

If your mental and emotional wellbeing is threatened, your brain's number one priority is still survival and it will automatically look for ways to fight or escape these threats. Alternatively, the fear of what you're facing can lead you to avoid the truth or to shut down, because otherwise you would be overwhelmed. To protect you, the 'freeze' mode then comes into play.

At any time, depending on what you're facing and your past experiences of traumatic events, you may experience fight, flight or freeze impulses simultaneously or in various combinations. One moment you could be ready to fight, the next you want to run away. Or perhaps on hearing your diagnosis, your mind blanks out and you freeze but in the next instant you choose to focus on practical matters.

Examples of Short- and Long-term Survival Mode Symptoms

Fight

- Your jaw is tight or you grind your teeth.
- You put on a brave face and get on with life.
- You want life to continue **exactly** as it did before.
- You may go into problem-solving mode and become overly practical.
- You have problems eating or digesting food and your stomach is tied up in knots.
- You become angry, irritable or defensive with others.
- You are frustrated with yourself whenever you feel down, tired or emotional.
- Fighting helps you feel less overwhelmed and more in control.
- Paying attention to your feelings is judged to be self-indulgent and pointless.
- You are primarily focused on 'being/thinking positive'.

Flight

- You feel trapped or become fidgety.
- You put a mask on and run away from any emotional pain or uncomfortable thoughts.
- You tell yourself that you don't have time or energy to deal with this.
- You put on a brave face, act 'strong' and get on with life.
- You distract yourself by being busy.
- You exercise excessively.
- You daren't stop because if you do, then you might just get upset – and you don't want that!
- You avoid talking about your cancer because it's too scary or because you want to avoid the topic altogether in case you get upset or it brings back painful memories.

Freeze

- Fear leaves you numb, stumped or speechless.
- You hold your breath.
- You disconnect from a part of your body.
- Your mind goes blank.
- You feel confused and decision-making is harder.
- You feel stiff or heavy.
- You have a sense of dread.
- You tremble or faint.
- You struggle to get out of bed or to do anything.
- You feel totally helpless or want to give up.
- You find it difficult to motivate yourself.
- You feel that your life has paused or is unreal. You're 'spaced out'.
- You might not want to know too much about the cancer or treatment and leave it to the professionals.
- Your anxiety levels are higher than usual.
- Your focus shifts to the bigger picture and you struggle to pay attention to everyday tasks.
- Your cancer defines you and you struggle with your self-image.
- You may be preoccupied with 'What if it spreads or comes back?'

The survival response is usually helpful, and in the short term it has the important and useful task of keeping you alive and helping you to deal with difficult situations. You do need to have some fight to get through the shock, decision-making, treatment and so on. But if your brain stays stuck on high alert, it's difficult for its other emotional and rational activities to function as they should. Your cognitive capacity is noticeably reduced and there is literally little space for you to feel and think clearly. It's no wonder that indecision and an inability to focus on routine matters is a common experience for anyone facing cancer. People describe it as 'brain fog', 'fuzzy brain' or 'washing machine brain'.

Physiology of Survival

When you're threatened or your mind perceives danger, the amygdala, the part of your brain that plays an important role in processing emotions, sends a distress signal to the hypothalamus. The hypothalamus, your brain's central command, communicates with the rest of your body via the autonomic nervous system, which controls your body functions such as your heartbeat, breathing, blood vessels and blood pressure.

With the alarm raised, the hypothalamus signals to key organs of your body and hormones are released into your bloodstream to make you ready to fight or run away. Your heart beats faster, your blood pressure goes up and you start to breathe more quickly. Your lungs take in extra oxygen that is pumped to your brain and you become more alert. Your senses are heightened, your focus is sharpened onto the threat and your awareness of pain lessens. Blood is redirected away from non-essential areas like your gut to your muscles and limbs so they are ready for action. Your fine and complex motor skills are impaired. You are now fully prepared to react to the danger.

Once the danger has passed, your body goes back to normal.

Our bodies are not designed to live constantly in a state of hyperalertness. An obvious example of the survival response is the well-documented fact that your gut processes are affected and become less efficient during an emergency. With an ongoing threat like cancer, it's therefore important for you to override the survival switch to restore your peace of mind; if you're stuck in survival mode in the long term, the stresses and strains can lead to psychological and physical ill-health.

How do you manage the mental response? This is what this book is designed to guide you through. It will develop your understanding of what's going on so that you know when it's OK to be in survival mode and when it's detrimental to your wellbeing. The exercises in the workbook (Part 3) will also give you the practical steps to take to achieve clarity and peace of mind.

Emotional Response to Cancer

The moment you suspect or hear that you have cancer, you experience a change in how you perceive yourself and how others perceive you. It's only natural. Often, it's a seismic change and the sense of loss is obvious. If it's a subtle shift in perception, it is nevertheless a change that includes some form of loss, however small.

Life Losses

Loss usually arises from a change in your life, where something is now different, not as it was. This could be the loss of a person (e.g. death, divorce/separation, children leaving home); losing something you value (e.g. your pet, a treasured possession, trust in a person); or a significant change in your circumstances (e.g. loss of health, losing/changing jobs, moving home, change in income).

Even a change for the better, such as coming to the end of your chemotherapy, involves some form of loss. For example, although you may be glad and relieved to have come to the end of the treatment, you might feel sad because you'll no longer see your favourite nurse who helped you through the hard times or you now face a waiting game until your next consultation which means there is a new routine that you now have to adjust to.

Loss of Health

With cancer, you are obviously dealing with loss of health. I have observed that cancer patients often only consider the headline 'Loss of health' and think that once their treatment is over, they can simply focus on regaining their health. However, underneath this headline there are many subtle losses, some of which you may not be aware of, and these can have a substantial effect on your wellbeing. Being aware of hidden losses is key to understanding the emotional responses to cancer.

As an example, the table below shows the different losses reported by the 40 cancer patients surveyed for this book.

Losses reported by respondents to survey	
Loss of energy	87%
Loss of confidence	59%
Loss of focus or ability to concentrate	59%
Loss of motivation	51%
Loss of income	49%
Loss of sex drive	46%
Loss of tolerance of others	44%
Loss of identity/sense of who you were	41%
Loss of self-esteem	38%
Loss of social network	26%
Loss of hope	18%
Loss of weight	2%

Essentially, cancer means that you lose a lot of what you considered to be 'normal' for you, so the list above is by no means exhaustive. I know that after reading this, you can come up with many more examples. And clearly, some are interlinked or can lead to other losses: if you lose your ability to focus or concentrate fully, you will struggle at work, which means that you might have to give up work, work part-time or even lose your job. This could then lead to a loss in income, a loss of confidence in your professional ability, a loss of tolerance of others, a loss of your work-based social interaction, a loss of purpose (if you don't have a job), and so on.

What's more, many of the losses listed can be broken down further into other hidden losses that are affecting how you feel physically, mentally and emotionally. Let's consider a loss of sex drive. It's understandable that initially this may come about because of your physical condition as you are fatigued, have physical pain or suffer a dysfunction as a result of the treatment. Or if you're like a friend of mine, 'I frankly have more important life-threatening things to be thinking about!'

Imagine, however, that your treatment is over and further down the line your physical strength and energy come back but you still experience a lack of libido. What's going on? It may be a number of hidden losses: loss of confidence in your physical attractiveness to your partner or others because of your scars; loss of interest in your relationship because you have a new perspective on life and maybe this is no longer the relationship for you; loss of interest in sex because you are focusing all your energies into a new cause or project; and so on.

Loss of Identities

A major intangible loss is the loss of your various 'selves' or identities. Throughout life, you naturally identify yourself by your job titles, your relationships, your interests, your lifestyle, your achievements, your disappointments, your religion, your beliefs about life, and so on. Cancer, being potentially life-threatening, will affect how you see yourself and will challenge the identity labels you may have used previously: a strong parent; a supportive wife/husband; an athlete; a healthy person; a problem-solver; an independent person who can cope with whatever life throws at you; a survivor; etc. There is no question that you will feel some psychological fallout from losing one or more of your identities.

Cancer Losses

In a nutshell, cancer not only involves coping with the physical disease and treatments – it also means experiencing and dealing with a web of hidden losses that will affect how you view and live your life.

It could be argued that some losses may be for the better. Say you were in an abusive relationship and the person left as a result of your illness, or you decided to leave. Or perhaps your experience has inspired you to set up a support group or to fundraise for a charity. These are clearly positive changes. However, if you reflect and look beneath the surface, these gains may be masking other losses.

In the example of the abusive relationship ending, you would still experience a broken heart (even if you are relieved to be free) and in the case of the fundraising, you would need to check that it is not simply a distraction activity so that you don't have to consider painful feelings.

The table below gives some examples of losses taken from the experiences of those I've interviewed and my own. There are exercises in the workbook (Part 3) designed to help you identify your cancer losses.

1) What changed?	2) What was lost?	3) What was it replaced with?
Had to rely on hospital team and help from family and friends	Sense of independence	Vulnerability • I'm vulnerable • I'm dependent • I might die
Medical team missed my cancer first time round	Trust in medical system	Cynicism or Doubt • Can I trust what they say in the future?
No 'proper' physical exercise for six months	Identity as a fit and active person	Frustration • I'm 'sickly' and incapable • I'm always tired
Body is no longer healthy	Trust in body	Fear • What if the cancer comes back? • Am I more likely to get other types of cancer? • What else will go wrong with my body?
Stopped dating/Strained intimate relationship	Confidence/ Self-worth	Self-loathing • Who wants someone with an unknown future? • I'm a liability • I'm ugly/scarred/damaged

1) What changed?	2) What was lost?	3) What was it replaced with?
Unable to do planned activities with my friends	Sense of belonging and common bond	Disconnectedness • I'm out of the loop • I'm in a different place
White noise in head; inane songs going round and round; washing machine brain	Peace of mind	Discontentment • Inability to focus or concentrate • Frustration with my limited capabilities
Having to go back to work	Motivation	Apathy • What's the point?

Clearly, some will be minor losses and others more significant. For example, the loss of trust in my body was only a fleeting worry but I felt the loss of independence keenly for months. Additionally, every individual will respond differently to the same event as illustrated by the stories in Part 2.

Loss and Grief

Every time we experience a loss, there is an emotional response: grief. Most people only associate grief with bereavement but it is in fact our natural reaction to any and all losses, including the hidden and intangible losses you face with cancer. It is not only those who have terminal cancer who grieve. Anyone who has or has had cancer, as well as their close family and friends, will also experience grief – because life has changed.

Grief happens whether or not the change is planned or unplanned, conscious or unconscious, because it is present whenever you are adjusting to a new situation. Its intensity will depend on how significant the change is, what else is happening in your life, other stresses, your previous experience of other significant losses and how much support you have access to. Whatever your situation, recognising your emotional response and taking steps to grieve are key to your whole recovery and moving forward from cancer.

Why, however, are most people surprised and confused when they experience loss? Why do people squirm when they hear the word 'grief'? Perhaps it is because in industrialised societies, life is rarely organised to support you in times of suffering.

Grief in Industrialised Societies

These days, in modern industrialised societies, communities no longer grieve openly and handling grief is not taught in schools. Grief is therefore not something that the general public know a great deal about and so you learn by mirroring what others around you do. What you may not realise is that most people you're copying don't have a clue about grief and are themselves just getting by, doing the best they can. It is often a case of the blind leading the blind, but down a potentially emotionally damaging and life-limiting path.

Grief is the messy, unpredictable and painful emotional response to loss and if you live in a culture that is driven by efficiency and productivity, grief is often considered to be unwanted and inconvenient. Any emotional pain or unpleasant thoughts are to be avoided or dealt with behind closed doors. In public, it's all about showing that you're on top of things and in control.

This pervades all aspects of life, including when you have a serious illness. When very sick people are cheerful and independent, we admire and praise their 'strength', determination and ability to bounce back quickly. Being emotional, especially expressing 'negative' feelings, is commonly viewed as 'being weak' or 'losing your composure'.

On the whole, your friends and family may not be comfortable hearing about the mental difficulties you face with cancer, the emotional roller coaster you are on or your increased sense of vulnerability. It's not because they don't care, but it can make them feel useless and frustrated that they can't fix things.

Except for the minority who are openly compassionate, kind and comfortable talking and hearing about honest vulnerability, most of your friends or family will either pity you or be terrified when they find out you have or have had cancer. Some people wince when I mention that I had cancer, some stop talking to me and some move away as if I'm giving out contagious vibes.

From reading people's posts on social media and on cancer forums, I know that this is sadly a very common situation for those who experience cancer. Many say how surprised they are by who does and who doesn't come forward, especially that their best friends have suddenly stopped phoning or coming round. Although there may be good reasons why that happens, it is nevertheless heartbreaking to experience this. It's a loss.

Cancer brings you face to face with your own mortality; the same goes for your nearest and dearest. There is grief here too. Sadly, discussing mortality is often taboo and considered to be morbid. It may even be that it's you who isn't comfortable with this topic.

All of this means that in mainstream Western society, you are more likely to ignore, suppress, avoid or fight grief. The implications of suppressing grief are discussed next.

I'm Fine (Not!)

As I pointed out earlier, most people only want to hear about how well you're fighting the disease and how much things are looking up. Society wants you to say you're 'fine' so people can get on with their productive and efficient lives. They negate the grief that you are feeling with socially accepted adages that they have heard others use or that they have themselves been told in times of difficulty. These are not helpful when you are in grief. Here are a few that might sound familiar:

'Don't worry; worrying doesn't get you anywhere.'

'Think positive.'

'Give it time. Time heals.'

'Just let it go.'

'Move on; it's done and dusted.'

*'Come out for a drink and drown your
sorrows. You'll feel better.'*

*'Don't feel anxious. You should be grateful
you survived; others didn't.'*

'If you worry about the cancer coming back, then it will!'

'Don't be blue. You should be happy that it's gone.'

The most unhelpful doctrines that are spread by society are that you should focus on keeping busy, control your negative feelings, carry on with life as normal and just let time heal your grief. Grief doesn't work like that. If, after cancer, you cope by repressing, avoiding or ignoring the emotional fallout, it will simply fester and intensify.

Society's ill-informed views of how you should feel and think after cancer can be damaging and impair your psychological recovery and in turn impact further on your physical health. If your emotional burdens aren't recognised and supported by others, they will go underground and you will either struggle in isolation thinking there is something wrong with you or you will stifle your emotions. Neither is healthy in the long term.

Going Underground

Isolating yourself is a common response when those around you aren't able or willing to let you grieve fully and openly. Alone, you are more likely to see it as a shameful or an unnatural state to be in. You tend to worry more and more about what's wrong with you because you're not feeling like people think you should feel. These thoughts go round and round and round. The feeling of being utterly alone in your anguish feeds your grief and isolation further. Your mental health might deteriorate and if left unchecked, you may develop anxiety disorders or become depressed.

Alternatively, you may do what makes society (and you) feel more comfortable – you bury, ignore or avoid your grief and just get on with life. 'I'm fine,' you say, 'no drama here.' You might knowingly pretend that you're OK and mask your grief in stoicism.

Unresolved Grief is Like Boat Leaks

You might, like I did for 30 years, actually fool yourself into thinking that all is well and blindly get on with life. It can seem that the emotional pain has gone as you get used to the loss, but unless you have actively grieved, the suppressed emotional pain stays there and will surface months or years later when you experience another major life challenge, or a series of significant losses. I've heard hundreds and hundreds such stories.

Imagine that each time you suffer a loss it's like getting a hole in a boat. The water that flows in is your emotional response, your grief. And then you choose to ignore the leak or pretend it's not there. Over time the water will continue to gather and the leak may get bigger and bigger. As you go through life, you will experience other losses, so more holes appear and more water accumulates – until you start to sink. It could be months, it could be years, but the water will keep building up in your boat until you address the leak – or sink.

This is certainly what happened to me. For most of my life, I believed it was weak to show feelings and stifled any grief, but after a series of major losses later in life, the buried emotional pain from my childhood resurfaced; the emotions hadn't gone anywhere and they were just as intense. This will be the same for anyone who doesn't grieve at the time of a major loss.

Another example is a client telling me that as a result of past talking therapy for his depression, he had been left with emotions that weren't there before. However, by doing the time-map exercise in Part 3, he realised that the emotions had always been there but he had buried and ignored them. He also discovered how suppressing his grief had limited and impacted on his life for 40 years, especially his intimate relationships.

So based on my own experience and having supported hundreds of grievers over the years, I know that emotions don't just go away like that. Unlike physical wounds, time and rest will not heal you emotionally. Do not 'give it time'. Time does not heal. You need to take action and actively grieve or work through Part 3 of this book to let go of any suppressed grief.

Emotional Rehab

Grief has a purpose. Grief is your natural emotional rehabilitation so if you don't allow it to happen, your full psychological recovery is compromised. If you stop yourself grieving by burying, avoiding or ignoring the feelings, then you stop your ability to have a clear-out and to recover naturally. The repressed emotions then come out sideways. Often, they are expressed in destructive behaviours such as social isolation, aggression, comfort eating, binge drinking, addictions or obsessive behaviours.

Just like the body's immune system helps you recover physically, grieving is the body's way of helping you recover emotionally and mentally from change and the associated losses. Imagine how ill you would be if you stopped your immune system working! And now perhaps you're not so surprised that mental health issues are on the rise in industrialised cultures? All those leaky boats...

Grief is Not Neat

Another common myth is that there are tidy, linear stages of grief (see box below). If only life were that neat! As discussed earlier, grief is predominantly messy, unpredictable and painful. You can't foresee what feelings will come up, when they will come up, how intense they will be and how long they will linger. Grief can therefore leave you feeling overwhelmed, like you're on an emotional roller coaster, or the emotions may hit you in waves. You can also feel numb or empty. It most certainly is not orderly.

Stages of Grief

Elisabeth Kübler-Ross published her book *On Death and Dying* in 1969 which set out the Five Stages of Grief for those who were dying: denial, anger, bargaining, depression and acceptance. These stages were later adapted for those who were bereaved in her book *On Grief and Grieving*, co-written with David Kessler.

Since then, these stages have been very misunderstood and misused by those who wanted a neat solution to grief. The stages are not meant to be logical steps that all grievers follow; instead, they are tools that should be used to help frame and identify their feelings as they respond to loss. Both Kübler-Ross and Kessler have stressed that grief is unique to the individual and that there is no prescribed order.

If you'd like to find out more, go to http://www.ekrfoundation.org/ and https://grief.com/the-five-stages-of-grief/.

This messy nature of grief arising from significant loss explains why, too often, people only address the leaks when they have already started to sink and are exhausted by the effort of having to stay afloat. Like dealing with the boat leak, it would obviously be much easier for you to face the grief when it first arises. You start by recognising that your emotional responses to cancer are normal and natural. To be emotionally and mentally healthy, grieve as you go.

Grief v Survival

Facing cancer usually means that your head and your emotional heart are in very different places and pulling you in various directions. You've experienced a traumatic change and not only are you automatically in hyperalert mode, but you are also grieving. To complicate matters, your brain sees grief as a threat to your mental and emotional wellbeing and so your survival impulses stay activated. This can lead to a loop between your grief and your hyperalertness, each feeding off the other. Your mind is focused on protecting you from pain and suffering whilst your heart is in turmoil. They are in conflict.

The chances are that your head is leading the way and dominating your efforts to recover because you are most likely accustomed to relying on your intellect to fix other problems in your life (e.g. finances, planning, DIY, career decisions, etc.). Since society generally discourages emotional expressiveness and vulnerability, you may be disconnected from your feelings and not used to paying attention to them. If you find yourself thinking or saying *should, shouldn't, must, mustn't, have to, ought to, oughtn't to* and other similar words, those are clear examples of where your head is overruling your heart. This is conflicted head–heart talk.

To tackle the psychological impact of your experience, it's important for your head and heart to be working together. If they stay in conflict, it will obviously be hard for you to find peace of mind.

Head-Heart Conflict

It's worth discussing head-heart conflict a little bit further and considering what is going on in your life that feeds this clash.

In recent years, the number of people diagnosed with mental illness has increased; there is more anxiety, stress and unhappiness. Your mental state is influenced by a combination of biological, social and psychological factors.

Indeed, I have observed that a lot of mental distress is caused by a head–heart conflict, fuelled by unhelpful beliefs about happiness, success and the 'perfect life'.

Such beliefs are influenced by the outlook on life of those around you – your family, friends, community, the media, online connections, etc. That's because you live by the rules and beliefs that are held to be true by the company you keep.

Let's have a look at the three most common unhelpful beliefs that can keep people stuck in a rut and affect their wellbeing. [Note: if you would like to explore your beliefs, there are exercises in Part 3 to guide you.]

1. Unhelpful Beliefs about Success

Mainstream society's view of success is often linked to materialism and status – money, big house, nice car, 'happy families', job title, amazing holidays, etc. Popular magazines and TV shows are devoted to external matters like beauty, financial success, social status and possessions. This idea of 'the good life' is amplified on social media, with photos of friends smiling, seemingly popular and in beautiful locations.

If you live in this idealised world and, say, you lose your job then you are more likely to swallow the pain even though your status, identity or self-worth are negatively affected. You also probably won't allow yourself any time to pay attention to what's going on inside – it's best buried and forgotten.

Repeat this for the numerous other losses you encounter in life such as cancer, relationship break-ups, bereavement, falling out with good friends, death of a pet, children leaving home, etc., and you have a store of unresolved grief. Your head is focused on achieving material success but your heart is holding on to past disappointments and hurting. You are brokenhearted by life's disappointments that have mounted up but your head is disconnected to your feelings.

In itself, material success is neither good nor bad. The question is whether you acquire these at the cost of your overall wellbeing. There are obviously people who have achieved material success and maintained their physical, mental and emotional health, but based on the hundreds of people I've worked with and looking at the lives of the people around me as well as my own, I'd say that most of us are out of kilter.

Is your life awry? Is your definition of success balanced?

2. Unhelpful Beliefs about the Perfect Life

The mainstream belief, fed by misunderstanding and misinformation, is that trials and tribulations are not part of what life should be. They are seen as inconvenient, unwanted and abnormal obstacles that get in the way of the 'idealised normal' life and are to be avoided or fixed so you can continue with 'normal' life. The common view is that if you have lots of trials and tribulations, then there's something wrong with your life – and therefore you!

As I've mentioned several times before, loss is part of normal life and it is inevitable that you will face challenging situations, suffering and darkness at various points in your life. The key is to acquire the knowledge and skills to help yourself through the easy times, the tough times and all the variations in between. As the quote at the beginning of this part said, 'All we can do is learn to swim.'

Setbacks are part of a fulfilled and content life, not interruptions to a perfect life.

Are you striving for an unrealistic perfect version of life that simply cannot exist?

3. Unhelpful Beliefs about Happiness

Clients often tell me that all they want in life, or the most important thing, is to be happy. If this is you, be aware that your mind is likely to read your ambition as 'I must be 100% happy.' I know this is perhaps not what you intended, but the belief that your subconscious mind forms will be along the lines of needing to be happy **all** of the time.

Another possibility is that you do actually believe that you must be 100% happy; if so, it's likely that you have spent years searching for the secret.

I've heard a life coach say that his objective is to make his clients become 100% happy.

What's wrong with wanting to be happy all of the time? Firstly, it implies that you have control over life, and this is not possible. Bad, sad and ugly events will happen to you that are beyond your immediate control, like cancer.

Secondly, you're setting yourself up for failure as each time you are not completely happy or are dissatisfied with life, the battle between your head and heart is fuelled. Anxiety increases and you wonder, 'What's wrong with me? Why can't I be happy?'

Instead of aiming for complete happiness, consider being grateful when things go well and being accepting and emotionally aware when things don't go to plan.

A Note on Mental Health, Emotional Health & Grief

Your mental health relates to your ability to function in your everyday life and to make a contribution to your community. It is also connected to how much self-compassion, self-love and self-care you have.

Your emotional health is about your ability to understand, to respond to, and to be at ease with the whole range of your emotional reactions to life events. It does not mean 'Am I happy?' – emotionally healthy people still feel stressed, angry, unhappy and sad but they are comfortable with how they feel.

There is a lot of discussion and more openness about mental health these days and I'm very glad about that. It's really important to remove the social stigma surrounding mental illness and for the right support to be made available to those who suffer. However, there are two consequences of this increased interest in and awareness of mental health that I need to highlight in this book because the most common thing I hear from grievers is, 'I think I'm going crazy. I must have depression.'

1) Emotions Matter

The media spotlight on mental health implies that only the mind is involved and therefore the solutions can only be found there too. Of course, the professionals know that this is not the case, but the lay person who hears 'mental health' does not know any better. When grievers experience strong and scary emotions, they are more likely to then panic and feel that there is something mentally 'wrong' with them.

What's more, you can be mentally healthy but emotionally unhealthy; for 30 years, I functioned, contributed and loved myself and yet I wasn't at ease with my feelings (or others'), and my suppressed grief simply accumulated as I experienced more losses. I would like to see the use of 'mental and emotional health' as the two are inexorably linked and it's time we got comfortable with feelings. Emotional health matters!

2) Grief and Depression

If you have experienced loss and you're grieving it can feel a lot like depression, but it isn't. Grief is not a mental health issue; it's about your emotional health. Grief is a normal and natural response to loss whereas depression is a clinical diagnosis. It is true that mental illness can develop if grief is suppressed over a period of time; and that's another good reason for you to attend to the holes in your boat at the time they happen.

If you're uncomfortable with messy feelings, it is understandable that you will suppose that your grief is an unnatural medical problem and look for a quick fix that is painless. You are also likely to want to numb painful feelings rather than face them, and reach for anti-depressants. I'm not against such medication as I think that it can be helpful in some situations. The grief, however, is still there – numbed. And there is no technology to selectively numb emotions; if you numb sadness and heartbreak, you also numb joy, love, gratitude, etc.

Tip: Unless you have been diagnosed by a doctor, I encourage you to avoid saying that you're 'depressed'. Instead, use the exact words to express how you feel: sad, frustrated, down, low, unhappy, miserable, fed up, etc. This way, you can address it honestly and appropriately as grief.

Positive Thinking and Mindfulness

Two current trends that can potentially disconnect your mind and your feelings are 'positive thinking' and 'Mindfulness'.

Positive Thinking

A common piece of advice given is to 'stay positive' when you're struggling with life, such as in these Instagram quotes: 'Positive thoughts lead to a happy life' or 'Positive thinking will lead you out of the darkest of times'.

The danger is that you interpret this advice as 'I must always think positively, regardless of what life throws at me', which can then lead you to believe that 'Negative thoughts and feelings are inappropriate and won't help me when things go wrong' or 'I must never focus on the negative as I will attract negative results'. I've had people say this to me and I've seen it online in various guises.

You may also form a belief that positive thinking **alone** will fix your struggles or help you deal with your emotional and mental turmoil. Sadly, it won't; not when you find yourself in a traumatic situation or facing your own mortality.

I know, because I did positive thinking for most of my 20s and 30s but still discovered that I had a load of unresolved grief. It just meant that I buried everything that wasn't positive. I know I'm not the only one; I've come across many grievers who have a similar story.

If you're grieving, simply saying to yourself 'think positive' is asking your brain to override your feelings; this isn't helpful. It's also unkind because you will beat yourself up when you can't think or feel positive because you're overwhelmed by grief.

It also leads you to feel like you've done something wrong when you are faced with a life-changing situation. Knowingly or not, you might think, 'I got cancer because I wasn't positive enough' – not true and not helpful.

It may just be semantic, but I prefer to talk instead about having an **optimistic or hopeful attitude** to life. I have found this to be a much more useful outlook to have. It will help you to remember that although right now you may be feeling awful, you know that there is still a lot of goodness in your life and that this feeling is temporary. All feelings are temporary.

Clearly if you have a hopeful attitude, you are more likely to recognise the good things in your life, such as love, kindness, compassion and joy, even in the darkest and most painful moments. Importantly, being optimistic still means that it's OK for you to feel sad, angry, frustrated, etc., in a given moment. It doesn't negate your negative emotions.

Be optimistic. Be hopeful.

Mindfulness

Mindfulness is a powerful tool in its original Buddhist philosophical context as it includes practising loving kindness, altruistic joy, compassion and equanimity. There are three elements to Mindfulness practice:

1. knowing and training the mind,
2. developing insight into suffering and impermanence, and
3. freeing the heart from attachments and misery.

Mindfulness as practised by Buddhists therefore doesn't mean that you can't be in touch with your negative thoughts and feelings because the key principles are that there is no judgement and no resistance. There is no need to decide if it's good or bad. When using Mindfulness, it is fundamental that any thoughts and emotions are allowed to arise freely and without judgement or attachment. In this context, the technique is very effective for everyday life.

Because of this, it has risen in popularity and it is now found everywhere, but sadly, not always taught properly. The prevalent quick-fix versions usually only include the first element of Mindfulness practice: knowing and training the mind. This means that it is often used as a distraction technique to override negative thoughts and feelings.

I know about many wellbeing courses, blogs and articles that encourage you to ignore negativity through mindful drinking, walking or observing a raisin or some other object. Whilst this might bring some tranquillity at the time, it is superficial and doesn't last. This could lead to further angst as you may then think, 'It's not working for me; there must be something seriously wrong with me!' Yet more food for the head–heart conflict.

Additionally, my personal experience is that even if done properly, Mindfulness, as with positive thinking, will not address historical unresolved grief. For a couple of years, I practised the technique correctly, guided by Buddhist monks and nuns; I certainly felt calmer and more content. However, when I experienced a major loss, 30 years of unresolved grief started to leak out. I was shocked and disappointed because I thought I had acquired the right skills and was 'sorted'.

My experience is mirrored by other grievers I've talked to; I have learned that it is necessary for grievers to express and release their unresolved grief first (i.e. have an emotional clear-out), before practising Mindfulness in its complete form.

Authentic Mindset

I have also found that when dealing with the psychological impact of cancer and other losses, the most useful attitude is an **authentic** one. This allows you to be human first and foremost. You give yourself permission to be honest about how you feel, what you think and where you're at right now. Feeling good is OK, feeling bad is OK. And even better still, try not to label your emotions as good or bad – they just are what they are.

Being human means feeling a range of emotions and being vulnerable. Don't resist and don't cling to them; simply accept. This may be scary, painful and unfamiliar. It will certainly require you to have courage, to be committed and to be truthful to yourself. It is worth it though as facing the psychological impact of cancer and the associated grief with an authentic mindset will start to release your emotional pain.

If you acknowledge and accept the psychological pain, you will gain a new level of intellectual and emotional maturity and will be better able to deal with the complexities of life and future losses.

Being Emotionally Healthy

When you face a major trial like cancer, it's not unusual for you to stop and re-evaluate your priorities. You are facing your mortality, and maybe not for the first time. It's natural that you take stock of your life. This can happen without you even being aware of it. It's part of grief: you question your life's purpose and the meaning of life.

Sometimes, cancer can rupture your life. It can be a seismic shift in your being, your assumptions, your values, your beliefs and your priorities. It may be a less dramatic transformation but the cancer experience will alter your perceptions as if you have new spectacles and notice things that you didn't before.

As I mentioned before, when I was diagnosed with cancer, I remember feeling like someone had pressed 'Pause'. Other people's lives were going on around me, but I was suspended and my life was on hold. Then I felt a shift coming on but I had no idea where I would end up and that frustrated me. For many months, I was adrift; everything was up for review and I felt lost and struggled to gain clarity about what to do next.

Your emotional and mental response to cancer is not something that has to be solved. It is neither good nor bad; it just is. Don't fight it. As they say, 'You fight life, it fights you back'. This isn't referring to you fighting **for** your life. What we're talking about here is not opposing your natural innate ability to deal with what life throws at you, such as your instinctive grief after a diagnosis of cancer. It's about your head not drowning out your heart. It's about you not fighting yourself.

Embrace your thoughts and emotions regardless of the 'flavour'. Discovery involves being familiar with your thoughts and feelings rather than being critical. Let it flow. Don't try to second-guess it, press 'Fast Forward' or stop it. Let yourself grieve. If you're not sure how to do this, then download my free e-book *Coping With Cancer: 7 Steps To Deal With Anxiety and Fear* which guides you through how to face grief (http://www.altereddawn.co.uk/books).

What seems to matter most to humans who face a life-changing situation is love, compassion, kindness, contribution and connection with others. What do you want more of in your life? What do you want less of? What do you fundamentally wish to change? These are some of the questions that you are encouraged to reflect upon in Part 3 of this book.

The next part includes a number of stories from people who experienced cancer and raises the question, 'What is normal?' It is my hope that reading them will give you some useful insights as you face your situation.

PART 2

STORIES
OF NORMAL

The purpose of a storyteller is not to tell you how to think, but to give you questions to think upon.

– Brandon Sanderson

The most common question cancer patients ask themselves and their medical team is, 'Is this normal?'

Whether it's your body's physical response to the treatment, your psychological reaction or the behaviour of your family and friends, you will inevitably wonder whether what's happening to you is OK and is normal.

From my work with grievers, I know that there is no 'normal' so I wanted to interview a range of people to illustrate how different our cancer experiences can be. Eight people volunteered to be interviewed, coming from three sources:

1. People who responded to a social media survey on the emotional impact of cancer and agreed to be interviewed.
2. People who contacted me after seeing an article in my local newspaper about my e-book: *Coping With Cancer: 7 Steps To Deal With Anxiety and Fear.*
3. People I knew.

The stories are transcripts of the interviews, edited for cohesion and approved by each person. Their own words have been used and the stories therefore reflect their individual personalities and attitudes to life. None have been changed to fit or support my beliefs or views.

Different levels of anonymity were agreed; some were happy for their real name to be used, others not. To respect the interviewees' privacy, I haven't indicated which names are real, nor given out their age or location. However, apart from Rhonda who lives in the USA, all the interviewees live in the UK.

Sadly, not as many men as women came forward and no-one living with cancer or with a limited life span volunteered to tell their story. I'd love to include other stories in future editions of this book and would love to add the voices of those not represented here. I'd also be really pleased to hear from people in different parts of the world to include their experiences.

I've also included my own story at the end of this part and provided you with the emotional truth of my account. I hope that this will ignite greater awareness in you of your own psychological response to cancer. This awareness is fundamental for the letting go process set out in Part 3, which helps you work towards your own recovery and improved wellbeing.

Our stories show that our personal circumstances are quite different and although there are some generic commonalities, there is a wide range of different beliefs, responses and reactions. I hope that you will find them helpful and that it will reassure you to know that there is no prescribed way to think or feel. You will also notice that the strategies that helped us to get through the cancer experience were also diverse.

May these stories give you the confidence and courage to work your own way through your experience and accept your own normal.

Robert's Story

Diagnosis

I was on holiday at the end of 2015 and I had a cough, a cold and a sore throat. My neck swelled up hugely. The same day I came back from holiday, I was admitted to hospital as an emergency and they took out a big cyst from the side of my neck. During the procedure, the surgeon saw something at the base of my tongue and took a biopsy but neglected to tell me.

The next week, I went to my follow-up appointment expecting to discuss the scar from the cyst removal. Instead, they told me that the results of my biopsy had come back and it was positive for cancer. That was the first I'd heard of a biopsy and the whole prospect of cancer hadn't even crossed my mind. I was there on my own and it was all a bit of a shock! It turned out I had a malignant growth at the very base of my tongue in my throat beyond normal vision.

I went back a couple of days later, with my wife to support me, and the oncologist told me I'd have to have all my back teeth out because I needed radiotherapy and that can affect the integrity of the jaw bone. He said I'd need to have daily radiotherapy five days a week for six weeks and a couple of chemotherapy sessions to help things along.

At this point, I fainted – which was rather embarrassing! They very nearly called the crash team as they thought I'd had a heart attack. It was absolutely overwhelming; so much information was being thrown at us and I just couldn't take it all in. I think *that's why I fainted and it took me a while to assimilate what I'd been told. The room was full and very hot and the consultant, I found out later, is not well-known for his bedside manner. Everyone else was kind though and made sure I was OK before being allowed to go home. I was also introduced to the first of my Macmillan nurses and she was incredibly supportive; just everything I could want.*

I then resigned myself to the process; it was a quite a relief to find that nothing was my responsibility any more. I am now in a system where everyone is doing the necessary jobs and all I have to do is make sure I'm where I need to be when I need to be. It was a real lifting of responsibility as I was now the one being taken care of.

Treatment

I didn't do any research because I worked as a financial advisor for the health sector so I knew a lot of hospital doctors, and I believe they know what they're doing and got where they are because they know what they're doing. I only allowed myself to be guided by the NHS and Macmillan nurses and no-one else. Challenging them wouldn't be beneficial to me.

I didn't have any side-effects from the chemotherapy but the radiotherapy was very unpleasant, particularly towards the end. It was really trying and I couldn't swallow water or anything really. I was in pain the whole time and on lots of painkillers. It was pretty dire and my nurse and consultant were concerned about my weight loss being too fast. I had to have a tube inserted into my nose (a nasogastric tube) and spent about eight hours each night with a pump giving me nutritious liquid food. I struggled to drink even 500ml of water a day so all my needs were met through this tube. When it was first put in, it was unbelievably uncomfortable, but like most things, you adapt over time. Once, it got blocked over a bank holiday weekend; I was totally reliant on it and so it was a panic for us. We had guests staying with us and we had to ask them to leave so we could go to the hospital and get it sorted. Throughout this time, the medical staff also needed to make sure that the tube didn't dislodge and reposition itself into my lungs. There were times when I wasn't sure it was still in the right place and that caused more upset and anxiety.

During treatment, my wife and daughters, my friends and colleagues were a tower of strength. They were supportive and offered to take me to the hospital visits;

everyone stepped up and I'm hugely grateful to them. My elderly mother felt guilty that she couldn't travel over to help out and because I couldn't travel either, she didn't see me much. I also refused to let my sense of humour be beaten and that kept me going.

The radiation made the jaw bone go into crazy mode and it kept growing sharp shards of bone through my gum which lacerated my tongue when I talked. I have to go to the dentist from time to time to get them ground down but hopefully it will settle down and happen less and less.

First Few Months Post-Treatment

A month or so after the treatment, I could swallow and things improved slowly. My saliva came back to a degree and I gradually ate custard and yoghurt.

There were times, lying in bed at 3am, when I thought 'it's all going to end' and I'd reflect about how I want to see my grandchildren grow up. At those points, I needed reassurance and my Macmillan nurse was my major form of support. She lifted me when ridiculous things went round in my head; stupid, tiny things that I couldn't get out of my head – 'washing machine brain' I call it.

I started using a Mindfulness book and CD that was given to me by the psychology team. I got halfway through but felt that I wasn't getting any further benefit. It had got me through a tough patch and I didn't feel the need to finish the course, but I did struggle. Since primary school, I've always had tasks to do and I always completed them. All of a sudden, I was floundering. Luckily, my nurse made me realise that there are no rules and it was OK not to see it through. It was a while before I realised that it was down to me and if I didn't do it, no-one was going to be upset!

Ongoing Monitoring

It's been quite a ride. I'm now officially in remission and now have bimonthly check-ups for the next five years.

What Helped

With hindsight, all the losses could be expected but at the time I was going through it, I knew nothing about what would happen. You don't know what 'normal' is – the Macmillan nurses must get so fed up with people asking! You just want to hear it's normal.

I did get professional support. I'm a huge advocate of mental health support and have always admired the psychiatrists amongst my clients. They were always the most pleasant people to deal with. When therapy was offered by the hospital, I thought, 'I obviously don't need it because I'm perfectly alright!' But I was curious as to what the experience would be like as a patient so I went ahead with the sessions.

It was just brilliant – and, of course, I did need it! It made a huge difference and made me less snappy with my family, less judgemental and softened my views on everything. Apparently, it softened my views towards my family (which I didn't realise was an issue!). The therapist coached me and it was just what I needed. No-one else had the ability to open the gate for me.

I'm very open about me having been helped and I now probably bore people about the benefits and changes it made to me. But here's the thing: if you have a bad tooth, you don't tie a piece of string around it and pull; you go to a dentist. If you have a bad ankle, you go to the doctor. If you have a problem with your head, you see the people who can help you with your head. It's no different.

Life Now

It's now September 2017 – I'm not where I was and nor will I ever be. As I have no saliva and can't open my mouth very wide, many parts of my life have been affected, like my ability to kiss, and there's a lot of food I simply can't manage. There's no way I could tackle a hot dog or apple. And that's for life. I can't swallow anything bigger than a pea so I have to chew everything to a pulp and it takes me a long time to eat a light meal. Restaurants are awkward as I get embarrassed about keeping others waiting for the next course. I don't have enough saliva to swallow everything properly so I have to have mouthwash with me. I only eat out with people I know very well.

Ironically, I'm now fitter than I've ever been since I left primary school because I lost 6.5 stones (41 kilos) and I can walk further and don't get hot and sweaty in the summer! My Type two diabetes has also gone.

I do have the odd 'wobble'. One time, I was on holiday with the family and we went to a pub that did glorious Sunday lunches. That got to me. I cried and felt that it's unfair. Why have I got this? The unfairness does get to me sometimes. It used to be almost daily, then the periods in between stretched and now it's every couple of months. I just tell my wife I'm having a bad day and we just leave it. We could probably talk it through but there's nothing new to be said. I know that it's OK for me to just realise I'm in it and wait for it to go. If it feels too long, I know I can go back to therapy. Just for today I'll live with it and the door to therapy is always open. It's a good safety net.

On a day-to-day basis, I don't think about the cancer coming back, but from reading blogs, I know it can come back. I would say that I don't fear cancer itself but the treatment is not something I'd like to go through again. Fear of recurrence is not a problem for me.

I find that giving back is helping my recovery. I now do voluntary work, helping the hospital cancer team and the GP. Helping my friend with cancer has enabled me to support and show compassion for someone else. It also made me realise that I should have asked for more help. When you give help, it's not just altruistic; it's a need that you have. I now know that it would have helped my family and friends if I'd asked for more help. It's a huge help for the people you love.

Advice to Others

So the advice I'd give anyone facing cancer is: ask for help and, more importantly, accept help when it's offered.

Petra's Story

Diagnosis

I noticed a change in the shape of my breast and at first thought it was cellulite. About six months later, in November 2015, I realised that something could be seriously wrong and went to the doctor. Within ten days, I had a mammogram and at the same appointment I was told that they were 90% sure it was cancer. This was a bolt out of the blue; I was the fittest I'd ever been and felt really well. I was quite tearful and kept asking myself, 'Why me?' and then I realised, 'Why not me?' as one in eight women will be diagnosed with breast cancer at some stage in their lives.

I wasn't bothered about dying but the thought of leaving my husband on his own really upset me. We had a trip to Venice already booked for our wedding anniversary and we made the decision to go – my husband initially didn't want to but I persuaded him. At that stage we had no idea of the extent of the cancer, or how long I had to live. We had a fantastic time!

Shortly after we got back and before my surgery, I had some great news – all the further tests had come back clear, so there was no indication that it spread beyond two lymph nodes.

Treatment

In December, just before Christmas, I had the mastectomy done privately and all my lymph nodes in my right armpit were removed. I then had six months of chemotherapy sessions starting in January 2016 and three weeks of radiotherapy in August. Although a couple of people encouraged me to have alternative treatments and therapies, I was in no doubt that I wanted conventional treatment as it was tried and tested and the long-term survival rate was good. In addition to the conventional treatments, I stayed as active as I could, and paid particular attention to my diet and mental state, in particular focusing on clearing any negative emotions in relation to the cancer.

I did lose my hair and needed a wig. I went out for the day with a friend and we turned wig-buying into a fun occasion. Finding a sense of humour in all situations and seeing the funny side of it was vital for me. I only wore the wig when I was with clients as I didn't want them to know. The rest of the time, I walked around without a wig. I also chose not to have a breast reconstruction – the thought of going through more major surgery was not appealing. I'm quite happy with my appearance and I now go swimming and to saunas without any prosthesis. I am lucky that my husband loves me as I am and has been very supportive throughout. But I am aware that he also needed support and it was just as bad, if not worse, for him.

What Helped

I'm an NLP (Neuro-Linguistic Programming) Master Practitioner. When I trained in NLP, it changed how I lived my life and taught me to focus my attention and energy on what I could control. I did have about three or four emotional clearance sessions with my NLP Coach which helped me to let go of a lot of negative emotion relating to this experience.

During my treatment and beyond, I focused on what I could control and read up on how to minimise the chances of recurrence. I exercise lots, eat a mainly organic plant-based diet and fast for 16 hours a day as there is anecdotal evidence that this reduces the risk of breast cancer recurrence. I also keep refined carbohydrates – especially sugar – to an absolute minimum. On top of this, I removed chemicals from my environment as much as possible and now only use organic cleaning products and toiletries. Paying attention to my mental state was also important and I monitored myself regularly.

Because of my background as a professional sailor, the chemotherapy didn't make me sick; apparently there is a link between chemo sickness and motion sickness, and I have never been seasick. I made the treatment part of my life and saw it as an interesting and different experience. Being fit also helped me get through the operation and chemotherapy easily and keeping to normality was my target. I know I was very lucky; I felt a bit tired at the end of it but that was about it.

I carried on working although I did no client-facing work during the neutropenic week. I also jogged for two to three miles, three times a week, during the chemo and radiotherapy. I continued flying my glider and instructing throughout. To me, continuing to exercise was a no-brainer and it wasn't so much a choice as a necessity. I did have the odd rest on the couch. My way of coping was to maintain as much normality as I could.

First Few Months Post-Treatment

People said to me that 'life starts again after chemo'. My life never stopped! For me, the chemo and radiotherapy were the easy bits. It was later things went wrong physically. No-one made me aware of the potential longer-term impact of chemotherapy and hormone therapy on tendons, muscles and ligaments.

I was put on hormone therapy (Letrazole and Zolodex) and six weeks later, I became unable to walk due to general joint pain and I developed a chronic soft tissue knee injury. By November 2016, I couldn't run or even walk the dog and that was mentally intolerable for me. My GP and practice nurses all kept telling me that it was because I was doing too much and I should rest!

I remember losing the plot with a pharmacist who told me that the joint pain was absolutely not a side-effect of the drugs I was on. Later that day, I spoke to my oncologist who agreed with me and suggested a three-month holiday from the medication. Within two weeks, the joint pain had gone and my knee started responding to treatment. I started running again properly in May 2017.

Looking Back

I really believe that my cancer was due in a large part to my past lifestyle. I used to have very high levels of stress, which I have now learned is highly inflammatory. I had in the past been really unhealthy as I'd been in a profession that involved a lot of social drinking for many years. I had made major changes to my lifestyle in the couple of years leading up to my diagnosis, and was very fit and eating healthily at the time.

Cancer teaches you who your friends are. Some people appeared to make a conscious effort to avoid me – I think they didn't know what to say. One of my best friends was conspicuous by her absence; she didn't ring or visit once. At the same time, a vague acquaintance is now my closest friend. She used to take me out to lunch after my chemo treatments and we'd have a really good laugh. Another very good friend also had cancer some years before, and she and her husband were very supportive too. It was helpful to be able to talk openly.

Life Now

Now it's October 2017 – I am taking Tamoxifen which is absolutely fine – no real side-effects at all for me (although everyone is different). Physically, I am back to the levels of fitness I was at before. It did take a couple of years for all the soft tissue niggles to clear – as well as physiotherapy I work out in the gym a couple of times a week to regain my muscular strength.

As a result of my experience, I have now become a personal trainer. I qualified in December 2017, and completed my GP referral qualification in April 2018. I now work with people in their 40s and beyond, and those with controlled medical conditions to help them become and stay fit and active into their later years.

I am passionate about the power of exercise, physical activity and healthy diet and lifestyle. I plan to do a cancer specialist course later in 2018 so that I can work with cancer patients – there is an increasing amount of evidence that exercise and physical activity significantly improves patient outcomes before, during and after treatment.

Advice to Others

I know that having gone through this has made me stronger. I would say to those who are going through cancer to focus your energy on what you can control. Stay positive, do your own research, go for the treatments – both conventional and complementary – which you believe are right for you. Question anything you are not sure about with regards to your treatment. Ask for a second opinion if necessary. But above all keep moving, go for a ten-minute walk, take the dog out or walk to the shops. And eat as healthily as possible, minimising sugar intake.

Mary's Story

Diagnosis

The first inkling that I got that there was something wrong was just before we moved house in late 2007. I just didn't feel right but I didn't know why. I wasn't experiencing any pain or anything significant. I went to the doctor and said that I was having stomach problems, but then I've always had gut issues. I thought I had some infection and the doctor thought it was probably Irritable Bowel Syndrome.

We moved home in early 2008 and when I registered at the new medical centre, I made a routine appointment to see a doctor. The day before my appointment, I had an anal bleed and the doctor referred me to the hospital with 'urgent' written across my form. Within a short time, I had my consultation and this was followed up with a colonoscopy.

They found the tumour there and then. My husband, Alan, came to pick me up and they asked to have a chat with us. They had also called down the cancer nurse. There I was sitting with Alan, the nurse and the endoscopist and they told me straight away that it was bowel cancer. They had caught it really early and it was very small but apparently very aggressive. They hoped it hadn't spread. I felt very much like a victim at the time, sitting there hearing the news.

Treatment

A few days later, on a warm, sunny day, the phone rang and it was the hospital asking me to come in for a pre-op assessment that day. I was then booked in very quickly for the surgery which took place at the end of August 2008. They were very efficient and I was looked after really well. The surgeon said all the relevant bits had been removed and were being analysed. Whilst still in hospital, they came back to me and said that it had spread to my liver and I had, I believe, five or six lesions there. I was told that I needed to start chemotherapy quite quickly.

I came home and while recuperating from the surgery and getting ready for chemotherapy, I woke up one morning with this pain and wondered if it was a heart attack... I knew it couldn't be though because if it was, then my heart would be in the wrong place! I then thought it was indigestion but it wasn't quite right. I called my doctor and he asked to see me straight away. By the time I returned from seeing him, the doctor had already arranged for me to go to hospital. So I was straight out of the door again and headed there. It turned out that I had a blood clot on my lung. I spent a week there going through lots of different tests.

About a week after I came out of hospital, I started the chemotherapy. My oncologist was lovely. He explained that they would be giving me quite a high dosage and the gist of it was that they would try to keep me alive! The chemotherapy was absolutely horrendous; they'd told me all the usual symptoms I was likely to get but I managed to invent a few more en route!

It used to make me quite ill – embarrassingly ill in fact. There were a few times when I didn't quite make it to the toilet on time. I was to have ten sessions; about halfway through I was kept in the emergency ward a couple of times because I was too ill to go home. It was very annoying. I was cross with the whole thing: about me actually getting 'it' and having to put up with this. It also seemed unfair that I got the cancer as I grew up on a Mediterranean type diet; I worked hard and ate good food.

At the follow-up consultation after Session three or four, my oncologist was away and the consultant who stood in for him told me I had six months to live! I thought, 'You must be joking! No!' I denied it as if I'd committed a crime.

The next time when I saw my usual oncologist, he said that it was 'touch and go' but he felt that I was starting to get onto the other side of it and he reassured me that he would do everything he could to make sure that I did come out on the other side. Around Session six, he then said that things were looking a little bit better and one or two of the lesions were much less than they were. We had to keep going.

The chemotherapy was making me feel worse and worse and there was this balancing act that I had to do. The lesions were starting to disappear but my reactions to the treatment were getting worse. My hands were red raw; my feet were red raw; I was losing sensation in my feet and in my fingers. I was nauseous all the time although I never actually vomited. The toilet was my best friend!

My husband, Alan, was very supportive but had to work during the day. It was towards Session seven or eight, I can't really remember any more, but I felt like I was imprisoned in my house. Most of the time, I was at home alone with my cat, George, and he was the only 'person' I spoke to all day. He also polished off everything I couldn't eat; he got fatter and I got thinner! It was Winter 2008/09; it was a fairly lonely experience.

I had two regular visitors. One was my cousin who was wonderful. The other was a lady I had only met a couple of times when I first moved in. She had got wind that I wasn't very well and knocked on the door to see how she could help. She just came regularly and chatted over a cup of tea and we talked about all sorts of things. It was nice to see a face.

Apart from those two, no-one else came to see me even though they knew I was ill. If they did come, they only came the once... so perhaps I scared them away. They told me afterwards that they didn't like to come in while I was ill. I wasn't infectious! I found that strange. And now when the boot is on the other foot, I make sure I'm there for others. I say, 'I'm here, what can I do? What do you need?'

I continued to do things. I had all sorts of things planned: an art degree and a lot of community work like working in the local charity shop and helping groups in the village. Alan was very supportive with that. It helped keep me focused and balanced. It was really hard but I think it was necessary. I didn't want to feel that the cancer had got the better of me and was ruling my life. I wanted to rule it. I don't suffer fools gladly and I saw the cancer as the biggest fool ever. How dare it!

In Spring 2009, my oncologist told me the good news that my bloods were much better; although my reaction to the treatment had been getting worse since Christmas, my blood counts had been steadily improving. He said we were nearly ready to stop. He reduced the dosage for the last two and finally said that the lesions had virtually disappeared. After the ninth session, I didn't need any more chemotherapy as the lesions would go of their own accord now – there was enough inside me to finish the job off.

Ongoing Monitoring

I had monthly consultations over the next six months, with scans, colonoscopies, blood tests, etc. Eventually I got the all clear and in the summer, the consultations were then pushed to three-monthly intervals. It went to six-monthly visits and then in due course, it was yearly, up until 2018. So that was for ten years.

I had a few hiccups along the way, when the oncologist saw something he didn't like, but it turned out OK. During this time, I've had two hip replacements and my back has had to be fixed and has been 'scaffolded'; these have been chugging along by the side of the cancer follow-ups. For the last three years, there has been nothing to report so they finally kicked me out (discharged) last month!

What Helped

Alan was quite shocked when I was diagnosed but he has been very level-headed about the whole thing. He kept me focused on doing things that I could. He was there whenever he could to take me to the hospital visits and shopping. The support I got from him was exceptional. He knows I'm a fiercely independent person and I like to do things my way (I'm a bit of a pain really!). I've been short-tempered over things and he got told off a lot when I was going through it. He sometimes couldn't do things right and I suppose I had to let fire at somebody and he was first in the line. We don't talk about his experience as he's a closed shop really. I know he didn't want to lose me and he was scared on that front.

Both my children were pretty shocked. I knew there would be an interesting reaction from them but I was surprised at how it turned out. I thought my daughter, who is the eldest, would be very keen to be in contact all the time and my son, who is a horizontally-laid-back individual, would just say, 'You'll be alright' and I wouldn't hear from him much.

Instead, my daughter didn't contact me; I think she was very scared and didn't want to know all about what was going on. It upset her. I didn't say anything to her and just let her get on as she needed to. She spoke to Alan a lot and got the information she needed that way. It's interesting that she has just helped one of her best friends through terminal cancer, helping her with all the practical matters and paperwork. I'm sure that if my daughter had lived close by, she would have done the same for me and organised me.

On the other hand, my son rang me every evening for a chat, told me about the grandchildren and other everyday things. We didn't always talk about the cancer and it was lovely to just chat. He was much more of a softie, a big teddy bear. He also helped his sister-in-law when she had cancer and took it all in his stride.

Other than my family, I didn't feel that I needed extra support, although the help I got from the two cancer nurse specialists at the hospital was invaluable. They were always openly available. Over the last few years, I have reported in to the nurses if there is something I can't understand. I don't have the fear of recurrence but I keep a very close eye on myself.

I did go along to a local cancer support group but I found the other people depressing and I couldn't cope with it. I didn't like it at all. I once went along to help and arranged to meet them but they didn't turn up!

Life Now

It's now July 2018 – a decade on, the cancer treatment has left me with quite a lot of curious little problems, which I'd rather weren't with me. My feet feel like I'm walking on gravel; my toes prickle right up to my ankle. I can't really feel my feet properly because the nerve endings have been compromised considerably so I have balance problems. The tips of my fingers are like little pads and feel dead although I can still feel things. It's odd. It makes fine motor work, like needlework, quite interesting at times. I get round that by using the side of my fingers. Luckily, I can still paint and do arty things I enjoy.

As the day progresses, I also get very tired still. Since the cancer, I can't sleep very well either and sometimes I have trouble getting to sleep. I don't know why.

I'm not sure if it's linked, but my teeth have got progressively worse and worse. I've always been scrupulous about my teeth. Some people I've mentioned it to say that chemotherapy can decay your teeth prematurely. I also have tinnitus which started about five or six years ago and it gets worse towards the end of the day when I'm more tired. I've also had trouble swallowing which could be related to the chemotherapy so I had an operation earlier this year to stretch my throat.

My gut is unpredictable and if I'm a bit wound-up about something, it can be a bit embarrassing. It worries me when I travel that I will need the toilet quickly. It can suddenly happen just like that. Doing weekends away can be difficult and I do get myself wound-up. I did a two-day course away from home recently and I had to take anti-diarrhoea tablets rather frequently. I do worry whether I will actually reach my destination without needing the toilet. I have to figure out my journeys, particularly in the mornings. I can whizz about locally without any issues – because I know where the toilets are.

When I was going through chemotherapy, I always had to design my journeys to make sure that I drove past places with public toilets, like garden centres and supermarkets. I have a little emergency bag in the car in case I'm stuck anywhere. My gut is a problem but I've adapted so I can still do things. I used to drink alcohol, not particularly heavily, but I've not drunk in the last ten years. I just can't face it anymore.

Advice to Others

If I were to give any advice to someone who had just been diagnosed, I'd say to chat to someone else who has had cancer and to keep going with what you like to do – but tailor it so that you're not overdoing things and overexerting yourself. Just think about the various processes you go through in organising your life and try and make them meaningful – but again don't do too much. It's difficult to balance.

Be as clear as you can about what you are going to focus on. When I was going through chemo, I set myself a small target every day e.g. make a cake, change the bed, hoover, sewing – things that made me feel like I'd achieved something.

Susan's Story

Diagnosis

In February 2015, I was referred for a lump but it wasn't biopsied and deemed to be a normal lymph gland. Six months later, I was on a second fast-track referral and biopsies were taken. I was diagnosed with invasive lobular breast cancer with two tumours at the beginning of September 2015. There was a cancerous tumour on the same site plus another identified elsewhere.

My memory of the weeks following diagnosis was that of decision-making.

It was decided that I met the criteria for Oncotype testing (gene profiling of the tumour tissue). The test gives a personal recurrence score result providing information about the chances of the cancer returning and the likelihood that you might benefit from chemotherapy.

Immediately after being diagnosed I remember expressing some strong feelings against chemotherapy. I had watched four friends go through the rigours of treatment and all had died within two to five years; it seemed pointless. I guess I was assuming the same scenario for myself. However, my perspective changed.

By deciding to take the test I had to accept that if my score came back as low risk recurrence (and therefore minimal, if any, benefit from chemotherapy) then chemotherapy wouldn't be an option even if I wanted it. I had to ask myself how I would feel if I couldn't have chemotherapy.

Other factors in part prolonged the time it took to agree my treatment plan. There seemed to be lots of queries along the way resulting in additional scans all of which clocked up more waiting time. It felt like an incredibly protracted period and according to my Breast Care Nurse, it was unusual. A further week of waiting seems crucial when you are at the stage of having been diagnosed with cancer but with no clear idea of what next.

The next step was in fact influenced by my recurrence result score which came back indicating moderately high risk. For me this was my guide to go for chemotherapy in a kind of 'belts and braces' way.

Treatment

I had surgery in October 2015. Again, more decisions – trial lumpectomy versus mastectomy and, if the latter, reconstruction options. It went on. I felt so grateful for the time the phenomenal Oncology Plastic Surgeon and Breast Care Nurse gave me at this point.

Decision-making in the early days caused me the most stress. There were times when I think I would have welcomed a return to medical paternalism! I remember on one occasion a very measured response, 'We would be looking to get the best outcome for you' pre-empted the 'What would you do if it was you, your mother, sister, auntie?' scenario. Maybe this was a reflection of my stress at the time. I recall being told, 'The most important thing is that you do the right thing for you. You will know.' I found it incredibly hard. I'm not sure I did know, but somehow decisions were reached.

I immersed myself in studies, research articles and statistics and listened to the experiences of others to the point that I felt I had as much information as possible. Ultimately this did help me reach decisions albeit at the eleventh hour.

The regime of cancer treatment and the side-effects were a real shocker at times. Feelings of independence and confidence took a real hit. I did experience low mood for a couple of days after every round of chemo and then it would lift. Along with this there were also feelings of guilt which I have never really understood. Maybe it was something to do with the post-fallout of decision-making stress.

What I have learned is that with decision-making comes a level of responsibility to accept ownership. Relationships changed and there was also a feeling of letting people down in some way. I remember waking up the morning after the first round of chemotherapy feeling as if I had been run over by a bus and thinking what the hell have I done, what have I got myself into? Those feelings passed.

I had Deep Vein Thrombosis (DVT) within the first five days of chemo starting and subsequently needed to inject daily for the next five months. It felt like adding insult to injury. I loathed doing it and, unlike the injections that had to be done after every chemo, I never mastered a pain-free technique. I had to go to another hospital every week for my PICC (Peripherally Inserted Central Catheter) line care. The two nurses there were always so supportive and sympathetic. That helped. They were fabulous in every way and actually were unexpectedly the best support throughout treatment.

Looking Back

Family and friends and colleagues flocked in around the diagnosis 'shock horror time'. In this early stage I think there is a sense of relief when people see that you are not in emotional meltdown and open about things. There were some who couldn't cope with the situation beyond the familiar and safe territory of surgery and there were times when I felt I had to make things easier for them. Tiring! There were also the well-meaning platitudes like 'they can do amazing things now'. In the early days, innocent but naive comments were irritating.

A diagnosis of cancer exposes a vulnerability in others previously not seen. Two people who I am very close to simply couldn't cope and disappeared. Both are masters of 'burying one's head' however. For one it was a case of history repeating itself – another friend dying. The other later confessed she thought she was going to lose me. People had different reactions and needs. This was really noticeable with each of my sons. The youngest asked more questions and wanted more frequent 'check-ins' and has continued to do so whereas the others were very much on a need-to-know basis.

Then there were those who were able to stick alongside for the long slow journey after all the initial fuss died down. I am lucky to have so many good friends around me. There were three friends in particular who understood the situation from the start. In our work, we had all experienced being with people going through difficult or life-changing situations and were familiar with viewing things from a medical model perspective. There is a level of understanding and honesty amongst us which made it feel easy to be open about possible outcomes and prognosis and other information that influenced my decision-making. I will always be thankful for our shared sense of humour too.

Looking back, I feel that I made the right decisions about both the surgery and chemotherapy particularly knowing that some metastasis on one lymph node had been found.

Being faced with your own mortality is the most frightening thing. It reframes everything. I had to adjust so the cancer experience became do-able. Adjustment does happen with time although that's not to say it's easy.

A diagnosis of cancer and its treatment affect so many aspects of your identity. I was told I would start to lose my hair after the first round of chemo. At first I wasn't sure if I wanted to have a wig or not but after an appointment with the wig-fitting service at the centre, I changed my mind. For me, coping with hair loss wasn't a huge deal although I do remember very clearly feeling shocked the day it started coming out in clumps. Time for a very short haircut! I preferred wearing a scarf in preference to the wig but there were some situations when the wig was more appropriate and I could blend into the crowd more easily. It suited me to have a choice.

Losing my hair meant a series of adjustments to a new identity – first hair loss, then 'scarf head' as it affectionately became known amongst friends and family, then braving it going out without a scarf in the early days of regrowth and finally new hair post-treatment. I often still don't recognise this 'new me'.

Another change that caused the need for further adjustment came when the offer of voluntary redundancy presented itself unexpectedly. I was planning to return to work a few months after chemotherapy and radiotherapy had finished. It was a huge dilemma, more decision-making. At the time I remember feeling angry that I had been forced into the position of having to make another decision. It felt wrong to have not been able to achieve either a return to work or plan a departure. I guess there is an element of lack of being in control here somewhere. In many ways it felt *as though I had slid out of work through cancer treatment and then slid into some unknown distant place never to return again!*

What Helped

In my experience there was invaluable support from the Breast Care Nursing Service in the early weeks around the pre-treatment plan decision-making. The Breast Care Nurse Specialist was there at the point of diagnosis and at every appointment with the Surgical and Oncology Consultants – as a kind of silent partner to listen in on the consultation and to then go through information after. Amazing. It wasn't all heaviness and agonising over decision-making – quite the opposite at times. There was a shared humour that I so appreciated. While I recognised her remit was essentially to be a key point of contact in those early days and to provide me with as much information and explanation as needed so that I could make an informed choice about treatment, it felt like a massive gap in contact after this.

I am lucky to live in an area that happens to have a charity cancer support centre within the hospital grounds. It's open to anyone receiving a diagnosis of cancer and also anyone whose life is affected by cancer. It always felt such a welcoming relaxed haven. It offered a wonderfully holistic approach to support and even something as simple as having somewhere quiet and nonclinical to sit before or between appointments was lovely.

After round three of chemo, I hit this massive wall. Things felt very different. Unlike the previous rounds, the chemotherapy cocktail hit didn't lift. Things felt very black. I felt out of my depth. It took a lot to ask for help – I was on the other side of the table this time and in the moment it was devastating to be told it would be a month before they could offer an appointment.

However, when I got there, counselling was good. There were quite a number of demanding things going on in my life aside from cancer which were a huge draw on my physical and emotional energy. It really helped to talk about this new situation that I had found myself catapulted into and about the stresses and strains it was placing on the extended family dynamics. During treatment, beautiful things made me incredibly emotional and also very sad. Everything felt more intense then. It was good to talk about the frustrations and sadness and to laugh because amongst all of the undesirables, there really were some funny times. Essentially it helped me reframe things.

I accessed other support services at the centre such as the art group. It was great to do something new and spontaneous and creative each week. Six complementary therapy sessions were also offered to us and our partners/significant others. Those sessions were such a treat and wonderfully relaxing.

A weekly Mindfulness drop-in group offered time to practise Mindfulness-based practices which I already had some experience of. I found Mindfulness helpful as a way of reducing anxiety and stress in difficult moments. By focusing on the moment it stops the big stories developing. There was something unique about practising it as a part of a group.

At a final Well Being After Cancer Treatment session, a paper by Dr Peter Harvey 'After Treatment Finishes – Then What?' was mentioned. I really found it interesting and useful to view the recovery process in the three stages he describes.

Sharing experiences with others who truly understand – that's what works and makes a difference and that's what the centre gave me.

Very shortly after treatment finished I was contacted by a friend who urged me to go on a four-day residential course – 'A Time to Re-Tune' based around Mindfulness. My husband came too. It was a unique experience for us both and a chance to share our thinking in a way we hadn't done before. Too often the focus is on the person with the cancer and partners can get sidelined. It certainly felt like this for me. I think we both learned some things about each other that we didn't know before and we both benefitted; however, I think I would have been in a different place had it been possible to do it later after I had a bit of a breather. My head was still in 'treatment land'. What the time did allow me to see is that I hadn't allowed myself to stop and just be.

Life Now

It's now September 2017 – I don't regret the decision to take the redundancy and see it as an opportunity for new things, a new phase in my life. Throughout the year of treatment and for two years prior to this, I had been looking after my father who had cancer and dementia. He died in 2017 so again, new territory. I am now feeling I have a chance to think and plan beyond the short term.

Events of the last two years are beginning to feel like a distant memory. The side-effects of long-term medication and regular monitoring and hospital appointments are reminders and a pull on your attention but I feel as though I have moved to a place where the whole cancer experience is on my radar but not dominating my everyday thinking.

Advice to Others

Talk, and ask for and get as much support as you need around decision-making – although I do recognise that not everyone needs it. I encourage others to access as much specialist support and information as they need. Above all, it's do-able and you do get through it. This is just a period of your life, a difficult one, but you can come out the other side.

I now understand 'being kind to yourself' a little better and how important it is to allow yourself to feel whatever you're feeling. My fundamental message is, 'It's OK and will be OK'.

Tony's Story

Diagnosis

About a week before Christmas 2008, I registered with a new doctor as I'd just moved house. I mentioned that I'd had some rectal bleeding but that my previous doctor had said there was nothing wrong. He told me to hop up on the bed and had a look. He then said, 'Stay there; I'm calling an ambulance.'

'What?!' I asked, shocked. 'You've got a real problem,' he said, 'and I don't know why your previous doctor chose to ignore it for so long.' I was taken to hospital as an emergency and underwent a colonoscopy. When I woke up in the recovery room, I was told that they hadn't been able to do the procedure because my colon was completely blocked.

I was still in a daze but remember being in total shock. Luckily my late wife, Bridget, was with me and together we took in the 'What happens now?' discussion. At this point, I was stunned and a lot of thoughts came to mind: 'What about my wife? What am I leaving behind? I need to get my house fit for purpose. How long have I got? How am I going to best use it? What can I do in that time? What haven't I done? What would Bridget like to do? What would we like to do together?' All these flashed through my head.

I was scared; if I was going to go quickly, I wanted to use the time to close things off properly rather than abruptly. Essentially, I needed to know how long I had and to plan the best use of that time.

It was all very quick – bang, I was out of circulation. I immediately stopped my consultancy work – if I had limited time left, I didn't want to spend it working. My family were shocked, especially Bridget who had lost her father to cancer when he was in his 50s. We didn't ask our children for help as they lived far away and it all happened so quickly that there wasn't much time for them to really do anything. The two of us felt that we had all the resources we needed to cope with this.

I remember thinking how incompetent and arrogant my former doctor was; a simple blood test could have caught the cancer earlier. I've always tried to look after myself and had sought expert help from him but he had given me terrible advice. Over the previous five years, I had been to see him lots of times because I had been bleeding from the rectum and finding it hard to go to the toilet. He'd made me feel as if I was being silly – he'd been a doctor so long, he was the expert. He'd said it was something like piles and nothing for me to worry about, so he didn't refer me for any further checks. He really should have retired earlier.

Interestingly, I've since had similar experiences with a few other doctors for other health issues; the ones who have the 'I know best' attitude are arrogant and are not willing to listen to me. I now always get a second opinion if I have any health concerns that are dismissed by a doctor.

Treatment

I had an operation to remove part of my colon a few days after the New Year. I didn't really have time to prepare but I knew it was fairly critical. I didn't know what the outcome would be, didn't know what the broader scenario was, and it felt like I was just going straight in.

A few years before, I'd ruptured my spine and had missing discs and a trapped sciatic nerve. Lying on my back all day long after an operation would be horrendous so they had to give me some special pain relief like opium. The operation was successful and I had a nurse by my side 24 hours a day for the first two days.

At the end of the first week, the doctors were ready to discharge me but I was all swollen up and told them I didn't feel that brilliant. Within an hour of their rounds, I was violently sick and brought up 16 litres of bile! It turned out that they'd been feeding me the wrong food; my stomach and gut were not in a condition to cope with normal food. There was no dietary advice in the hospital back then. Wholemeal bread and salads may be good for you, but not after a bowel operation as the gut has to work too hard.

As a result of this, I had to stay in one extra week. I eventually discharged myself because I ended up with gout as the uric acid had been building up in my body as it struggled to digest the food. I knew that I would be better off at home where I could control what I ate and handle the gout with my local doctor's help.

First Few Months Post-Treatment

For the first six weeks, there wasn't much external support around: no-one to talk to or to get advice from really. It was hard as there were lots of things I couldn't do physically, like driving, lifting, walking the dog, shopping, etc. It's fine if you have the resources to get someone in, but if not, it must be very difficult because you're on your own maybe and end up doing things you shouldn't really do.

Then someone in my choir told me of a local bowel cancer support group that he'd joined, called the Semi Colon Group. This had been set up by one of the nurses in the hospital but she was really stretched and struggling with her caseloads. I went along to the first meeting and found that they were about to close down because there weren't enough helpers.

I agreed to be Vice-Chair only to find out the next day that the Chairman had decided to resign! Two weeks later, the Secretary resigned too, then the Treasurer and other members. It was now down to me to keep it going. As a former Chief Executive of a local authority and having worked as a consultant with charities on large-scale projects to deliver services nationally, re-forming the group wasn't a problem for me. The medical side of the health system had worked and saved my life; I could now use my knowledge and skills to put something back. I was very happy to do so.

At this point, I still didn't know if I would need further treatment like chemotherapy or what the prognosis was. I wanted to know how long I had to live and was doing a bit of bargaining with myself, 'Just give me 12 or 18 months so I can go about enjoying that with my family.'

Luckily, I didn't have to worry as they'd caught the cancer just in time. I then went to the hospital's post-cancer course which was held over six weeks. Meeting people who had different forms of cancer was very helpful, particularly meeting those who were still living with cancer. Seeing someone who had been given 18 months to live and watching how they were making every moment count was inspiring. But some were struggling and a couple weren't able to, or didn't wish to, pick themselves up. They felt sorry for themselves which actually stopped them from applying the positive techniques that would help them move forward. They didn't even try. I think that instead of saying, 'I can't walk 100 yards' just set a smaller goal. If I'm unable to walk to the corner of the road, I walk ten yards and build up slowly.

Getting the right dietary advice was a struggle for me. I didn't know what I should or shouldn't be eating. I eventually got it sorted. I also got advice from a dietician because the painkiller for my back problems made me put on weight and I wanted to keep it under better control.

Ongoing Monitoring

Subsequent colonoscopies found polyps but I'm not worried as long as they catch them in time and whip them out. If there is no follow-up, I wouldn't know. That's why the monitoring shouldn't be hit and miss. After the five years of routine monitoring, the system isn't as good as it should be and I'm often not told about any future follow-up appointments so there is doubt in my mind.

This needs improving to help to reduce doubt and worry about recurrence. If one cell grew bad once, then why not any cell at other times? I would most definitely rather be checked out regularly and know if anything was wrong now so that I can do something about it. I think it's important to be in the driving seat and take responsibility and follow these things up.

Looking Back

I know that I was very, very lucky. The tumour was 4.7cm long and I think that within a week or two, it would have grown through the bowel wall and infected the lymph glands. I wouldn't be here now because once it spreads there isn't much they can do.

My lifestyle back then was such that I didn't eat properly on a regular basis. I was catching food when I had the opportunity in between meetings which would go on into the night! I think I could have looked after myself better although I've got no idea if it would have made any difference with me getting cancer. I suspect not, but I do wonder. On the plus side, I wasn't overweight; I was active and fit.

The cancer forced me to look at my future years and to use them to the best of my ability to do the things that I never had the chance to whilst I was so busy working hard. It was a chance to catch up on the things that I'd missed and to learn new skills. It was both a shock and an opportunity for me to think, 'What would I like to do with the rest of my life? How do I want to do it? How do I best use my remaining years?' It was a real wake-up call.

What Helped

Bridget was amazing. She came from a medical background and was very understanding and caring, and someone I could always talk to. She knew me better than I probably knew myself as we were childhood sweethearts and had been married for 49 years. I was lucky to have her. Sadly, I've since lost Bridget.

From the courses I've attended (a pain clinic and the post-cancer programme), I know that talking is very important; it's helpful to talk to others who have had cancer. It helped me to put it in a bigger context than myself and I wasn't quite so focused on myself. I realised many things: I'm not alone; I'm not the only one; there is nothing to be ashamed of; and there's very little I could have done to stop getting cancer. Learning from others about how they coped is beneficial; if they can do it, why can't I? It helped me to move forward as there is no reason why cancer should stop me enjoying the rest of my life regardless of what future treatment is needed.

Joining the Semi Colon Group, meeting people who had actually been through it and seeing that there is life afterwards, even 20+ years on, also changed my perspective of my life expectancy. I learned new skills and had new challenges which helped me to not wallow or worry about things. After ten great years, the group has folded, because just like when I first joined, we didn't have enough new volunteers and we were spread too thinly. I'm sad about the group closing down as our trained volunteers helped many people.

It's priceless having someone on hand who is trained to support you through the diagnosis and treatment and to help with the practical everyday things while you recover. The group supported mostly women and the men who came forward had usually been 'sent' by the nurse at the hospital or encouraged by their wives who wanted them to take better care of themselves. It may be part of the male psyche to bury their heads to certain bad news. I don't think men cope with grief that well. They don't like bad news and tend to ignore it or let it wash over them rather than deal with it. I think they tend to run away from things like that. Maybe they don't want to bother or worry others or hope that it will go away. It's fairly common. My father-in-law was like that. He didn't tell anyone he had cancer till it was really bad and he only had a month to live.

From the awareness campaigns we've done, men say they don't need testing and have even refused to return stool samples. Maybe they are ashamed, especially if they then have a stoma bag. Cancer is simply cells in the body going bad, in which case, you have nothing to be ashamed of; so then, why not talk about it? We found that if they were buddied up with a volunteer pre-operation and had a chance to chat to someone that had been there, they were more likely to be open afterwards as they realised they weren't the only one and that many people go on to live for years and years.

I hope that the British National Health System can provide this kind of personal post-treatment support because at the moment, they don't in my local area. Over the years, it has been hit and miss, because when budgets are limited, it's the discretionary services like this which get cut back. It'd be far better for them to say they aren't doing it, and hand it over completely to the third sector. This would ensure that the after-treatment support is consistent. It's really important and much better than people burying their cancer experience and just going to their doctor for pills.

Another thing that helped me was to focus on what I could sensibly do at the time and to make changes so that I could carry on doing things. One critical example was controlling my weight as I know that being overweight brings other health complications and would restrict me from doing the things I want to do.

Life Now

It's now August 2018 – I'm enjoying life. I met and fell in love again with a wonderful woman, Pam. She had lost her husband to cancer and it hadn't been easy for her. We're now celebrating six happy years, so for me, there has been a beautiful rainbow at the end of all the hard times.

I think about what I'd like to do that I haven't yet done and go and do it. With Pam, I continue to enjoy living: I go sailing, I sing, I travel, I learned the guitar, I've played in a samba band and at a jazz festival, I've learned mahjong, and more.

Advice to Others

Find out more. What are the implications of your cancer? It's likely that your cancer is not life-threatening to the degree you think it is. Get as much advice as you can. Don't hide from it but find out actively what you can do. Look at what help and support is out there and ask for it.

Rhonda's Story

Diagnosis

In November 2014, during a routine mammogram, a new 3D machine found something under my arm. I scheduled a biopsy and it was discovered that I had Follicular Lymphoma. Follicular Lymphoma is a low-grade, slow-growing cancer and I was asymptomatic in that I had no symptoms apart from a few enlarged nodes. I didn't follow any active treatment. During the summer of 2016 through to the fall of that year, I was experiencing severe stomach pains. I thought it was an ulcer. I was under a lot of stress: my sister had died from an overdose; my mother had passed away eight months later; I was taking care of my father; and my husband, who has Stage 4 malignant melanoma, was in treatment every two weeks and had several surgeries that same year.

In October 2016, I made a visit to see my family doctor and a subsequent scan showed that my Follicular Lymphoma had transformed into a diffused large B-cell Lymphoma which was very aggressive. I needed to start treatment immediately and I chose the Cancer Treatment Centre of America. The best thing about this centre is that whenever you are scheduled for tests and scans, you meet the team on the same day so you don't have to wait for weeks. My medical team consists of a haematologist, an oncologist, a naturopathic doctor, a nutritionist and a nurse case manager and I meet them all at the same time, every time I visit.

The new scans found 30 lymph nodes were affected; one had turned into a six-inch tumour that was sitting on my lower bowel, and that's what was causing the pain I thought was an ulcer.

Treatment

The treatment was dose-adjusted EPOCH chemotherapy which was made up of four different types of chemotherapy. Treatment required that I stay as an in-patient at the hospital five days at a time where the chemo would run continuously for 24 hours a day over those days. Then I'd go home for two weeks and come back again for another five-day stay. Each stay was considered a cycle. I went through six cycles, which ultimately turned out to be more than 600 hours of chemo.

When you're told that treatment needs to start immediately, it's hard to wrap your head around that. How would I adjust my life around this? How could I possibly spend five days at a time in the hospital and even the thought of having to be an in-patient was difficult for me. I was angry that it was happening and I was desperately trying to figure out how I would readjust my life and how could I fit this in.

Then I just got sad. I was in the hospital at Thanksgiving and over Christmas. I was tired. I was angry that I wasn't my full self during those times and towards the end, I so desperately wanted to run away from it. By the fourth cycle I had to really push myself and convince myself to just get back to the hospital. In the fifth cycle I think I cried the entire 45-minute drive to the hospital.

The second cycle scans showed that 95% of the cancer was gone but I still had to finish the six cycles. There were some dark hours around the time I had to go for the fourth cycle; if I could have run away, I would have. By the time the full treatment was done, I was completely in remission.

I had extreme fatigue during my treatment. I love to cook, and I'm a caregiver and a nurturer but during my treatment, just standing in my kitchen and cooking was so tiring. The fatigue was like nothing I'd ever experienced before. I had mouth sores and diarrhoea immediately following each treatment, which would last several days. I look after my young granddaughter once a week and although there were points when I was very fatigued, I didn't want to give that up so it was challenging at times.

My sons and husband visited and a few friends also visited, but mostly I didn't want friends seeing me like that. I turned people down when they asked to come visit. I now know how those animals feel trapped in a zoo. I'm naturally the hostess and love to entertain but I didn't want to do that in the hospital. I wasn't dressed in my regular clothes. Keeping a sense of humour is important and I'd tell friends not to come and see me in hospital – wait till I'm home and can put a bra on!

First Few Months Post-Treatment

As soon as I finished treatment in February, a friend introduced me to a plant-based supplement and that made a huge difference. I began drinking a moringa supplement daily and detox tea every other day. At my three-month and six-month check-ups, the naturopathic doctor, oncologist and nutritionist were surprised at my high energy levels. They had been certain that it would be six months to a year before I would get my energy back to this level.

Before the cancer, I worked 32 hours a week. I didn't work at all during the chemo because my company gave me short-term disability payments which meant that I was on full pay for the first 12 weeks. I couldn't take this intermittently as it had to be taken all at one time. The chemo was so exhausting I couldn't go back to work after three months and went on long-term disability. I was off work for seven months.

I went to visit my workplace a month before I was planning to go back. At that point I had no eyebrows, no hair and no eyelashes. Losing my hair was devastating and a struggle as I lost that image of myself. My company was very gracious and understanding. They suggested I come back one day a week and work up to my normal hours. But within four weeks of taking the supplement I felt ready to go back full-time.

By the time I went back to work, my eyebrows, eyelashes and hair had started growing back. My hair is now grown back although I'm not embracing all the curliness of my hair! My fingernails and skin are also in good condition and I also attribute that to the supplement.

I'm a technical trainer and instructor and I love working with people. But in the months before I went back I wasn't sure I could face people. I was afraid to get up in front of people. At the time I thought you couldn't look at me and not know that I'm a cancer patient, and I didn't want people to feel sorry for me. I worried a lot about that and I even entertained the idea of changing careers, maybe something I could do from home. But I'm glad I didn't and I'm even proud that I pushed myself to step forward. Working with people has helped my recovery. I'm exactly where I need to be.

Ongoing Monitoring

I'm still clear and there is no evidence of the disease. The follicular part could still affect me but we've conquered the large beast – at least I hope so.

Do I worry about the cancer coming back? No. Having cancer wasn't the worry and the cancer coming back doesn't worry me much. Going through chemotherapy scares me the most. I was afraid that my husband, whose prognosis in March 2014 was a one-to-three-year life expectancy, would die before me. I worried about having to go through chemo without him. He's my greatest supporter; I could not imagine how I would have gotten through any of this without him by my side. Now that I'm through the chemo I don't even want to think about the cancer coming back.

Looking Back

Now, I look back and I see that I've moved forward and I don't want to go back there. I've always been a thankful person but now I'm even more grateful. There has been stress caused by illness and death but it hasn't changed me at the core in terms of who I am. I feel stronger than I was before, I feel more resilient and I can keep getting up when life knocks me down. I'm grateful.

What Helped

The Cancer Treatment Centre treats the whole person. Every day I was in the hospital, I was able go to Mind and Body where they have acupuncture, reiki, meditation, massage and lots more complementary services. There are also psychologists, counsellors and chaplains. All these services were available to me at any time whether I wanted to take advantage of it or not. A nurse case manager handles all the scheduling for every appointment. Having to only work with one person when scheduling relieved a lot of stress. I also met with the pastor every day that I was in hospital.

Deep-breathing meditation helped me relax while I was in the hospital. Although my hospital room was lovely, I felt trapped in my room: no plants, no animals and no children under six which meant that my granddaughter couldn't visit. I was hooked up to the chemo through a port in my arm so I couldn't move about much. They were long, hard days; the meditation helped.

My husband is a warrior and is still working through his treatment. He's on immunotherapy one hour every two weeks. He's doing well; he's in the 1% that hasn't had any serious side-effects. He has experienced fatigue too but not to the extreme I did. At first, he was sceptical about taking the supplement and detox tea. After a while, he stopped taking them but when he felt so fatigued again, he started up again.

I have a very large extended family and I have two grown sons. Nothing has changed in the way that we deal with each other and our family time. My family and friends have always been supportive. I do worry for my children as they have two parents with cancer and I wonder how they deal with it emotionally.

Life Now

It's now September 2017 – I think a lot more about my purpose. While I was going through treatment, two friends I knew died from cancer. One was a 53-year-old family friend and I couldn't attend his funeral as I was in hospital. The other was a co-worker who was 49 years old who left behind his wife and young son. So I do wonder: Why did I survive? Why am I still here and they aren't?

My faith has without doubt helped. I don't know what caused the cancer and focusing on 'Why' doesn't help me. I look forward. I also get out and exercise more and eat more healthily.

I've always felt that life is beautifully brilliant and then there are things in life that are just brutally random. Cancer is just one of those brutally random things and was just something I had to go through. All these life events: my sister, my mother and my husband – I just have to go through them and I've honestly always believed that everything is going to be OK. I believe that God guides us and that there's a reason for everything even if I don't quite know the reason yet.

Advice to Others

The key, I think, is to look forward and don't live in that moment of treatment. See yourself getting through that. I kept thinking 'I've got 300 more hours' instead of thinking about the 300 I'd done. Stay as positive as you can.

Meena's Story

Diagnosis

I feel that my doctor let me down. I had noticed a lump on my right breast three years before I was officially diagnosed with cancer. The lump came and went so the doctor said it was hormonal and didn't investigate further. A few years later, when the lump was present for the whole month and really painful, I was finally referred to hospital. Two weeks later, I had a mammogram. It's a bit of a blur to be honest, but I think they asked me to wait and then I had a biopsy there and then.

They told me that results had shown pre-cancerous cells so I thought it wasn't serious; it's not cancer, it's pre-cancerous. So I wasn't worried and when they asked me to come back a week later, I said I couldn't as I was busy at work!

Treatment

Just before my diagnosis, I had been violently mugged when I was out walking the dog. I ended up with a broken jaw which needed two operations. I was still recovering from that, but here I was a couple of months later undergoing several more operations to take out the growths. Initially, I didn't want the mastectomy as I was still thinking that it was pre-cancerous. Generally, I wish the hospital team had explained things better. I think they could have been a lot clearer and said, 'It's cancer.'

Eventually, I did have a mastectomy and fortunately I didn't need any further treatment as my lymph nodes were not affected. All along they told me that they would reconstruct with muscle from my back and I wouldn't need an implant but at the last minute, they said they couldn't as there wasn't enough muscle in my back. I had to have an implant.

Whether or not to have an implant is an important decision; I wasn't given enough time to think about it and there was no-one to talk to about the choices I had. They gave me lots of leaflets, but because I couldn't focus, I just put them to one side to be read later. I was only referred to support centres after my mastectomy! Talking to the nurse or someone who had had breast cancer when I had to make decisions would have been helpful because it was all unknown to me. I didn't know what to ask and what to expect. I needed to talk to someone about the pros and cons of having an implant. No-one mentioned the risk of the implant exploding! I had issues with the original implant because it was too heavy and it had to be replaced through yet another operation.

Looking back, I think I would have refused an implant. I think that implants have to be replaced every ten years, but no-one's talked to me about that.

In total, I had seven operations over the two years. It was a confusing time and I didn't know what to think. I fitted my appointments and operations around my job as I didn't want to take too much time off work because I was concerned about my finances and couldn't afford to be off. I'm a contract worker, so there is no sick pay. The medical team were sympathetic and made it work for me.

Looking Back

Apart from the implant, I felt that I didn't really have a choice with the other decisions; 'If you don't have the operation, your life is in danger' or 'There is the danger of it spreading so you need a mastectomy.'

I went to all my tests and consultations alone. I'm used to dealing with things myself so I didn't make much use of the cancer nurse specialist; obviously I now wish I had. At the time, I didn't realise that I could talk to her and she always seemed to be very busy so I thought it best to handle things myself.

I was much more emotional and was often in tears in the hospital waiting room, especially when I kept needing operations. It just seemed to drag on. For those two years it seemed like all I did was hang out in hospitals, either having an operation or going to follow-up appointments. I remember sitting in a waiting room crying because I couldn't see an end to it all.

I felt spaced out by the experience of having to face things I've never had to. How do I deal with this? What compartment do I put this in? I have at times felt like a fraud because I didn't need chemotherapy or radiotherapy. It seemed that others would see it as less serious.

I didn't consider talking to a helpline or contacting a local cancer group. I was all over the place so hadn't thought about outside help; it's also not who I am, so it never occurred to me. If I'd been made aware, I'd have thought about it. I did ask for counselling after my treatment but never got a call back, so I gave up.

What Helped

The things that helped me were having my kids around. This was important. Their support was lovely and they looked after me well. They helped by walking my dog when I couldn't and were on hand to give me advice on diet.

I did also use the cancer centre at the hospital and had some massages and some yoga sessions. That was really good to have, although I found it difficult to fit in as I was still working.

Life Now

It's now June 2018 – recurrence is something I think about. Will it come back? Whenever I experience pain or tenderness in my breasts, I get concerned. I don't want to go through it again. But overall, there has been no major negative impact on my life as I'm the sort of person that keeps going and continues to live life as normal. I do, however, recognise that there was a subtle change underneath.

Once the treatment was over, I knew it wasn't business as usual for me. I now think more about my life, how I want it to be and what I'm doing with it. I make more conscious decisions and no longer drift along. I'd say it woke me up and I became more health conscious. I'm a calmer person who no longer feels the need to rush around.

I know I have a choice in how I behave and prioritise having time to myself; I now consciously slow down and meditate. To me, people living on a constant treadmill is unnatural.

Advice to Others

My advice to anyone diagnosed with cancer is to speak to someone who has experienced cancer and talk things through with someone. It will help you get your head around it.

June's Story

Diagnosis

It was almost a relief when I was told I had cancer. For about five years, my blood pressure had been going up and the medication was slowing me down to the point of taking away my life; I had little energy and couldn't do much. I had a couple of strokes a few years ago, so my doctor said I needed to keep taking the meds.

In January 2017, I went on a juice diet to counteract the excesses of Christmas and the increasing lack of exercise. I had more frequent bowel movements and looser stools but I didn't mention it to the doctor for four months because I put it down to the diet. However, by April, I noticed that my stools had a strong 'off' smell and when I mentioned this to my doctor he referred me for further tests.

In the first half of 2017, two colonoscopies were abandoned because of my high blood pressure just before the procedure. I suggested to the consultant that this was being caused by the laxative as I am very sensitive to a lot of things. He dismissed this and said that it was because I was nervous. I knew this wasn't the case and when I had another pre-assessment appointment six months later, I told the nurse about my severe reaction to the laxative. It turned out that she had a drawer full of alternative options because that laxative '...doesn't suit some people'. The consultant never mentioned that was even a possibility! Why hadn't he listened to me? It could all have been sorted back in April, 20 weeks ago!

During the colonoscopy, I could see a black mushroom-type blob on the screen and I thought, 'Hmm, that's cancer.' When I came round from sedation, they asked me to see one of the consultants. The Macmillan cancer nurse specialist was also present and had a very serious face. I had processed the possibility of cancer after seeing the screen and just wanted it dealt with quickly, efficiently and unemotionally but it seemed to me they were interpreting my calmness as not understanding the seriousness of the situation.

We discussed treatment and I was told we were looking at major surgery. They needed to remove half of my colon, which was a shock and more extensive surgery than I had expected. I understood that my life was being threatened and that I could die on the table but I just wanted it to be dealt with. To me they seemed to be overly coddling and too full of sympathy and I didn't want that. I didn't need that. It felt like they just didn't understand that I understood what they were saying to me and the fact that I was taking the news in my stride seemed to make them uncomfortable as if they were waiting for an emotional reaction.

My husband had been waiting for me in the waiting room and I chose to tell him there and then by myself. Looking back, I think my husband wished he'd been offered the chance to ask his own questions.

The subsequent tests revealed that the tumour was at Stage 2 and probably two nodes were affected. I called the cancer 'Vance' as this was the autocorrect word that came up once when I mistyped 'Cance' in a web search. Vance surprised me and everyone else in the final histology as he was Stage 3 and four nodes were diseased – but no metastases.

Treatment

The pre-assessment appointment left me shaken. My blood pressure was high as usual plus the stress of facing a few hours of tests and being fiddled with. The nurse checking my results said that she couldn't possibly put me forward for surgery unless my blood pressure was considerably lowered. She said it wasn't good enough and made me feel both inadequate and unwilling to co-operate. I felt shaky and tearful after speaking to her; she wasn't looking at me as a patient or a person, but looking at my file and following a set of guidelines. I'm a strong woman but she ground me down that day. I felt 'got at' and this particular nurse made me feel guilty for not fitting into the norm. However, when I later saw the consultant, he was unconcerned and said he'd signed me off already. The stress placed upon me by this nurse had been totally unnecessary and was probably my most upsetting experience as a cancer patient.

The surgery was scheduled and everything happened quickly. I didn't want anyone knowing about my diagnosis or my planned treatment, not even my children. My husband went along with it, much against his better judgement. In hindsight, I realise that he would have appreciated support from family and friends. His mother had died of leukaemia while he was working abroad and no-one had told him she was ill. Asking him to do that to our children was unfair, but luckily, they were understanding and supportive when they were eventually told. He knew I needed to deal with this in my own way. I needed his strength and he gave that to me.

At that time, it was important to me that I did not have to deal with other people's reactions. I wanted to stay in my own little world where I was quite happy; I did not want to deal with misguided concern.

I was in hospital for 15 long days which I found difficult. The bed was uncomfortable, the routine a mystery and I couldn't eat properly. Looking back on it, I had a fairly rough ride at times although going through it step by step meant that it was all 'do-able'.

Six days after the operation, I had an anastomotic leak. When I asked how it happened, they said, 'It sometimes happens.' I wanted more information but I didn't get any. The leak caused an infection and I had tachycardia. I was given lots of antibiotics and ended up vomiting blood – it was an allergic reaction to one of the antibiotics. I was quite unwell and completely unaware of what was going on.

One night, I passed about two litres of blood. I was grateful to the nurses who cared for me and the professional way they dealt with the situation as they were very sensitive. When I asked what had caused the haemorrhaging, no-one seemed to have an answer. Again, they said, 'These things happen.' I felt I was being fobbed off.

I also had an abscess under the external scar and finally on the day of discharge the decision was made to make an opening and excise the contents of the abscess. Once discharged, I had a daily appointment with the surgery nurse and the community nurse. Every single day for two months, including over Christmas and New Year, the abscess was drained and the wound packed. At the time it seemed invasive and never-ending, but it proved to be a beneficial routine as it forced me to put on clothes and leave the house. To go out into the winter cold after being in a ward was refreshing and I saw that life was still going on. The nurses were kind, gentle, informed, encouraging and supportive.

My experience with the oncology team was not what I expected. At the first appointment the oncologist was running three hours late. As I was still raw from surgery, I went home. The following week when I did eventually see the oncologist, he was not prepared for the consultation in any way – he didn't know my name, my conditions, and hadn't read my notes. I had to spend the first 50 minutes of the hour I was allocated telling him my history. I had assumed he would have access to my notes and would have been ready for our appointment.

Chemo Or No Chemo

My initial response to my oncologist's suggestion to have chemotherapy was to say no because of any potential allergic reactions. He insisted chemotherapy was the only way forward. He had no notes or experience of my medical history, yet insisted I comply with his advice. Luckily the Macmillan nurse who was present said that I could start on a lower dosage to see how I responded and that reassured me slightly. Without her input the whole appointment would have been a waste of everyone's time. I came away disappointed and shocked at the ignorance and intolerance I received; I perceived this as unprofessional treatment.

I went off and did further research on the chemotherapy treatment he had suggested not only because I'm allergic to many things, but also because I experienced some peripheral neuropathy from the anaesthetic used during the cancer surgery. This caused my fingers to stick together like magnets and they were difficult to prise apart. When I drank, I got electric tingles on my lips and tongue. I discovered that the chemotherapy could lead to peripheral neuropathy in a more serious form and that it could stay for life, 24/7, and the pain could not be alleviated by any medication. I knew I needed more opinions.

I was stressed when doctors treated me as if I was unable to understand the correct terms for treatments, or even parts of the body. Their language and inferences seem to suggest they were not convinced this grey-haired old lady could go away and do proper research, talk to people and analyse the results.

Through contacts I elicited help from four oncology departments in different parts of the world to discuss my case and apply the 'mum' test: 'If June was your mum, what would you recommend?' The unanimous answer was chemotherapy. I also consulted a world-renowned oncologist privately who told me more about cancer and about my condition in six minutes than the health service had told me in six months! He recommended that I try just one of the chemotherapy treatments to see how it went and then review the possibilities.

Although everyone was telling me to have the treatment I was still undecided. Then I woke up one morning and surprised myself that in my sleep I had decided that I would try just one pill. But when I next saw my regular oncologist and he again recommended chemotherapy, I heard myself saying, 'No.'

With six oncologists telling me to have the treatment, I hadn't made this decision lightly. I had learned that due to my allergies, the first pill could kill me and I wasn't prepared to take such a chance. To my amazement, the oncologist said, 'I understand. I've actually seen the first pill kill somebody.' I went with my inner belief; chemotherapy was not the way forward for me and, so far, that has proven to be a good decision.

Ongoing Monitoring

To my relief, the CEA levels at my three-month check-up were fine and there are now no cancer cells in my body. I'm as likely to get it again as King Kong because it was a mucous cell carcinoma and it could have happened anywhere in the body. It's been taken out and it's gone. Recurrence is not something I think about. The doctor who does the follow-up consultations is great. He has a good attitude and encourages me to ask questions. He listens to me.

There has, however, been a complication – the infection I'd suffered in hospital increased the chances of getting a hernia. And I did get one; I call it 'Horatio'. The hernia consultant doesn't think it's a priority so now it's the size of a water melon. This is what I'm now having to deal with.

Looking Back

I feel a fraud because I didn't have chemotherapy and my cancer was dealt with quickly and it's gone. There are people facing metastases and other complications, even death, and they are the ones who, in my mind, are the real cancer patients. Mine was just a little thing that thanks to the expertise of the medical staff is now in the past. I knew it could kill me but I never thought it would. I just knew it was going to go away. I was never scared or anxious.

I know I was selfish putting the veto on people knowing – and as far as social media was concerned we had what we called a 'three-line whip' on privacy. When under threat of something that could kill me, I think I needed to bring my boundaries in and have this little bubble that I could have control of. It was my way of coping. I'm not a selfish person but I knew that I needed to act to protect my bubble even when this meant being selfish.

I am uncomfortable with the language used about cancer. I do not see treatment as a battle. Would you say that a broken leg is a battle? Cancer is no different. Over the years, I've had five basal cell carcinomas (BCC), a type of skin cancer, removed from my face and over three dozen from my body, and I now have another four waiting to be excised. It's a ten-minute job. It's not a battle or a war, it is a treatment. It's not logical to think cancer has invaded me because I'm not a good person or I need a lesson. It's just a fact of life. Things happen to you; you have no choice but to deal with them. For me choosing the positive way through made it easier and manageable.

I'm a very matter-of-fact person. I have done a lot of my own research and have several folders full of information. I was fully prepared for whatever happened. I may be grey but I have sufficient intelligence to assess complex information for myself. I've just written a paper for my local health board on the topic of keeping patients informed to improve clinical standards. One of the most important messages is, 'Talk to the patient, not the grey hair.'

We're all different, but surely there has to be a simple way of finding out our individual and specific needs. 'What do you need from me right now?' If the patient says, 'I don't need anything' then let them be.

The medical staff should deal with the whole orange, not just a segment. Each team in its own right is good but there seems to be no joined-up thinking or communication. Are my cancer team speaking to the hernia team? I have no idea. It would be useful to have just one point of contact for any post-treatment complications like my hernia. Instead, I've been passed from pillar to post. With several appointments at different clinics, there is often a lack of explanation. The letter just says that I have an appointment to see so-and-so but there is no information as to which department they are in and I'm left wondering, 'Who are they? Why am I seeing them? Do I wish to see this person?'

What Helped

My husband was a great help. When I got home from hospital every room in the house was filled with flowers – including the bathroom. Every time a vase faded, he replaced it right up to my birthday several months later. It was lovely. Lots of people sent flowers, cards and gifts. It was wonderful. It is a reminder that we all need those around us to express themselves and their thoughts and feelings to us when we are vulnerable – it really helped and reminded me I wasn't alone.

To help reduce and control my blood pressure, I had two Neuro-Linguistic Programming (NLP) sessions. This was brilliant and one of the best things I did. Pre- and post-surgery, the NLP Practitioner I saw was a really good backup, helping me to focus on what I could do. In the past, I've learned and used Brandon Bay's 'The Journey' which is a transformational and healing method. I have also practised yoga, tai chi and meditation. It is part of my life so I wasn't consciously using the techniques but was definitely aided in having them to hand in dealing with the cancer and rationalising what I could do to deal with it. It also helped me to keep positive and believe in myself.

In hospital when I couldn't concentrate to read a book or do Sudoku, I was able to write poems. Looking back, it's interesting to see how I felt at the time. I would recommend poem-writing as a tool to acknowledge dark and vicious thoughts and get them out. Sometimes random words make you realise an emotion, feel a feeling, admit a fear, recognise an outcome and sometimes introduce you to you.

Finally, what helped me was being fortunate enough to have a wonderful doctor who supported me, informed me and always got me copies of all the reports of tests I had undergone if and when I asked for them. I was never more than a phone call away from his know-how and his advice, and knowing he would be there for me gave me strength. I may be a strong woman but it is to all those who gave me their strength and their support I have to thank for coming through relatively unscathed.

Life Now

It's now August 2018 – I'm now fitter, healthier and better than before the operation. If it wasn't for Horatio, I'd be walking and swimming lots. One post-cancer limitation is that I've lost some freedom around days out and meals out. I have to think and plan carefully as the food passes through my system much more quickly.

My Advice

My advice to anyone recently diagnosed with cancer is to find out how threatening it is to your future. Is it likely to have spread? How serious is that? Then if you choose to put your head in the sand, do so. But don't just rely on one doctor, one opinion. Ask for second, third or fourth opinions. Be interested in your own health. Take some responsibility over what is going to happen to you; after all, the only thing in life we really own is 'our life'!

Taking small baby steps throughout, building up slowly each day and accepting temporary limitations all help in going from dependent patient to fully fit individual. Small increments will mean that you worry less and become more capable of dealing with what you're facing. Remember, the pathway ahead is yours alone and always remember that you CAN deal with whatever life throws at you.

With a smile on my face when I woke
up to be told 'it's all gone'

In the middle of me, a lacuna

They took the cancer.

My Story

Diagnosis

As I mentioned in my introduction to this book, I discovered that the tumour they found during the colonoscopy was cancerous because of the appointment letter with the cancer team the following week.

That Saturday night, reading the letter at home alone, this fear rose up, followed by a need to know more: What is bowel cancer? What can be done? What are my chances of survival? Will I need chemotherapy and radiotherapy? How long will I have to be in hospital? I was living a long way from my family; would I have to move? I spent the rest of the evening researching, finding out as much as I could.

I'm an information-seeker so I read and read and came up with a list of questions I wanted to ask the consultant. I was impressed by the cancer charity websites with their clear medical information and guidance on cancer diagnosis. The main relief at this point was realising that my chances of survival were high as the endoscopist had said the tumour was 'in the early stages' and I clung on to that. Having researched and reached this conclusion, I felt calm and was able to relax.

Now, how do I tell my family and friends? What words do I use? I made the decision not to tell anyone else that evening as I wanted to give myself time to digest all of this and frankly, I'd spent enough time thinking about cancer and I needed to switch off. The following day, I told my mum, my cousin and one close friend; that was all

I could manage. A big part of me was still convinced that the consultant would say it's not cancer so there was no point in alarming everyone.

Meena, the friend I spoke to (and who I also interviewed for this book), had had breast cancer a few years before and I found it helpful to hear about her experience, especially her advice about taking someone along to the consultations. I had planned to go alone as I'm fiercely independent and don't like to bother other people, but Meena, who has a similar self-reliant streak, said that she had gone alone to all her consultations and it's the one thing she would do differently. I was glad that I followed her advice as having my cousin by my side taking notes and giving me moral support before and after the consultations made it an easier experience. Especially for the first consultation when they confirmed it was cancer and there was no mix-up. It was real. Apparently I could get cancer and I had bowel cancer.

I then struggled with wanting to understand why I'd got cancer; what had I done wrong? What should I have done differently? In mulling this over, I became aware that I had unknowingly formed a belief that only people with a genetic predisposition or people with unhealthy lifestyles get cancer. Not so. Sometimes cancer just happens. Random. Bad luck.

When I read the information leaflet that lists the factors that put people at increased risk of bowel cancer, I didn't tick any of the boxes. Looking at the typical tell-tale symptoms, I only had one – a change in bowel habits, but I put that down to my worsening irritable bowel symptoms that I'd had since 2010, caused by work stress.

The situation I was facing was serious. I decided to take it step by step by step, and responded to what each test or scan revealed about my treatment options. In between, I continued working but there was an ongoing battle in my head because I was determined that the cancer wouldn't stop me – but I was struggling to focus. After a lot of self-resistance, I was forced to give myself permission to be OK with not achieving as much at work and just doing the minimum. I then had to warn my colleagues that I would not be able to work as efficiently as usual. Admitting this felt a bit like failure.

I also had a lot of 'cancer admin' to get through and my brain fog was constantly present. I did a lot more research about the tests and about diets that help the immune system. Then there was the job of having to respond to others as they heard my news. Apart from the medical uncertainties and decision-making, the one part I found most challenging and stressful was how others reacted when they first heard the news and then having to keep them informed.

My family and friends love me and obviously wanted to hear the latest after each test, scan and consultation. But I felt conflicted; I was grateful and knew that I was lucky that so many people cared and wanted to talk to me and to know how I was doing, yet I found it exhausting having to say things over and over again. I'd then feel bad about being so begrudging and start telling myself off, which left me even more emotionally drained.

At this point, post–diagnosis when I was having a series of tests and scans so that my treatment could be determined, I spent a lot of my time on the couch sleeping or watching something inane on TV because my brain was overwhelmed. And that was hard for me as I was used to being active and useful and here I was, having very little energy.

To stay sane, I had to accept that for now, I would have to slow down and train myself to be OK with functioning below par. But it took me a while to adjust to this as I'd often forget and resist how I was feeling.

I did get angry with a friend who would talk to me as if I was about to die, and was irritated by another who couldn't resist telling me about other people they knew who'd died. Really?! There were also those who said, 'Wow, you're so fit and active and you still got cancer. Just shows you, there's no point in exercising!' How is that helpful? I had to bite my tongue a lot. And my cancer experience has confirmed that there is a point to exercising and being fit because it means that when you're hit with a major illness, you are likely to recover more quickly from the treatment and experience fewer complications. Of course, being fit doesn't mean that someone won't face cancer or another major illness, or that there couldn't be complications with treatments, but I believe the odds are more in your favour.

I was also really conflicted when some well-meaning people would advise me to take a particular vitamin or wonder food as it would clear my cancer and I wouldn't need any treatment. Although I knew they were coming from a good place, the implication is that I got cancer because I hadn't been eating properly or nourishing my body. I found this both hurtful and irritating. It added to my existing self-reproach that I was to blame and by not eating correctly, I got cancer. It was really unhelpful and increased my stress levels.

Plus, facing a potentially life-threatening disease, would I take the risk of relying on vitamins or a particular diet to cure me? No chance! But I did eat simpler food so that my gut didn't have to work hard and my body could then focus on fighting the cancer and stopping it from spreading.

Treatment

In the end, I was lucky. After weeks of uncertainty, waiting for various scan results, it was confirmed that the tumour was contained in the bowel so the first step was an operation to remove part of my colon and review treatment options based on the histology of what was removed. A few weeks after the operation, I was delighted and relieved to be told that none of the nodes were affected and that I wouldn't need any further treatment. I was over the moon. Apart from the standard regular post-treatment check-ups, that was hopefully the end.

First Few Months Post-Treatment

Like most cancer patients, I was physically and mentally fatigued. I was recovering well from the operation, yet there was this incessant white noise in my head going round and round, not profound insights, just songs I'd heard or thoughts about an inane TV programme I'd watched. Although I am a regular and experienced meditator, I struggled to meditate. I struggled to focus at work. Was this what the nurse meant when she said to watch out for the psychological effects? What do I do about it? I asked the nurse for help and she put me on the hospital's post-cancer group course.

Looking Back

When people ask me about my cancer experience, I say that I was luckily unlucky: unlucky to have had cancer and lucky to have caught it early, only needing an operation and to have had an excellent medical team – many others are not so lucky and that complicates their emotional response to their experience.

What Helped

Talking with my cousin after each meeting about what the consultant had said and what that meant, helped me to deal with the early stages of the conveyor belt. She was the right person because I've known her all my life and I didn't need to wear a mask with her. I could be open and completely honest about how I felt even if it was negative, but at the same time, we often had a laugh and a giggle as we sat in the waiting area.

I'd given her a clipboard, paper and pen so she could take notes and we joked about how intimidating that might be for the consultant. It was a way for me to take control and having the notes helped with questions that cropped up afterwards as I couldn't always remember everything the consultant told me because of my foggy brain.

My family were also helpful in that they let me determine how I'd like to be supported. Mostly, I wanted to relax and recuperate after my operation so I turned down all offers to visit me because that would mean me having to make sure they were OK. My bowel movements were also not very 'pretty' for several weeks and I didn't want anyone else to witness this! The best way for me to stay stress-free was not to have visitors.

My mum did stay with me a few days after I was discharged and made sure that my first meal was a treat – delicious lobster! Friends in my village also popped round with soup and flowers. It was little things like this that meant a lot.

A week later, I was able to go back to my running club to help with the beginner's course as that involved sitting and talking; I could do that, although I wouldn't stay very long as the effort exhausted me. It was really good to have something to focus on though.

Being able to work flexibly was a huge help. I'd do a couple of hours in the morning, then rest for about four hours before doing another couple of hours. It wasn't only the physical exhaustion; my brain was fuzzy for several months. Gradually, I went back to working full-time.

The hospital's post-treatment course was really useful as it helped to hear about others' experiences and how they were coping. Although we all had different types of cancers and experiences, we were going through a lot of the same things. I was surprised by how much we had in common. The facilitators, especially the clinical psychologist, were very supportive and participants were encouraged to share their own truth regardless of what that was.

I was feeling like a fraud by attending these sessions as I was one of only two people who hadn't had chemotherapy or radiotherapy. I also felt that five months on from my operation, I should be back to normal so I was extremely frustrated with myself; after all, I had no reason to still feel under par. Being able to share this out loud with the group helped me to work through this and I was constantly reminded of how important it was for me to be kinder to myself.

In this group, people of different ages and backgrounds with different types of cancer reported a lot of very similar post-treatment challenges, particularly fatigue and a sense of loss/life-changing event. And that's when the penny dropped: **going through cancer is about dealing with a series of losses and the initial psychological impact is grief.** Now grief is something I know a lot about so I felt a great sense of relief as I was now on familiar territory and knew what to do. Phew, there was nothing wrong with me mentally!

Life Now

Since 2012, I've helped over 400 grievers through my voluntary work on a helpline and ongoing one-to-one support. I was aware that it's natural and normal for humans to grieve after a major illness, but finding myself in autopilot on the conveyor belt, I'd completely forgotten this.

Also, the term 'psychological impact' had thrown me as I was expecting to have some kind of mental breakdown; something abnormal and unfamiliar. Instead, what I was going through was grief, and once I realised this, I knew that I'd be OK as the emotional and mental turbulence of grief is something I've handled many, many times after other major changes in my life.

By amalgamating the experience and expertise I'd gained over the years, including my training as a Grief Recovery Method Specialist®, I helped myself. The process I used is set out in Part 3 of this book. In this way, I was able to regain my peace of mind and my emotional wellbeing within weeks. The white noise in my head faded away, I was able to meditate again and I went back to functioning fully at work.

As part of the life-changing experience of cancer, I also realised that I wanted to and could help others handle the emotional and mental impacts of cancer and other life-changing events. I formed a not-for-profit company, Altered Dawn CIC, with the objective of raising awareness of grief and supporting grievers. Grief is not just about death and dying. It's a natural emotional response to a significant change in our life.

In particular, I wanted to give cancer patients the know-how and support they need to secure lasting emotional and mental wellbeing. I've come across so many who are struggling to function or have suppressed their emotions. Cancer leaves us with grief and there's a lot we can do to help ourselves. I wanted to share my knowledge and tips to as many people as possible so in June 2017, I started researching and interviewing cancer patients for this book.

In the interim, I wrote some tips on how to grieve after cancer and in January 2018, I published a quick guide, Coping With Cancer: 7 Steps To Deal With Anxiety and Fear which is available at www.altereddawn.co.uk/books.

At the time of finishing this book in October 2018, I've had my second annual check-up and am cancer-free. I have my six-monthly appointment with the consultant next week, and yes, a part of me wonders if the blood tests will bring bad news. I feel optimistic and a bit anxious. I'm OK with that.

Wrap-up

As you know, I wanted to include stories of others affected by cancer because there is no 'normal'. That's why I won't be analysing the stories; it's irrelevant in this context. I do hope that you gained useful insights from reading them; I know I found them poignant.

I'd like to thank Robert, Petra, Mary, Susan, Tony, Rhonda, Meena and June for their time and for giving permission for their words to be used in this book. I know that when they read the typed-up transcript, they were moved by their own stories. They also noticed how far they had come since the original diagnosis and were grateful for their current situation. It was a privilege to connect with them and to be entrusted with their stories.

Finally, without analysis(!), the one thing I would like to highlight is that cancer changed the lives of each and every one of us. What about you?

If you're feeling that a life-shift is on its way, Part 3 is designed help you have a clear-out and figure out what you want.

PART 3

————————————

THE WORKBOOK

A little knowledge that acts is worth infinitely more than much knowledge that is idle.

– Khalil Gibran

Introduction

The previous two parts have provided you with information about how cancer has affected your life and your psychological wellbeing. Now it's time to take action.

This part contains a four-stage process designed to lead you step by step through a series of exercises so that you:

- identify your core beliefs and their helpfulness
- gain clarity about your life now and what you'd like to have
- let go of any significant mental and emotional pain attached to your cancer

The exercises are not necessarily new and it is likely that you have done some of them in the past. They are all tried and tested therapeutic and coaching tools that have been used effectively over many years in different contexts. The time-map technique is one I first devised in 2009 when I was reflecting on traumatic events in my life; it's an amalgamation of a timeline and a mind-map. They are all exercises that I've used personally and with clients to good effect.

In this workbook, I have ordered and adapted these techniques to create a transformative process that is relevant to those affected by cancer. The process is underpinned by my knowledge and expertise of grief and experience of helping grievers. If you were to come to my two-day workshop, this is the process that I would guide you through. I've included it in this book for those who are unable to come along or would prefer to work through it themselves.

You must complete all four stages in order to gain clarity and find peace of mind. Here are the stages and exercises:

Stage 1:   **Mapping Your Cancer Experience (2 hours)**
Exercise 1: Mapping the Facts – What, When, Who, How?
Exercise 2: Identifying Your Losses
Exercise 3: Mapping Your Mental Responses
Exercise 4: Mapping Your Emotional Responses

Stage 2:   **Discovering Your Guide to Life (50 minutes)**
Exercise 5: Recognising Your Default Position
Exercise 6: Identifying Your Core Beliefs
Exercise 7: Assessing Your Beliefs

Stage 3:   **Taking Stock (1 hour 45 minutes)**
Exercise 8: Checking In
Exercise 9: Assessing Your Life Now
Exercise 10: Reflecting on Your Life Now
Exercise 11: Establishing Your Desired Future

Stage 4:   **Letting Go (1 hour 30 minutes, plus 20 minutes for sharing)**
Exercise 12: Expressing How Others Made You Feel
Exercise 13: Expressing How You Feel About Yourself
Exercise 14: Adding Your Helpful Beliefs
Exercise 15: Adding Your Desired Future
Exercise 16: Sharing Your Release Letter

How to Use the Workbook

There are spaces in the book for you to write your answers. If you'd prefer not to, then please go to www.altereddawn.co.uk/crc to download the worksheets. For the time-map, you will need some blank pieces of paper and four different coloured pens.

You will gain the most benefit by putting aside a whole day or two half-days and working through all four stages without any external distractions. Working through the complete process in this way ensures that you are more likely to stay in the 'self-discovery' mode and it's easier to maintain momentum.

Perhaps take a break away from home to ensure that you will not be interrupted. If it isn't practical or possible for you to do all four stages, then work through one stage at a time in order, leaving a gap of no more than one or two days to ensure that you don't lose impetus.

In between the stages, I encourage you to take a break (30–40 minutes); do something else that is enjoyable and relaxing, such as gardening, walking, cooking or whatever makes you feel relaxed.

If you find that you struggle to complete the workbook or your life is not organised in such a way that you can spend enough time on yourself, then do consider joining me on a two-day workshop where I can guide and support you through the exercises. The workshops are designed to give you a safe environment to show up, have difficult conversations and practise vulnerability and courage. You can get more details at www.altereddawn.co.uk.

This process will require your commitment and effort. The exercises are designed to facilitate deep reflection and are likely to be emotionally demanding.

Warning: Facing uncomfortable dark scary thoughts and feelings is part of the letting go process and is normal. However, if you have a medically recognised history of mental illness or any other medical conditions that mean you are more likely to harm yourself, don't do this workbook alone. The exercises could take you to some challenging places so it's best to discuss it with your medical team and follow their advice.

Principles

For this process to work, an authentic mindset is essential. I have therefore set out the underlying principles that you need to follow when undertaking the exercises. This will ensure that you are working on the truths of your cancer experience which in turn means that the exercises in this workbook will be more beneficial to you.

It's important to be honest about the thoughts and feelings that you are facing or have experienced. You may be wearing a mask to function in life, but for the sake of the exercises in this workbook, take it off and be honest with yourself; otherwise you are working on a lie which will be of little benefit to you.

Principle 1: Recognise the Good, Bad and Ugly

As discussed in Part 1, life is not 100% good or happy. Neither is it 100% bad or miserable. Normal life is somewhere in between. The bad times are not interruptions and inconveniences to your perfect, happy life. Scary life-changing challenges, utter bliss and the various levels of pain and joy in between are normal life. The truth of your experience will therefore always include good, bad and ugly times; it's life.

To be authentic, you need to acknowledge the whole range of events and responses, regardless of whether you deem them to be good, bad or shameful. You may find this tricky.

If you're currently feeling overwhelmed by the diagnosis, living with terminal cancer or a whole series of things has gone wrong, you may struggle to find anything positive to say. Similarly, if you've perhaps moved on and life is good, you may think that there's no point in raking up what you put behind you or you have a belief that it's not helpful to dwell on the negative. Or you may be scared. This means you will be resistant to considering the painful aspects during the exercises and it's therefore likely that you will skip the bad parts completely or miss the really painful elements because you are subconsciously only committed to giving them a cursory glance.

However, if you don't fully consider the dark and ugly aspects of your cancer experience, you won't be able to fully address them. Remember the analogy of the leaky boat in Part 1; for this process to work, it's imperative that you acknowledge and express both the positive and negative elements of your experience.

Principle 2: Practise Courage

To be able to let go fully, you will need courage.

Courage originates from the Latin word 'cor' which means 'heart' and here's the Collins Dictionary's definition:

> *'Courage is the quality shown by someone who decides to do something difficult or dangerous, even though they may be afraid.'*

I've chosen this word carefully because sometimes working through these exercises can be hard when you come face to face with something difficult, uncomfortable or scary. I can't predict which exercise will be tricky for you and it may be that none are. More often than not though, there will be at least one exercise that you find challenging because after all, you are exploring your emotional wounds and delving into the pain. Understandably, your default defensive cynicism or rebelliousness might kick in and you may be tempted to abandon that exercise or the process.

If you find yourself in this place, it's an indication that there is something important that has to come out. Instead of giving up, see this as confirmation that you're on the right track and keep going. Recognise it for what it is – resistance. Perhaps your survival impulses have been reactivated. Stay committed to the process because it will help to liberate you from what's been holding you back.

If you find yourself overwhelmed, know that this is also a defence mechanism. It's your mind's way of flagging up that there is something you've buried or avoided and have previously decided not to feel. See it as a sign that this exercise is exactly what you need to be doing.

In the first part of this book, I highlighted the survival instinct to fight, freeze or run away, and that the key is to face your suffering by allowing a dialogue between your head and your heart. The work you are about to do will expose your vulnerability, your shame, your fears and your suffering. Be OK with this; tap into your courage and approach these exercises with an open heart and mind. It's what you need to do to find relief and move towards peace of mind.

Sit quietly and focus inwards. Listen to what your heart is saying. Find out which emotions are present. Is there fear, anxiety, sadness, etc.? Make friends with them without judgement or criticism. Soothe yourself: 'It's OK to feel the way I do.' Take a short break (up to 15 minutes) if you need to and then come back to the exercise.

Principle 3: Don't be Perfect

When writing down your answers to the exercises, it is not important for you to remember every single detail. Perfectionists will find that challenging and will be tempted to produce a beautiful time-map and written responses. But the objective of this process is for you to find the key pain points and release them. It is not about producing an accurate and detailed report of your cancer experience.

Also bear in mind that there is no need to worry about spelling, grammar and punctuation! This process is designed so that even those of you who are not keen on writing will still benefit from completing the tasks.

I've suggested timings for each exercise as a guide. If you find that you're spending a lot longer, check whether you're going into too much detail. It may also be that you're actually analysing your experience – you don't need to do that because analysis means the brain is taking over the process; you want to turn down the volume in your head so you can hear your heart. It may be tricky for you, but do avoid analysing when writing your answers.

Assuming that you follow the first two principles of being truthful about the light, dark and greys in your life and that you work with an open heart and mind, the significant events, people, thoughts and emotions will come up first. They are the ones that matter.

It's possible that you may forget something that was in fact particularly important; that's fine, you can add it later. Or maybe you've completely forgotten what you thought or felt at the time; that's OK too. You work with what you can remember.

There is no extra benefit to be gained in being perfect.

Stage 1:

Mapping Your Cancer Experience

Allow two hours.

We start by creating a time-map of your experience using the facts. A time-map is a combination of a timeline and a mind-map. It's not possible to reproduce my whole time-map in this book, but an example of my cancer time-map can be found at www.altereddawn.co.uk/tm. As you progress through the different exercises in this stage, you will be adding thoughts and feelings.

Why a time-map? The physical act of creating your time-map declutters your mind and turns down the chatter. There is something very powerful about putting what happened, how you felt and what you thought down on paper. Here's why:

- By recording it on paper, especially using colours and symbols, you are providing your mind with a way to organise and make sense of your cancer experience, as well as giving it the opportunity to have a clear-out.

- You will notice patterns and underlying issues more easily and will therefore get to know yourself a lot better.

- It can also give you a bit of distance between you and your experience as you are looking at it from a new perspective – it's there in front of you rather than going round and round in your head.

- It's a quick and easy method – you only use dates, words, symbols and colours. It doesn't have to be pretty, perfect or presentable. The time-map is for your eyes only. Do feel free to be creative, but remember that this is a working tool, not a piece of art for display.

- Once you've completed all four stages of this process, I recommend that you don't keep your time-map. Commit now to destroying it at the end; this will give your subconscious the permission to write everything down, even scary or shameful information, without the fear of someone finding your time-map in the future.

It's not unusual to forget some events, even ones that were particularly traumatic at the time. That's normal. You can add them to your time-map retrospectively. Work through all the exercises in this stage in one sitting.

This stage may bring up some unhappy memories and emotions; do not be concerned. It's OK to feel what you feel. These may be troubling you because you have buried them, so it's important to stay committed to this process. These painful thoughts and emotions need to be acknowledged and released. Read Principle 2 and find your courage again.

You are now ready to begin.

Exercise 1:

Mapping the Facts – What, When, Who, How?

Time: 45 minutes

You will need:

- A piece of A3 paper. If you only have A4, then tape two pieces together. If you find that you need more paper, just tape on more sheets.

- Coloured pens – four colours minimum. I've suggested colours to use (black, green, red, blue) but feel free to use whatever colour you like.

- Note: The aim is to record the key events that stick out for you, not a detailed blow-by-blow report of every single incident or person. If you can't remember the names or tests, it's fine. Just put a question mark or a symbol of your choice.

1. Using a black pen, with your paper in landscape format, draw a line in the middle from left to right. You are going to use this line to mark down what happened, when and who was involved.

2. On the left hand side of the line, write the date when your cancer experience started. This could be when you first had an inkling that something was wrong with your body (e.g. symptoms), or if you had no idea there was anything wrong with your health, it could be when your doctor or the hospital highlighted that there was something that needed further investigation.

3. On the far right, put today's date. It goes without saying that your cancer experience doesn't stop once the treatment is over. Note roughly where the half and quarter marks are so that you have an idea of where events will go on the timeline.

4. Mark the significant events that occurred onto the line and write a short label of the event. Alternate between writing above and below the line so that you have plenty of space to add other bits of information. Dates are optional; the focus is on what happened, not necessarily on what day.

   Examples of significant events include: symptoms, CT scan, colonoscopy, endoscopy, consultations, significant phone calls or appointments, finding out that it's cancer, breaking the news to family/friends/work, chemotherapy, radiotherapy, operation, other health issues, complications, side-effects of treatment, going back to work, regular check-ups, new job/hobby/interest, moving home or other changes, etc.

5. Still with the black pen, for each event add a short line and label to record anyone significant who was involved, e.g. spouse, parents, friend, nurses, consultants, etc. If it's a whole team of people, just write the name of the team. If a particular person was significant then write down their name. You are likely to end up with more than one name – so just keep adding lines with name labels as necessary so it branches out. If you went to particular appointments or medical procedures alone, note this.

   Note if the person or team was supportive by putting a symbol next to them; it could be a tick or a smiley face. If they were not supportive, add an appropriate symbol such as a cross or an unhappy face.

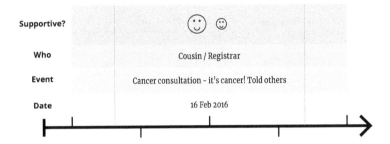

6. Next, with the black pen, for each significant event, note down what you did in response to the event and add the name of anyone involved. For example:

   • Did you keep your cancer diagnosis to yourself or talk to someone?
   • Did you isolate yourself, share your experience with others or join a support group?
   • Did you cry?
   • Did you keep busy?
   • Did you spend a few days in bed?
   • Did you research your cancer or did you prefer not to know too much?
   • Did you trust or challenge the medical team?
   • Did you exercise?
   • Did you focus on your kids or work so you didn't have to think or feel?
   • Did you drink more alcohol?
   • Did you meditate or use an alternative therapy?
   • Did you eat more or go on a special diet?

   Was there a particular person or group that helped or didn't help you with your response? If so, add an appropriate symbol next to them.

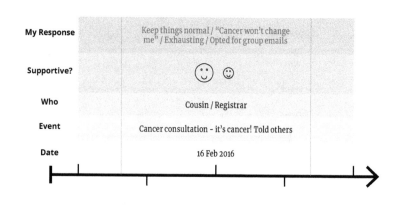

My Response Keep things normal / "Cancer won't change me" / Exhausting / Opted for group emails

Supportive?

Who Cousin / Registrar

Event Cancer consultation - it's cancer! Told others

Date 16 Feb 2016

Exercise 2:
Identifying Your Losses

Time: 25 minutes

We discussed the hidden and intangible losses we face from cancer in Part 1 and I gave you some examples. In this exercise, you will identify your losses and what you have been left with as a result.

1. Look through the events on your time-map and note your answers to the following questions:

    *   What changed?
    *   What did you lose?
    *   What was it replaced with?

    Note the answers on your time-map with a red pen.

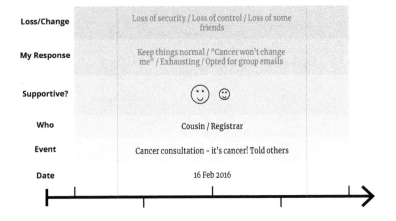

Loss/Change	Loss of security / Loss of control / Loss of some friends
My Response	Keep things normal / "Cancer won't change me" / Exhausting / Opted for group emails
Supportive?	☺ ☺
Who	Cousin / Registrar
Event	Cancer consultation - it's cancer! Told others
Date	16 Feb 2016

Exercise 3:

Mapping Your Mental Responses

Time: 20 minutes

You will now consider your mental responses. You may find it helpful to reread the section on mental response in Part 1.

1. For each significant event, ask yourself:

   • What were my thoughts at this point?
   • What survival symptoms kicked in?

2. Note them down on your time-map using a blue pen.

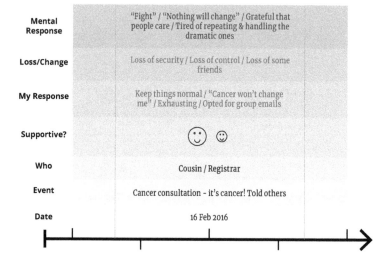

Mental Response	"Fight" / "Nothing will change" / Grateful that people care / Tired of repeating & handling the dramatic ones
Loss/Change	Loss of security / Loss of control / Loss of some friends
My Response	Keep things normal / "Cancer won't change me" / Exhausting / Opted for group emails
Supportive?	☺ ☺
Who	Cousin / Registrar
Event	Cancer consultation - it's cancer! Told others
Date	16 Feb 2016

Exercise 4:

Mapping Your Emotional Responses

Time: 30 minutes

It is time to identify the different feelings that arose during your cancer experience. Emotions may include gratitude, relief, joy, fun, love, anger, fear, frustration, numbness, emptiness, isolation, heartbreak, sadness.

If you are doing this exercise several months or years after your diagnosis, don't be surprised if you can't remember exactly how you felt. Do not force it. It may be that you just have no need to release it at this point. Equally, don't be scared to delve deep and unearth difficult, painful and undesirable emotions. The aim of this exercise is to identify them so that you can acknowledge and release them.

Don't judge whether or not you ought to have felt how you did. Just note the feelings as best as you can remember. You may find that you have conflicting feelings around the same event. For example, when I realised that it might be cancer but in the early stages, I felt scared, relieved, sorry for myself and annoyed with myself in the same instant. I also felt numb and nauseous. I had also hoped it would be Stage 1 or 2 cancer so when it turned out to be Stage 3, I was disappointed. I was also relieved that it wasn't Stage 4.

You may need to dig a little deeper to identify buried emotions and pain. Be OK with getting out of your comfort zone. Be OK with feeling vulnerable and emotional. Be courageous. You are simply expunging suppressed grief.

Tips if you become overly anxious

If at any point your levels of anxiety increase, recognise the feeling(s) and take a short break. Anxiety is a sign that there is an emotional response or bundle of feelings that your brain has deemed to be a threat, maybe because they are scary, unwanted, uncomfortable or unfamiliar. Your brain has therefore decided that you should be protected. When anxious, people typically avoid a situation or distract themselves so that their anxiety reduces. Remember that this is a short-term benefit; in the longer term, it is not a useful strategy for you.

Note what triggered it and remind your mind that scary, unwanted, uncomfortable or unfamiliar emotions are to be expected in your circumstances; after all, cancer is a potentially life-threatening disease. If you're living with cancer, this is likely to be very challenging but you will gain a lot of benefit from recognising your emotional responses even though you are still under threat.

Sit quietly and say hello to your anxiety. Speak to it, soothe it as you would an injured child:

'I'm not under threat right here, right now. It's simply a memory. I am honouring the emotional pain that I experienced at the time so that I can release it, and my mind can be more peaceful. It's OK for now.'

Then, once your anxiety subsides, continue with the exercise. If it doesn't subside, talk to a friend, use a local cancer support group, call a cancer helpline or feel free to contact me at info@altereddawn.co.uk.

Take a deep breath and calm your mind. This is the time to let your heart speak.

1. Using a green pen, add in the emotions you felt at the various points of your time-map. Put all the feelings, regardless of whether you judge them to be positive or negative.

2. Vary the size of your writing according to the intensity of the emotion felt. If it wasn't particularly strong, just write a small label; if it was an overwhelming feeling, then write it in very large letters. In this way, you can see at a glance very clearly which emotions were strongest at which point.

3. Are there any occasions where you buried, avoided or ignored your emotions? Note this on your time-map.

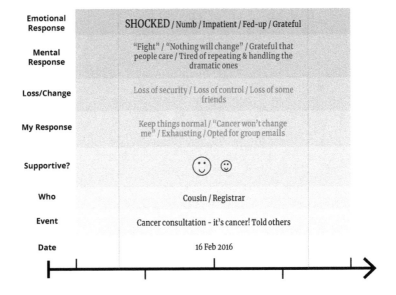

Emotional Response	SHOCKED / Numb / Impatient / Fed-up / Grateful
Mental Response	"Fight" / "Nothing will change" / Grateful that people care / Tired of repeating & handling the dramatic ones
Loss/Change	Loss of security / Loss of control / Loss of some friends
My Response	Keep things normal / "Cancer won't change me" / Exhausting / Opted for group emails
Supportive?	☺ ☺
Who	Cousin / Registrar
Event	Cancer consultation – it's cancer! Told others
Date	16 Feb 2016

Working on your emotions can be exhausting and leave you feeling drained. That's normal.

Congratulations on completing the first stage and mapping your cancer experience. **Take a break of 30–40 minutes before moving on to the next stage.** Do something else that is enjoyable, gentle and relaxing, such as gardening, walking, cooking, listening to music, or whatever makes you feel relaxed.

Stage 2:

Discovering Your Guide to Life

Allow about 50 minutes.

You will need:

- A pen
- Some paper or downloaded worksheets if you don't want to write in the book itself.

When faced with a life-threatening situation, your mind is influenced by what you've learned in the past. Your brain's response is automatic and is based on what you believe to be true about life and how to deal with life.

Your response is pre-programmed by something you were once told (usually by someone significant in your life) or an event you experienced in the past. In working towards releasing painful emotions and gaining greater peace of mind, it is necessary for you to gain a deeper understanding of yourself and what makes you tick.

Let's therefore do a quick exercise to explore your brain's default position.

Exercise 5:

Recognising Your Default Position

Time: 10 minutes

In this exercise, for each line, write the first thing that comes to mind. Do not think, analyse or ponder. What you want to find out here is your instant and automatic response, your default position so to speak. As with previous exercises, there is no right or wrong answer. The quicker you write the response, the more useful and truthful the answer will be to you.

1. Cancer _____

2. Death _____

3. Being strong _____

4. People think cancer _____

5. Having cancer means _____

6. Being sad _____

7. I always cope by _____

8. I think emotional people _____

9. A person who falls apart in a crisis _____

10. Being ill _____

11. Being healthy _____

12. When I see other people struggling emotionally _____

13. When ill, my father would _____

14. When ill, my mother would _____

15. People who cry _____

16. My friends _____

17. When I am upset _____

18. I don't deserve _____

19. The best way to deal with cancer _____

20. Courage means _____

21. When I'm happy _____

22. When I have a problem _____

23. Good mental health _____

24. Being in control _____

25. Relying on others _____

26. My family _____

27. Being vulnerable _____

28. Being independent _____

29. Looking through my mother's eye, being emotional _____

30. Looking through my father's eye, being emotional _____

31. Life always _____

32. Coping means _____

33. When I'm worried _____

34. Cancer causes _____

35. I got cancer because _____

36. Being emotional means _____

37. I handle pressure by _____

38. Grief _____

39. When I'm afraid _____

40. Asking for help _____

Beliefs

The exercise you just did will help to reveal your core beliefs. The Oxford Dictionary defines 'belief' as:

> *'Something one accepts as true or real; a firmly held opinion.'*

Throughout your life, you will have developed a number of core beliefs, which underpin how you view the world and make sense of what's going on around you. It's your internal guide to life and it moulds your life as illustrated below.

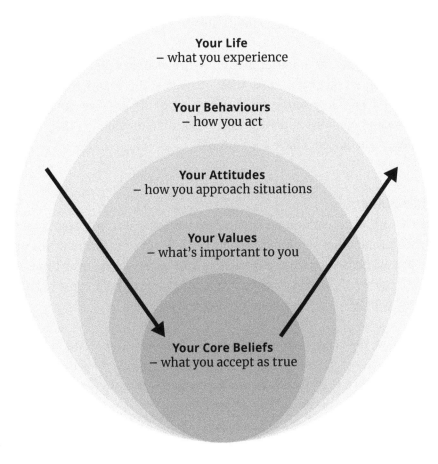

Your Life
– what you experience

Your Behaviours
– how you act

Your Attitudes
– how you approach situations

Your Values
– what's important to you

Your Core Beliefs
– what you accept as true

Your experience of life is affected by how you act in different situations, i.e. your behaviour. How you behave is influenced by your attitudes to life, other people and to yourself. In turn, your attitudes are guided by your values or what is important to you, which are shaped by what your mind believes is true or real – your core beliefs.

By the same token, there is a feedback loop in that your resulting experiences may reinforce your beliefs, values, attitudes and behaviour; or it could change them.

For instance, before experiencing cancer, I'd had little contact with the NHS (British National Health Service) and I trusted the service. When I was treated for cancer, I was lucky in that I felt well cared for and the operation was successful. It's no surprise that I still trust the NHS and my original belief that the health system is great was reinforced.

Now consider some of the stories in Part 2, where people's experiences weren't good and they felt let down on several occasions; the degree to which they now trust the health system is much reduced and they are now more likely to ask for second opinions and push for testing than previously. Their beliefs, attitudes and behaviours have been altered.

Conditioning

Your core beliefs are based on what you have learned from parents, peers, instructors and other significant people you encounter throughout your life. They are also based on your experiences and observations over time. This means that there is always a good reason as to why you have come to believe what you believe – it's social conditioning and learning.

What's more, if you learned your belief from somebody important in your life or because you experienced a significant life-changing event, you will hold on to the belief more strongly and view it as 'the absolute truth', especially if you were young at the time the belief was formed.

Often these beliefs are developed unconsciously in that you aren't aware that a situation or person has influenced your internal guide to life. More importantly, unhelpful beliefs can be life-limiting. For example, your beliefs about expressing emotions will define how you respond when you are faced with the messy emotional experience of grief and they will determine whether you are generally at ease with being down and being vulnerable.

Here's a good personal example: during my teens, 20s and 30s, emotional people made me uncomfortable and I actively avoided them. I didn't 'do emotions' and thought touchy-feely people were uncool and needy. This was based on beliefs that formed in my subconscious mind as a result of my brother dying suddenly when I was 13.

At that point, I looked around me and no-one in my family showed much emotion; the beliefs that I developed were: 'Strong people don't show emotions', 'The best way to deal with a death is to keep busy and not think about it' and 'When the going gets tough, the tough get going.' The last one was from a film in the 80s which reinforced what I'd learned. I imagine that if I'd had cancer during this time, my default response would have been, 'Show no emotions, keep busy and get on with life.'

When faced with a significant situation like having cancer, you will automatically fall back onto your core beliefs about how you should cope, and your thoughts and behaviour will reflect these beliefs. It makes sense therefore that you now pause and reflect on the previous exercise to figure out what your internal guide looks like.

Exercise 6:

Identifying Your Core Beliefs

Time: 20 minutes

1. Look at your responses to the previous exercise. Are there common threads running through your answers? These will be your core beliefs. You may find it useful to think in terms of these categories:

   * My beliefs about cancer/illness
   * My beliefs about coping
   * My beliefs about emotions
   * My beliefs about life

   Here are some examples from my list to start you off:

   * Cancer happens to unfit people.
   * Cancer is mostly a genetic predisposition.
   * I handle pressure by withdrawing and eating crisps and chocolate.
   * I think emotional people need to be heard.
   * When ill, my mother would keep going.
   * When ill, my father would sleep.

2. Add them to the first column in this table and number them:

My Beliefs	Who/Where From?	Helpful?
1.		
2.		

My Beliefs	Who/Where From?	Helpful?
3.		
4.		
5.		
6.		
7.		
8.		
9.		
10.		
11.		

3. Next, if you can, identify who you learned this belief from. Or was there a particular situation that led you to this belief? Complete the second column of the table (leave the third column blank for now).

Exercise 7:

Assessing Your Beliefs

Time: 20 minutes

Now let's consider how your internal guide to life shaped your attitudes and behaviour during your experience of cancer and whether they in turn have been altered by cancer.

1. Look back at your time-map and your table of beliefs:

    * What are the links between your core beliefs and your cancer experience?

    _____

    _____

    * Can you link any of your thoughts, feelings and behaviours to a particular belief or set of beliefs?

    _____

    _____

    * Can you identify any other points when your beliefs about being emotional influenced what you did during your cancer experience?

    _____

    _____

2. To help you to recognise any trends, note down the beliefs on your time-map in blue pen. If you don't have much space on your time-map, then simply write down the reference number of the belief as given when you filled in the table.

3. Now take a step back from the details of the time-map and look for any patterns.

- What can you see?

  _____

  _____

  _____

- Is there a dominant belief or a set of beliefs that recurs?

  _____

  _____

  _____

- Have any changed as a result of cancer?

  _____

  _____

  _____

4. If you can, decide if the belief has been helpful or unhelpful to you during the cancer and note it in the third column of your beliefs table. There is no right or wrong answer; it's just your current view. If you're not sure, just put a question mark.

- Has it served you well or has it limited you?
- Is it a supportive belief or a rule that you beat yourself up with?

Well done for completing the second stage of this process.

Take a break of 30–40 minutes before moving on to the next stage. Do something else that is enjoyable, gentle and relaxing, such as gardening, walking, cooking, listening to music, or whatever makes you feel relaxed.

Stage 3:

Taking Stock

Allow up to about 1 hour 45 minutes.

You will need:

- A pen
- Some paper or downloaded worksheets if you don't want to write in the book itself.

Now it's time to look at what is going on right now in your life so that you have greater clarity about what is working, what isn't working and what you'd like to be different. Essentially, we are talking about an inventory of your current life and what you would like to change.

The four exercises in this stage will give you a baseline measurement that you can use to compare against a few months down the line. Knowing what you'd like to change in your life is part of your recovery. Having your end goal in mind will also help you keep on track towards greater peace of mind.

As mentioned already, introspection is key to the process of letting go and changing things that are limiting you at this point in time. Resistance to change is normal. If you find yourself making excuses or putting off a specific exercise, stop and ask yourself, 'What's going on?' 'What am I afraid of?' 'Why am I afraid?'

Again, there are no right or wrong answers and this is a series of subjective assessments. The only instruction is to be honest with yourself. This is the right time to reveal things you might not admit to someone else – or to yourself.

For those living with cancer or with a limited time to live, this can be a tricky stage to complete. You may notice a lot of anger or sorrow; it's OK. Note them down and do your best to flow through the exercises. If a particular exercise is too distressing, reach out for support. It's also OK for you to skip it. You could perhaps come back to it later, or not. I leave it to you to decide what's right for you.

Exercise 8:

Checking In

Time: 15 minutes

For the purposes of this activity, just look at what's happened in the last two weeks. The aim is to identify your current situational triggers and response patterns.

1. Find a quiet, comfortable space where you won't be disturbed. Tap into your thoughts and feelings and mull over these questions.

    Over the last two weeks:

    *   What's been going on?
    *   What's upset you or hurt you?
    *   What's made you happy?
    *   When have you felt anxious, overwhelmed or numb?
    *   When have you felt OK, happy or at peace?
    *   What thoughts are going round?

2. Use the table below to jot down your answers to the questions – don't analyse or think too hard. Take about ten minutes to list the significant answers. Let it flow naturally from the heart. Use extra paper if you need to.

    If you can't think of anything, then have a break. You've picked up this book and are working through the exercises; that is an indication in itself that there are things you want to look at or that you're struggling with. Perhaps you're not ready or you feel confused or overwhelmed right now. Don't get bogged down; take time out. If you can come back to it after a short break, do so. Otherwise, over the next few weeks, bear in mind this exercise. Pay attention to what's going on and then put some time aside to quickly note this down.

Over the last few weeks, what thoughts and feelings have been preoccupying you? What are you struggling with? What has been working?		
Your situation: • list events where you've felt down, upset or not in control • list times when you felt good, calm or had a laugh	Your emotions: what were the main feelings you experienced?	Your thoughts: what did you say to yourself?

3. Once you've drawn up your list take about five minutes to look through it and consider the questions below. Note down your answers.

- What jumps out at you?

_____

_____

_____

_____

- What patterns do you see?

_____

_____

_____

_____

- Is there anything that surprises you?

_____

_____

_____

_____

The Wheel of Life

The Wheel of Life is a useful self-assessment tool that is widely used; it's a simple yet powerful diagnostic tool that gives you an overview of your life today. Clearly, our perception of how we're doing can change from day to day, but we are not concerned about this; we simply want to take a snapshot of 'now'.

I have adapted this wheel to show the ten areas of your life that are most likely to be impacted by your cancer experience:

1. Family & Friends
2. Intimate Relationship
3. Physical Health & Body
4. Spiritual Health
5. Emotional Health
6. Mental Health
7. Belonging
8. Fun & Leisure
9. Work
10. Finances

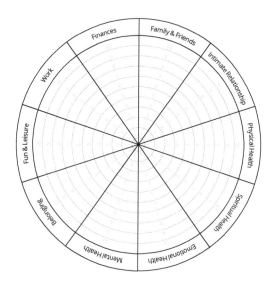

If you feel that one category is not relevant to you, take it away or change the heading. Likewise, if there is a category that you think is missing, go ahead and add it in. You may also split categories if it makes more sense to you, for example, separating 'Family' from 'Friends'. This is your wheel; feel free to change it so that it works for you.

Most of these life areas are fairly self-explanatory but some warrant further explanation.

- Intimate Relationship – this is your primary physically and emotionally intimate relationship which includes your spouse, partner or other significant person in your life.

- Spiritual Health – this includes your values, beliefs, principles and morals. Whilst it includes religious faith, it is also relevant to those without any religion.

- Emotional Health – this does not mean 'Am I happy?' This is about your ability to understand, to respond to, and to be at ease with your emotional reactions to life events. Are you comfortable with feeling the full range of your emotions, both positive and negative? Remember, emotionally healthy people still feel stressed, angry, unhappy and sad. Are you able to empathise with others?

- Mental Health – this covers your ability to function at work, play or rest and to make a contribution to your community. It also relates to how much self-compassion, self-love and self-care you have. Do you see yourself as being a valuable person in your own right? Are you kind to yourself? Do you accept that you have faults and are not perfect?

- Belonging – generally, this considers how much you feel that you belong, and are valued and are accepted by others. This could be by your neighbours, particular groups you belong to (including virtual groups), your wider community, etc. Do you feel connected and well supported? The amount of giving that you do and your contribution towards others and your communities is also relevant here.

- Work – if not applicable to you, then replace the heading with one that makes sense to you, e.g. Parenting, Studying, Retirement, Volunteering.

Exercise 9:

Assessing Your Life Now

Time: 30 minutes

This is a quick assessment of your life so you don't need to spend more than 15 minutes on filling in the wheel.

1. Working on one segment at a time, complete the wheel. For each category, ask yourself the following questions:

   * What would a satisfying life look like or feel like for you in this area?
   * For this area, how satisfied are you at this point in time?
     Choose a value between 1 (very dissatisfied) and 10 (fully satisfied). Use the first score that comes to mind, not the number you think it should be.
   * Draw a line across the segment based on the score you chose.
   * Move on to the next category and repeat the steps above until you've completed all ten areas.

Life Balance

The purpose of the wheel is to show you how balanced the whole of your life is today. It highlights any areas of your life where you may be giving too much of yourself at the expense of other parts of your life. For example:

   * Are all your needs currently fulfilled in the right way?
   * Are you working too hard?
   * Are your family relationships neglected?
   * Is your spiritual wellbeing your main focus to the exclusion of having fun?

- Are you putting your family first but forgetting about your own wellbeing?

It is common that when one or two areas of your life become the focal point, the others suffer and your wheel is out of balance. If your wheel looks something like the example below, it cannot roll forward smoothly. Your life will be a wobbly, bumpy and uncomfortable ride.

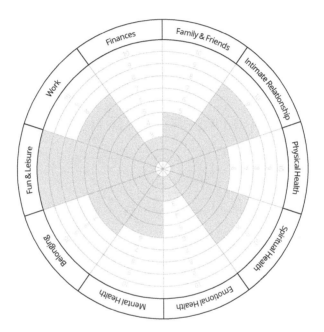

Your objective is not necessarily to get to a score of 10; it's a subjective score anyway. The idea is to adjust your areas of focus so that you achieve a more balanced wheel. You may need to change how you spend your time, effort and resources and pay more attention to areas you're currently neglecting. Your goal is to focus on achieving balance and therefore a greater 'wholeness' to your life.

2. Look at your wheel, consider these questions and note down your responses. Allow up to 15 minutes.

- How do you feel about your life as you look at your wheel?

_____

_____

_____

_____

- Is there anything that surprises you?

_____

_____

_____

_____

- If there was one key action you could take that would begin to bring everything into balance, what would it be?

_____

_____

_____

_____

Exercise 10:
Reflecting on Your Life Now

Time: 20 minutes

This exercise will help you to contemplate if and where you are currently struggling and to discover whether your existing beliefs, behaviours and attitudes are limiting you. It focuses on your struggles so that you gain a better picture of what the costs are to you and those around you.

1. Look back at your responses to Exercises 8 and 9, and answer these questions:

   • What are you currently struggling with?

   • What are these struggles stopping you from being, doing or having?

   • Are any of your relationships suffering? Explain.

   • Are you underperforming at work, in your studies or with your everyday duties? What's the impact?

   • Are you experiencing any additional physical health issues? How is that affecting you?

   • How well are you looking after yourself?

   • Bearing in mind your understanding about your core beliefs, are any of them limiting you?

   • What attitudes are keeping you stuck?

   • What behaviours are unhelpful to you now?

Exercise 11:

Establishing Your Desired Future

Time: 40 minutes

If you have limited time left, this exercise might be hard for you to do. Just answer as honestly as you can and focus on what you want your life to be like in the time you have left. Maybe it's to have more fun, to be more connected with those around you, to have a good death, to share your story, to campaign and make a difference, to find peace of mind, etc. Perhaps your hope is to have certain things in place for your family and friends. Whatever your circumstances, this exercise can still be of benefit to you.

It can be challenging to contemplate your own mortality so if you need extra support, reach out to me or to others around you.

1. With the answers from Exercises 9 and 10, consider what you'd like your future to look like, feel like or sound like in terms of your physical and psychological health:

   - What do you want to have in your life to improve your physical wellbeing?

     _____

     _____

   - What do you want to have in your life to improve your mental wellbeing?

     _____

     _____

- What do you want to have in your life to improve your emotional wellbeing?

  _____

  _____

2. Next, mull over these questions and note your answers. These are some of the most useful coaching questions for focusing on the future. However, if any are not relevant to your situation, feel free to skip them.

   - What area(s) of your life would you like to improve?

     _____

     _____

   - What would you like to have instead?

     _____

     _____

   - What needs to happen so that you can have this?

     _____

     _____

   - What options or possibilities do you already have to make these happen?

     _____

     _____

- What would you like to have happen? Can it happen?

_____

_____

- How could you reallocate your time, effort and resources to make it happen? Be realistic about what is achievable and sustainable for you.

_____

_____

- What help and support will you need from others to make changes and be more satisfied with your life?

_____

_____

- What area(s) of your life is/are working well for you? Do you want more of this?

_____

_____

- Who or what has helped? Can you transfer this across to other parts of your life that you'd like to change?

_____

_____

- What small action can you do in the next week to take you one step closer to your goals?

  _____

  _____

3. Finally, write down or record a statement for each one – your goals. Be as specific as possible and use 'power' words like: I promise..., I commit..., I choose to..., I decide..., I prioritise..., etc. You will come back to these answers in Stage 4 so keep hold of them.

   For example, for several years, the most important goal for me has been to maintain my peace of mind. Here are some examples of my statements:

   - I commit to take better care of my body, my emotions and my mind.

   - I promise to be kind to myself.

   - I prioritise activities like meditation, walking along the beach and connecting with supportive friends.

   - It's OK for me to just stop each day.

   Write your statements here:

   _____

   _____

   _____

   _____

   _____

   _____

_____

_____

_____

_____

_____

_____

_____

_____

_____

_____

You're now over halfway and hopefully have a greater insight into what happened, where you're at and your hopes for the future.

Take a break of 30–40 minutes before moving on to the next stage. Go for a walk, meditate, do some gardening, read the paper; do whatever helps you to relax.

Stage 4:

Letting Go

Allow about 1 hour 30 minutes (plus 20 minutes for sharing).

In creating your time-map during the first stage of the process, you recorded what your mind and your heart have experienced since you first became aware of the cancer. In Stage 2, you identified your underlying core beliefs that influenced your responses and also whether they were helpful.

During the third stage, you developed a picture of what's been going on in your life, where you're currently at, and what you would like to have in the future. You have taken stock of where the cancer experience has led you.

It's now time for you to make peace with your cancer experience by recognising and articulating its psychological impact on you. This is a crucial stage that will ensure that you go forward free of the mental and emotional conflict.

In this final stage, you will draw upon your answers from the first three stages to draft a release letter that communicates the truth of your cancer experience. You will then complete the letting go activity by reading your letter out to another person, and I will explain later how you can do this anonymously.

If you haven't done this type of activity before, just trust the process. You've come this far and have done a lot of hard work. This is just another step for you to take. You may or may not find this process emotional. As with all the other exercises, be OK with whatever comes up.

If you're stuck, please contact me at info@altereddawn.co.uk.

The Release Letter

Why write? Research by psychologist James W. Pennebaker and his colleagues has demonstrated that the act of writing down your experience of a life-changing event will help to free you from the mental and emotional turmoil going on inside you. This type of writing has been shown to function as a psychological release and improve health.

Additionally, I recommend that you now commit to destroying your letter once you've read it out which means that your self-censorship switch is off. Your subconscious mind is therefore free to express everything it needs to because it will not be assessed or criticised. My clients find this very liberating and transformational.

You have already done most of the hard work – your efforts in creating your time-map and exploring your core beliefs have prepared you for writing your release letter; you now know what you need to say about the emotional and mental roller coaster.

'Write hard and clear about what hurts.'

– Ernest Hemingway

If you prefer, you can use a computer to type what you want to say; however, I find that the most effective method is to write by hand. If you are unable to write, then the next best thing would be to record your answers instead. In this case, your computer or phone should have a speech-to-text feature that you can use. This will ensure that you are then able to see your own words; seeing your words in black and white is an important part of the release process. You want to end up with text that you can then read back.

If you're not keen on writing, you will naturally have reservations at this point and may even contemplate stopping. Stick with it. What you write is for you and no-one will be judging your composition, spelling, grammar or punctuation.

The Principles – A Reminder

For this final stage, I recommend that you reread the Principles at the beginning of Part 3.

Remember, to regain your peace of mind you will need to disengage or turn down your survival response in your head and to grieve fully and authentically from the heart. So instead of fight/flight/freeze, you choose to 'face' your emotional pain – gently.

The key to this part of the process is to acknowledge and express not only the good, but also the bad and ugly elements of your time-map, paying attention to the most significant messages. To be authentic, you must recognise and express all flavours. It may be that you have more of one than the other; that's fine. But make sure you acknowledge at least one good, one bad and one ugly response. You may be caught up in the pain of your experience and find it difficult to see any examples of a good feeling. But they are there: perhaps someone was kind to you, your loved ones gave you a hug, or your grandchildren made you laugh. Quieten your mind and you will find them.

Similarly, if you are one of those who had a generally positive experience, or you are keen to leave the past in the past and not think about anything negative, it is equally important for you to find the painful responses because they are there. Burying, avoiding or suppressing them is not useful to your health in the long term. Calm your mind and you will find them.

If you still struggle, then read the stories of those I interviewed for this book in Part 2. They are all completely different but in each one, you will see that there were good and bad times. The aim is for you to air your joy, pain and all the other emotions in between.

Focus on What Was Significant

In letting go, you only need to express your significant emotional and mental responses to the cancer experience. Those of you who are detail-orientated or perfectionists may be tempted to get bogged down in the detail and want to put down every thought and emotion that you lived through, which would probably take you much longer than the suggested timings. I would discourage you from doing this because if you are taking longer, the chances are that you are overanalysing; this is not necessary.

Instead, I suggest that you stick to the time given and focus on the major events. You want to be focusing on the things that jumped out at you as you worked through the previous three stages.

Forgiveness

The objective of this workbook is to help you regain peace of mind so that you can go forward free of the psychological fallout of cancer. However, you can only regain tranquillity if you forgive.

Some of the situations you've had to go through may have left you with psychological wounds that make you now feel hurt, bitter and angry. There is often an element of loss involved, particularly a breach of trust, and in those instances, grief will be present.

Forgiveness is the act of forgiving and starts with you making the decision to do so. Some find it easier to forgive than others, but it is always possible to forgive because it is a conscious choice.

It doesn't have to mean forgetting or overlooking the harm that was done to you, or staying friendly with the person involved. Instead, it is about acknowledging the grievance, the emotional pain caused and releasing any resentment or thoughts of revenge whether the person deserves it or not. If you forgive, you will enjoy a kind of peace that helps you go on with life.

*'To forgive is to set a prisoner free and
discover that the prisoner was you.'*

– Lewis B. Smedes

If you are unable to forgive, it is probably because you are holding on to a judgement you have made: it's unfair, it's wrong, it's outrageous, it's evil, it's illegal, it's incompetent, it's rude, etc. It is therefore important for you to stop judging. If you're stuck, it might help you to develop more empathy by looking at things from the other's perspective or by reflecting on times where you've hurt others and have been forgiven.

Important note: you should never actually tell the person that you have forgiven them as they may not even be aware that they upset you. Forgiveness is an inside job; it's a wholly internal process to set your 'prisoner self' free and there is no need to discuss it with those involved.

If you find, like me, that you struggle to forgive yourself, then tap into some self-compassion: Imagine that a kind and loving friend is looking at your situation; it's unlikely that they would berate you or make the wound and pain worse. They would comfort and soothe you and give you a big warm hug. Do the same; be kind and compassionate to yourself.

Should you be completely stuck and find yourself unable to forgive the person or situation, I recommend that you still write a statement that reflects your wish to be released from the prison. For example, 'I forgive (_____) so that I don't carry this (pain/resentment/hatred, etc.) forward with me into the future' or 'I forgive (_____) so that I am released from this (pain/resentment/hatred, etc.)'.

Preparation

You will need:

- Your time-map (from Stage 1)
- Your helpful beliefs (from Stage 2)
- Your desired future (from Stage 3)
- Some blank paper to write down your statements
- A pen

Find a quiet spot where you won't be interrupted or distracted. Make yourself comfortable and settle down. Proceed with self-compassion, an open heart and an authentic mindset.

When looking back at your time-map, just review the events that produced a big emotional response for you and that you put in large letters. Note recurring patterns and trends, if any. Don't judge yourself. You are telling the truth for that particular point of your life, so even if you now know that it was wrong or ridiculous, don't discount the emotion. It is still valid.

See my example about the colostomy bag below – I now know my response was ridiculous, but this is the genuine response I had. It is important to honour your authentic response **at the time** without the censorship of today's rational perspective because your aim is to release any strong emotions that you have consciously or inadvertently buried.

Similarly, you don't need to analyse why someone said what they said or why something happened the way it did. It isn't helpful in this context because it's how you felt at the time that needs to be aired. It's not the 'rational you' that needs to be heard; it's your emotions and vulnerability that need exposure.

It is also natural that you can feel conflicting thoughts and emotions about the same person or event. For example, while recovering from my operation, I was in an antiquated bed with an air mattress that had an extremely noisy pump that moved air through the mattress in waves (presumably to prevent bed sores). It kept me awake and it made me nauseous. At the time I was really fed up with it. But at the same time, I was very grateful to be on a ward and that my operation hadn't been cancelled because of a bed shortage. (In the UK, this is a common occurrence!)

You may be tempted to skip out bits because you're embarrassed or don't want others to know. **The button you need to press to release the pain of your cancer experience lies within your vulnerability. It is not possible to truly let go unless you are working from your vulnerability.** It's OK to show and give voice to your vulnerability – you will be destroying all written evidence once you've completed the process.

You are now ready to begin drafting your release letter. There are two aspects that you need to cover: others and you. We start by looking at how you felt about other people.

Exercise 12:

Expressing How Others Made You Feel

Time: 30 minutes

1. Looking at your time-map, reflect on the most hurtful or amazing things about others that you'd like to recognise. Ask yourself these questions:

    *   What would you like to say to particular people, groups or institutions? Or perhaps to a specific situation you found yourself in?

    *   Is there anyone you'd like to apologise to, show gratitude or to say thank you to?

    *   Is there any anger that you need to vent? Any fear or frustrations?

    *   Is there anyone in particular, or groups of people, you'd like to forgive? (See box about Forgiveness.)

    *   Was there anything else that generated very strong emotions such as hate, love, bliss, etc.? *I hated it when.../I loved it when...*

2. Write statements based on your answers. Where relevant, note who or what you are talking to. Use this template to help you draft what you want to say, but do amend the structure to suit what you need to communicate.

    To X, when (insert event) happened, I felt (insert your feelings) and I thought (insert your thoughts).

    To X, I (hated it/loved it/enjoyed it...) when...

To X, I (thank/forgive/am grateful...).

Tip: Leave generous gaps between your statements so that you can add to or modify them if necessary when you pull things together later. This is a working copy so there is no need to be neat and tidy.

Here are some examples of statements. The first three are mine and the last one is made up based on someone else's experience.

> *'Adam, I want you to know that I was disappointed, hurt and exhausted by your reaction to my cancer news. You made it about you, your fears of cancer and dying, and your stupid questions made me angry. I forgive you so that I am free of this anger and disappointment.'*

> *'Mum, I loved it when you bought some lobster for my first proper meal after my operation. Even though I was feeling rotten from the drugs, it cheered me up, made me feel cared for and reminded me that I was loved. Thank you.'*

> *'To my antiquated hospital airbed, I forgive you for making me feel nauseous which made me stay in hospital an extra day. I was really down and miserable about that. I am grateful that I had a bed and that my treatment wasn't delayed.'*

> *'Consultant X, I hated the way you told me the news without any compassion as if you were telling me the weather. I feel very bitter and hurt by your attitude. You left me shocked, scared and feeling alone. I forgive you so that I don't carry this pain forward with me into the future. I am thankful for your cancer expertise and that you saved my life.'*

You will see from my examples that it is OK to have conflicting feelings about someone or something at the same time. That's normal.

Exercise 13:

Expressing How You Feel About Yourself

Time: 30 minutes

1. Look at your time-map and consider any important losses or gains (i.e. changes) in your relationship with yourself. These questions should help:

   - What would you like to say to yourself?

     ○ Do you wish to apologise to yourself? Or to show gratitude? Is there any anger, fear or frustration?

   - Is there anything you'd like to say to your body? As above, think of apologies, gratitude, anger, etc.

   - Do you need to forgive yourself or your body? (See box about Forgiveness.)

2. As before, write statements, along the lines of this template. Where relevant, note who or what you are talking to:

   To X, when (insert event) happened, I felt (insert your feelings) and I thought (insert your thoughts).

   To X, I (hated it/loved it/enjoyed it...) when...

   To X, I (thank/forgive/am grateful...).

Here are a couple of examples:

> 'When I was told it was Stage 3 and it was suspected that the nodes were affected, I was gutted and anxious; these things don't happen to me. When the consultant said that there was a high chance that I would need a colostomy bag, I was both horrified and terrified, and thought I'd be better off dead.'

> 'To my body, I apologise for not paying attention to the symptoms. I forgive you for getting cancer and I know that cancer can just happen – it's a random life event sometimes. I'm sorry that I was cross with you for a while. I'm grateful that you have recovered so well. I promise that I will keep looking after you by staying active and eating healthily.'

It might feel ridiculous to write to your body or as in my case, to my hospital airbed! But it is essential to recognise the things you need to say. With the airbed, it meant staying in hospital for one day longer than the goal I'd set myself. However irrational it sounds now, at that time it added to my sense of loss: loss of control and loss of my self-image of being a fit and healthy person. I was also very upset with my body and every time I saw my scar, I felt cross.

Know that despite these being intangible losses, you still experience their impact and the associated emotional pain and mental confusion. For cancer, I know that these intangible losses are particularly important as they can lie hidden and fester away, limiting your capacity to live fully.

Exercise 14:

Adding Your Helpful Beliefs

Time: 15 minutes

Look back at your beliefs table from Stage 2 Exercise 6 and select the helpful beliefs that you intend to take forward. Likewise, if there are unhelpful beliefs that you would like to change, rewrite them and add them in here. Incorporate them into your statements or simply list them at the bottom of your letter.

Exercise 15:

Adding Your Desired Future

Time: 15 minutes

Having expressed your thoughts and feelings about what's happened, it's now time to include your hopes and priorities for the future. In Exercise 11, you identified what you would like to have in your life so that you improve and maintain good physical, mental and emotional health. Add these at the end of your letter.

Tidying Up Your Letter (Optional)

You now have a letter that expresses your emotional and mental experience of cancer. Depending on how many alterations you have made, you may choose to rewrite it out neatly. This is optional. This letter will not be read by anyone so it doesn't matter how scruffy it looks or how coherent it is. You will, however, need to be able to read it out.

Congratulations on completing your letter. Having been through this process myself, I know how much commitment and effort it takes. If you like, give yourself a round of applause or a pat on the back; I always do!

You can now destroy your time-map and notes. Just keep the letter as the final step is to read it out loud. It isn't necessary to do it straight away. Please read the box on Sharing before you take a break.

Sharing

The action of working through this process and writing your letter will have given you a greater awareness of yourself, what you experienced, your beliefs and what you would like to have going forward. This in itself is clearly valuable to you.

In order to wholeheartedly let go of the emotional and mental pain of your cancer experience, it is necessary for you to communicate what you felt and thought to another human being. Time and again, my clients are astonished at the deep sense of release and relief they feel after reading their letter. They say that the letter-writing is therapeutic but reading it out loud to someone else is even more powerful.

Why is this? Because you need to be heard. Your heart needs to be heard. Your turmoil and vulnerability need to be heard. Your hopes and fears for the future, however short, need to be heard. This is what completes your process of letting go.

The Listener
Who you choose to read your letter to is important. It can be tricky to find a good listener because most of us like to fix others, and analyse and solve their problems, and we just love to be helpful. But there is no problem to be solved; you simply have a need to express what's been going on internally, that's all.

In an ideal world, where you are allowed to be your vulnerable human self and to be authentic, you would share with your nearest and dearest, and they would hear you without judgement or criticism. They would not tell you how you should or shouldn't be feeling. They would not give you advice or some logical explanation that negates your feelings.

In reality, how likely is that? Cancer is such an emotive subject; it makes us and those around us face mortality and change. So it is unlikely that your close family and friends will be able to stay detached and focused solely on hearing you and nothing else.

As an alternative, look around you and see if you can find someone who could just hear you as you read your letter and maybe give you a hug at the end if you need one.

If you can't find a good listener, or want to keep your anonymity, use a cancer helpline or a mental wellbeing helpline. These are staffed with skilled listeners and you're free to simply offload. It might feel strange at first, but they are trained to put you at ease and will give you the time and attention you need to share without judging you or wanting to fix you. Just call and tell them that you've written something that you'd like to read out to them.

Resistance

If you notice that there is resistance to the sharing part, observe why, if you can. Is it something you can face and push through? If not, then accept that you are perhaps not ready to share it. Store your letter securely so that if in the future you feel ready or meet the right person, you can read your words out loud. Do not let your resistance to sharing stop you from writing the letter. The action of writing the letter in itself will still be beneficial to you.

Take a long break before reading your letter. Go for a walk, meditate, do some gardening, read the paper; do whatever helps you to relax.

Exercise 16:

Sharing Your Release Letter

Time: 20 minutes

If face to face, sit next to your listener in a safe, comfortable environment where you won't be disturbed. I'd avoid sitting directly opposite as it can feel a bit intimidating, like you're being observed. Remind them that they should neither comment on what you read out, nor advise. Also, make sure they do not touch you or try to comfort you physically while you read. It is important that you are able to read what you have to say without interruption. If you're on the telephone, make sure that you have privacy and are in a safe environment.

Feel the words as you read them.

As previously, respect whatever emotions come up when you read your words. It's OK, let it out. You may or may not cry; that's fine. You might or might not feel vulnerable; accept it. You could possibly feel overwhelmed, or not. Don't expect any particular emotion or response – life is not that neat. Have tissues to hand just in case.

Whatever comes up, keep reading until the end. Once you've finished, if you want to, ask for a hug. Do not sit and chat about your letter as you will end up analysing things. This is not helpful.

Thank your listener, go your separate ways and do something enjoyable or have a rest.

As soon as you can, destroy your letter so that it can never be read by anyone else.

What Next?

Having completed the workbook, you will feel a sense of release and relief. It may be straight after reading the letter, a few days on or weeks later. There may be other emotions too. Pay attention to them, observe them and be OK with them.

You are also likely to enjoy greater peace of mind because your head–heart conflict is greatly reduced. Knowing that you've let go of the main emotional baggage from the cancer experience, you are now freer to focus on your life, in the present and into the future.

I recommend that you repeat the exercises in Stage 3 every three or six months so that you can monitor how you're doing. I have been doing these exercises for years and find them useful as they help me to check in and make sure that I'm spending time and energy on what is important to me. It's a good way to ensure that the 'busy-ness' of life doesn't take over and that I maintain my mental and emotional wellbeing.

If you are living with cancer or it comes back, I would encourage you to complete the workbook again as needs be. However, it isn't necessary to go right back to the beginning; you can simply start your time-map from the date you ended and focus on the fresh emotional and mental responses you've experienced since you previously completed the process. It won't take as long to complete because the timescale should be shorter and you are also more familiar with the process.

Parting Words

I thank you for placing your trust in me and allowing me to guide you through your emotional and mental recovery.

I've enjoyed writing this book and hope that it has helped you. I would love to hear about your experience of using it as I am always looking to improve. Please do share your thoughts, feedback and insights by contacting me:

Email: info@altereddawn.co.uk
Phone: +44 (0)7742 236 970
Website: www.altereddawn.co.uk

Acknowledgements

A massive thank you to Robert, Petra, Mary, Susan, Tony, Rhonda, Meena and June for their time and for giving permission for their words to be used in this book.

I'm extremely grateful to Kathryn Kelly, Cecilia Dearing and Meena Hans for reading my first draft and helping me to organise my thoughts more coherently. Thanks also for encouraging me during the process when I doubted myself; I love you all.

To Karen Williams, Book Mentor at Librotas, who held my hand from the beginning to the end, thank you! I know that I would never have got very far on my own. Thanks also to the Author's Journey online community and the quarterly meetings, which helped by motivating me to keep going when I struggled or got distracted!

My thanks to all who have contributed their time and effort to take this book to print: Samantha Pearce at SWATT Books, Sandra Board at Sanded Script Editing & Proofreading and Louise Lubke Cuss of Wordblink.

And finally, thank you to those who pick up this book and use it. If you work through the book alone, know that I'm with you in spirit.

Services

Juliette Chan provides support and training for men and women facing significant life-changing events so that they can regain peace of mind, develop clarity and find their own unique way forward. She offers clients a safe space to have difficult conversations and to practise vulnerability and courage.

Cancer Roller Coaster Two-Day Workshop

Take time out and spend a weekend working through the exercises in the handbook, guided by Juliette. Limited to eight people, the workshops provide a safe and supportive environment for you to focus on your psychological wellbeing.

Grief Recovery Method® Programmes

- Helping Children With Loss Programme – a four-week training course designed to teach adults what to say and do, and what not to say and do, around children who have experienced emotional loss. A mix of teaching, group discussion and practical work.

- The Grief Recovery Method® Support Group Programme – an eight-week step-by-step course in how to take the actions necessary to recover from grief. It is not a drop-in group, nor is it counselling or therapy. It is a powerful, dynamic, sensible and accessible programme that is genuinely for anyone willing to take the necessary actions to help themselves.

- The Grief Recovery Method® 1:1 Programme – a seven-week step-by-step course in how to take the actions necessary to recover from grief. Available face to face or online.

Bespoke Support

Tailored training and support for individuals, groups and businesses looking to help people deal with loss and life-changing events, such as cancer and other major illnesses, bereavement, pet loss, job loss, bankruptcy, and so on.

Retreats

Please check our website www.altereddawn.co.uk for dates or to subscribe for our updates.

About the Author

Juliette Chan specialises in helping men and women through the emotional and mental impact of their cancer experience. She has helped hundreds of grievers since 2012 and is an Advanced Grief Recovery Method Specialist®. Following her personal experience of the cancer conveyor belt in 2016, Juliette was able to use her expertise and experience of handling grief to help her cope with the psychological aftermath.

She is now on a mission to help others to not only deal with the psychological turmoil, but also to find peace of mind and clarity so that they can turn an extraordinary experience like cancer into an extraordinary life.

Juliette published a free e-book in January 2018, *Coping With Cancer: 7 Steps To Deal With Anxiety and Fear*, which sets out how those who have been affected by cancer can grieve. It is available at www.altereddawn.co.uk/books. *The Cancer Roller Coaster* is her first print book and is based on her two-day workshop.

Juliette runs webinars on the topic of cancer and grief. She is also an engaging speaker and trainer and if you are involved with a not-for-profit group, Juliette is happy to present free of charge.

Index

Lightning Source UK Ltd.
Milton Keynes UK
UKHW032200010221
378068UK00007B/981